DICTIONARY OF MARKETING TERMS

CONTRIBUTORS

Paul F. Anderson
Alan R. Andreasen
Arnold M. Barban
Donald J. Bowersox
Victor P. Buell
Gilbert A. Churchill
Dorothy Cohen
C. Merle Crawford
William R. Davidson
George S. Day
David L. Huff
Harold H. Kassarjian
Warren J. Keegan
Bernard J. LaLonde

William Lazer
Gary L. Lilien
Kent Monroe
John R. Nevin
Jerry C. Olson
J. Paul Peter
David C. Schmittlein
Don E. Schultz
Donald L. Shawver
Orville C. Walker
Barton A. Weitz
David T. Wilson
Yoram J. Wind

EDITOR

Peter D. Bennett

Published by The American Marketing Association

LIBRARY OF CONGRESS
Library of Congress Cataloging-in-Publication Data

Dictionary of marketing terms / editor, Peter D. Bennett.
    p. cm.
    ISBN 0-87757-194-5
    1. Marketing—Dictionaries. I. Bennett, Peter D.
HF5415.D4873 1988   88-24116
658.8'003'21—dc19   CIP

Preface

Human communication is never simple, and is often complicated by the fact that there is less than complete agreement on the symbols that are the building blocks of communication. The terminology of a profession, or of an academic discipline, is a major part of the shared set of symbols by which persons in the profession, or discipline, communicate with one another.

Marketing, of course, is both a profession and an academic discipline. Marketing has been blessed by a particularly close relationship between the practitioners who make up the profession, and the educators who carry prime responsibility for the advancement and development of the discipline. That close relationship has been fostered and enhanced by the American Marketing Association (AMA), which is the result of a merger in 1935 between the American Marketing Society (practitioners) and the National Association of Marketing Teacher (NAMT, educators). Since then, the presumption has been that one terminology has been appropriate for both the discipline and profession.

Indeed, prior to the creation of the AMA by the merger, the NAMT formed in 1931 a Committee on Definitions. The central proposition was that the more precise the language of a group, the more clear will be its collective thinking, and the more accurate will be its communication. Quoting the committee, "When the members of the original committee began work in 1931, we hoped that we might achieve some degree of uniformity of usage among writers on the subject of marketing. We hoped we could avoid, in our discipline, the waste of paper and ink which plagued the field of economic theory where at least a third to a half of the verbiage of many of the textbooks were devoted to presenting and defending the author's personal definitions of the terms he used." (from the Committee's 1961 report)

During the life of the Committee, under both the NAMT and the AMA, it issued three published reports, in 1933, 1948, and 1961. Throughout its life, the committee was chaired by the late Dr. Ralph S. Alexander of Columbia University. The last report was titled, *Marketing Definitions: A Glossary of Marketing Terms,* and was published by AMA. That report, in its printed form, was 24 pages long and included the definitions of 112 marketing terms.

In contrast, the current volume is several times that earlier version in terms of both pages and the number of marketing terms. The contrast is a result of the explosion of the language of a young discipline over a quarter of a century, as well as our purpose here to be more inclusive, as compared to the more limited scope of earlier publications.

That difference in the scope of the task caused a distinct difference in how this work was completed in contrast to the earlier works. For instance, the 1961 report was put together after asking about 74 AMA members to critique the 1948 report, suggesting changes and additions of new terms. The 11-person committee, after researching definitions of the added terms, were engaged "In a series of meetings that totaled about four or five working days . . ." to hammer out the definitions of the 112 terms. Attempting to follow such a procedure for the scope of the current work would have been asking the marketing community to wait another quarter of a century for our work to be finished.

The present publication actually started with the work of the 1980 AMA Ad Hoc Task Force for Marketing Definitions, chaired by Donald L. Shawver of the University of Missouri-Columbia. That group included the following individuals:

Victor P. Buell	University of Massachusetts
Edward W. Cundiff	Emory University
Thomas Greer	University of Maryland
Eugene J. Kelley	Pennsylvania State University
William Lazer	Michigan State University
Wayne Lemburg	American Marketing Association
Elmer Lotshaw	Owens-Illinois, Inc.
Vern McGinnis	Growmark, Inc.
Fred Reynolds	University of Georgia
Emily Tompkins	Journal of Marketing Research
John Wright	Georgia State University

That group, under Don Shawver's leadership, provided the base on which the current work is built. Starting with a list of over 1,600 terms, the group worked toward a goal of reducing the list to 500 terms. Once reduced, it was the intent of the task force to prepare a glossary using methodologies much like that of the earlier works. For various reasons, the work of that task force was not completed. While serving as the AMA Editor of Professional Publications, the present editor became committed to an approach that would provide the profession/discipline with a dictionary of marketing terms.

Early in the preparation of this dictionary, it was decided that the committee approach would not work. Instead, this is a compilation, a collection of definitions of marketing terms prepared by authoritative individuals in several domains and sub-sets of the marketing discipline/profession. The legitimacy, and authoritative character, of this work rests squarely on the expertise of the individuals who are its collective author. At the end of each definition is a set of initials, those of the author of the definition. Two definitions included in the book, that of **marketing** and **marketing research**, are those adopted by the Board of Directors of the American Marketing Association, and are marked [AMA]. The authors, and the particular marketing area in which they prepared definitions, are the following:

[PFA] Paul F. Anderson: Finance/Control.

Paul F. Anderson holds a Bachelor's degree in economics and an MBA from Kent State University. He received his Ph.D. from Michigan State University with a major in marketing and a minor in finance and in economics. He has published articles in such journals as *The Journal of Marketing, The Journal of Consumer Research, Financial Management, Engineering Economics, Accounting Historians Journal,* and *The Journal of Accounting, Auditing, and Finance.* He is a previous winner of the Alpha Kappa Psi and Harold H. Maynard awards, and is now on the faculty of Penn State University.

[ARA] Alan R. Andreasen: Social Marketing.

Alan R. Andreasen is Professor and Chair of Marketing at California State University, Long Beach. He has written and consulted extensively on social marketing, for such agencies as the National Cancer Institute, SOMARC (Social Marketing and Change), the Academy for Educational Development, United Way of America, and family planning programs in Egypt, Bangladesh, Pakistan, Jamaica, Thailand, Colombia, Mexico and

Peru. His articles include "Alternative Growth Strategies for Contraceptive Social Marketing Programs, "*Journal of Health Care Marketing,* (June 1988) and "Social Marketing: Its Potential for Child Survival, "*Academy for Educational Development,* (November 1987).

[AMB] Arnold M. Barban: Advertising.

Arnold M. Barban is Professor of Advertising in the School of Communication, The University of Alabama. He has co-authored four books in the field of advertising: *Readings in Advertising and Promotion Strategy,* 1968; *Advertising Media Sourcebook and Workbook,* 2nd edition, 1981; *Advertising: Its Role in Modern Marketing,* 6th edition, 1986; and *Essential of Media Planning,* 2nd edition, 1987. He served as President of the American Academy of Advertising in 1981-82, and was selected by that organization in 1986 as a Fellow; he is a member of the editorial boards of the *Journal of Advertising* and *Journal of Advertising* and *Current Issues and Research in Advertising;* is listed in "American Men and Women of Science" and "Who's Who in America." He currently is a member of the Council of Judges of the Advertising Hall of Fame.

[DJB/BJL] Donald J. Bowersox and Bernard J. LaLonde: Physical Distribution.

Dr. Bowersox is Professor of Marketing and Logistics at the Graduate School of Business Administration, Michigan State University. He is the author or co-author of seven textbooks and over 100 articles on marketing, transportation and logistics. He is a recipient of the Distinguished Service Award presented by the Council of Logistics Management.

Dr. Bernard J. La Londe is author or co-author of a number of books and is a frequent contributor to professional journals and the trade press. He has consulted for more than 40 *Fortune 500* companies, and lectured in Canada, Europe, Japan, and Australia. Founding editor of the *Journal of Business Logistics,* he has received a number of awards for his contributions to education and research, including the Council of Logistics Management's Distinguished Service Award.

[VPB] Victor P. Buell: Organization.

Victor P. Buell is author of *Organizing for Marketing/Advertising Success,* three marketing management books, an award winning *Journal of Marketing* article on product management organization, and editor of the *Handbook of Modern Marketing* containing six chapters on organization. He conducted two in-depth marketing organization studies for member companies of the Association of National Advertisers. He lectures and consults on the subject. Professor of marketing emeritus, University of Massachusetts, he is the former head of marketing for three major international corporations, former consultant with McKinsey & Company, and past president of the American Marketing Association.

[GAC] Gilbert A. Churchill: Marketing Research.

Gilbert A. Churchill, Jr. is the Donald C. Slichter Professor in Business Research at the University of Wisconsin-Madison. Professor Churchill was named Distinguished Marketing Educator by the American Marketing Association in 1986, only the second individual so honored; the award recognizes and honors a living marketing educator for distinguished service and outstanding contributions in the field of marketing education. He is a past recipient of the William O'Dell award for the outstanding article appearing in the *Journal of Marketing Research* during the year, and has also been a finalist for the award three other times. He is a past editor of the *Journal of Marketing Research* and is author of two leading books for marketing research: *Basic Marketing Research* and *Marketing Research: Methodological Foundations,* 4th ed., 1987, both by Dryden Press.

[DC] Dorothy Cohen: Marketing Legislation/Social Responsibility.

Dorothy Cohen served as Vice President of Public Policy for the American Marketing Association. She has written a column for the Legal Developments of Marketing section of the *Journal of Marketing* for every issue since 1963, and contributed to the "Legal News" column in the *Marketing News for many years.* She is the author of numerous articles on legal issues which have influenced both policy changes at the Federal Trade Commission and programs developed by the European Economic Community to eliminate misleading advertising. She is the co-author of *Modern Marketing* and the author of *Consumer Behavior* and *Advertising.*

[CMC] C. Merle Crawford: Product/Product Development.

C. Merle Crawford is Professor of Marketing at The University of Michigan. He has also served 10 years in industry in marketing research and product management. He was the Charter President of the Product Development and Management Association, and was twice elected vice-president of AMA. He is currently co-editor of Journal of *Product Innovation and Management,* and is the author of *New Products Management,* 2nd edition, 1987.

[WRD] William R. Davidson: Marketing Institutions (Wholesale/Retail).

William R. Davidson is co-founder and Chairman of the Executive Committee of Management Horizons, a division of Price Waterhouse. He was formerly Professor and Chairman of The Department of Marketing at The Ohio State University and has been a Visiting Professor at Harvard and Stanford Universities. He is a coauthor of *Marketing* and *Retailing Management* and is the author or co-author of more than 100 papers, monographs, or articles in professional or trade publications. He is past President of the American Marketing Association.

[GSD] George S. Day: Strategic Marketing.

George S. Day, Magna International Professor of Business Strategy, University of Toronto, has written extensively on strategic marketing topics, including books on *Strategic*

Market Planning, 1984; and the *Strategy and Marketing,* 1988; and has a forthcoming book, *Competing for Markets.* He consults extensively on strategy issues for companies and has taught on more than 250 executive development programs.

[DLH] David L. Huff: Geography.

David L. Huff is the Century Club Professor of Business Administration at the University of Texas at Austin. He is a specialist in the geographical dimensions of marketing. He has pioneered work on consumer spatial behavior, location decisions, and market area analysis. His publications on these subjects are quoted widely.

[HHK] Harold H. Kassarjian: Consumer Behavior.

Harold H. Kassarjian is a professor of Marketing at the Anderson Graduate School of Management at the University of California, Los Angeles. An author of numerous articles and several books, he has served as editor of the *Journal of Consumer Research,* and president of the Association for Consumer Research.

[WJK] Warren J. Keegan: Global Marketing.

Warren J. Keegan is Professor of International Business and Marketing at Pace University. He is the author of *Global Marketing Management,* 4th Ed., *Multinational Marketing Management,* 3rd Ed., and *Judgements, Choices, and Decisions: Effective Management Through Self-Knowledge,* and has published numerous articles in such journals as *Harvard Business Review, Journal of Marketing,* and *Journal of International Business Studies.* Through his consulting firm, he specializes in assisting clients in global competitive strategy formulation and implementation.

[WL] William Lazer: Environments.

Dr. William Lazer is the Eugene and Christine Lynn, Eminent Scholar in Business Administration at Florida Atlantic University and has served on the faculties of Michigan State University, University of Manitoba, Canada, and the University of Louvain, Belgium. He has published eleven books, and over 140 articles and monographs for professional journals and business periodicals. He is one of only two Honorary Advisors to the Japan Marketing Association and has lectured at scores of universities and educational institutions throughout the world. Dr. Lazer was a member of the Presidential Blue Ribbon Committee on Trade Negotiations under two U.S. Presidents and has served as Chairman of the Census Advisory Committee (Marketing). He was an advisor to the Office of the U.S. Price (Commissioner during Phase II, a delegate to the White House Summit Conference on Inflation and to the White House Conference on the Industrial World of the 1990's.

[GLL/DTW] Gary L. Lilien and David T. Wilson: Organizational Marketing.

Gary L. Lilien is Research Professor of Management Science in the College of Business Administration at Penn State University and Co-founder and Research Director of Penn State's Institute for the Study of Business Markets. He is the author of four books and over fifty articles, mainly in the area of business or organizational marketing.

David T. Wilson is Professor of Marketing, Co-founder and Managing Director of the Institute for the Study of Business Markets at The Pennsylvania State University. He has published over fifty articles and several books on business to business marketing. He is Vice-President of the Business Marketing division of AMA, for 1988-89.

[KM] Kent Monroe: Pricing.

Kent B. Monroe (D.B.A., Illinois) is Robert O. Goodykoontz Professor of Marketing, Virginia Polytechnic Institute and State University, Blacksburg, Virginia. He has pioneered research on the information value of price and has chapters on pricing in the text *Modern Marketing Management*, 1980; in *Marketing Handbook, Vol. 2, Marketing Management*, 1985; and in *Handbook of Modern Marketing*, 1986. He is the author of *Pricing: Making Profitable Decisions*, 1979. He has served as a consultant and regularly conducts executive education programs on pricing.

[JRN] John R. Nevin: Channels of Distribution.

John R. Nevin holds the title of Wisconsin Distinguished professor at the University of Wisconsin-Madison. He has been an active teacher and researcher in channels of distribution for approximately fifteen years. His research on the behavioral and legal aspects of channel relations has appeared in such journals as the *Journal of Macromarketing, Journal of Marketing* and the *Journal of Marketing Research*. Professor Nevin is on the Editorial Board of the *Journal of Marketing*. He has also served as consultant or expert witness for many organizations.

[JPP/JCO] J. Paul Peter and Jerry C. Olson: Consumer Behavior.

J. Paul Peter is James R. McManus-Bascom Professor in Marketing at the University of Wisconsin-Madison. He has published a variety of articles on consumer behavior, marketing theory, and research methodology. One of his papers received the William O'Dell Award from the *Journal of Marketing Research* in 1986. He has coauthored several textbooks including *Consumer Behavior: Marketing Strategy Perspectives A., Preface to Marketing Management, Marketing Management: Knowledge and Skills,* and *Strategic Management: Concept and Applications:* he is on the Editorial Review Boards of the *Journal of Marketing Research* and *Journal of Consumer Research*.

Jerry C. Olson is Professor and Chairman of Marketing and Binder Faculty Fellow in the College of Business Administration at Penn State University. He is co-author with J. Paul Peter of *Consumer Behavior: Marketing Strategy Perspectives* and has edited 3 other books on consumer behavior. He has served as President of the Association for Consumer Research. Professor Olson holds a Ph.D. in Consumer Psychology from Purdue University.

[DCS/YJW] David C. Schmittlein and Yoram J. Wind: Marketing Models.

Dr. Schmittlein's research concerns the development and application of models that improve marketing decisions. Since 1980 his research has appeared in major journals in Marketing (e.g., *Marketing Science, Journal of Consumer Research*), (*Management Science, Operations Research*), (*The Rand Journal of Economics, Journal of Business and Economic Statistics*) (*Journal of the American Statistical Association, The American Statistician*). He is an area editor for *Marketing Science* and editorial board member for the *Journal of Marketing Research*.

Jerry Wind is The Lauder Professor and Professor of Marketing. He has served as editor-in-chief of the *Journal of Marketing*, the policy boards of *Journal of Consumer Research* and *Marketing Science*, and served on the editorial boards of all major marketing journals. He is a regular contributor to the marketing literature (including 10 books and 200 papers and articles) encompassing marketing strategy, research and modeling. He has been an active consultant to many Fortune 500 firms utilizing marketing research and modeling. Dr. Wind is also the recipient of various awards, including the prestigious Charles Coolidge Parlin Award.

[DES] Don E. Schultz: Sales Promotion/Public Relations.

Don E. Schultz is Professor of Advertising and Director of the Graduate Program in Direct Marketing at Northwestern University's Medill School of Journalism. He was also instrumental in the development and design of Medill's graduate program in Corporate Public Relations. He is the author of several texts in the areas of advertising and sales promotion, including *Sales Promotion Management, Essentials of Sales Promotion, Strategic Advertising Campaigns, and Essentials of Advertising Strategy*. He is a frequent lecturer and consultant on advertising, sales promotion, and overall promotional campaign strategy for companies in the U.S. and Europe.

[DLS] Donald L. Shawver: Economic Terms.

Professor Emeritus Donald L. Shawver received his Ph.D. in Economics from the University of Illinois in 1951. He taught marketing to more than 20,000 students during five decades, from the 40's through the 80's. He served the American Marketing Association four years as Secretary-Treasurer, three years as Book Review Editor, and three years as Editor of Professional Publications.

[OCW] Orville C. Walker: Sales Management.

Orville Walker is Professor of Marketing at the University of Minnesota. Among his teaching and research interests are marketing management and sales management. He is the co-author of the books *Sales Force Management* and *Sales Force Performance* and has published a number of articles in the *Journal of Marketing Research*, Journal of Marketing, and Journal of Business Research. Among his current research interests are the determinants of motivation and performance among salespeople, and the design of incentive programs to improve the productivity of marketing and sales personnel.

[BAW] Barton A. Weitz: Sales.

Barton A. Weitz holds the J.C. Penney Eminent Scholar Chair at the University of Florida. Prior to his present position, Dr. Weitz has held a variety of sales and marketing management positions for high technology firms and has been a member of the marketing faculty at UCLA and the Wharton School. Dr. Weitz's research on personal selling and sales management has been published in leading marketing journals, and he is the coauthor of one of the most widely used personal selling textbooks, *Selling: Principles and Methods*. In addition to his academic achievements, Dr. Weitz has participated in a wide variety of sales management executive education programs including programs sponsored by Northwestern University, the Wharton School, AT&T and General Electric.

The bulk of the work of this group took place from 1985 to 1988, with Peter D. Bennett, Pennsylvania State University, acting as editor and task force chairman. Specifically, the steps involved in the preparation of the final product included the following:

1. The editor began with the 1,600-plus terms of the 1980 task force. From this, some terms were eliminated which were either redundant, or not in the domain of marketing. To this were added terms utilizing the "subject index" of several marketing texts.
2. The contributors selected for each sub-area took the list from their own domain, added and deleted terms until a satisfactory set was established.
3. Once the scope of the work was established, the contributors provided definitions for terms in their domain.
4. The editor was responsible for negotiating and eventually settling any "border disputes" among contributors. (The boundaries were clear in places, and fuzzy in others.) This involved discarding some definitions when two or more persons defined the same term in about the same way. It also resulted in the retention of two or more definitions of the same term when there were more than one meaning. In one case, the definitions of marketing models provided by Jerry Wind and Dave Schmittlein, it was determined that the complexity of the subject matter called for references to the literature for more complete guidance to the reader.
5. The editor was responsible for achieving consistency in format, punctuation conventions, etc. He was not responsible for adding to, subtracting from, nor in any other way changing the meaning of the definitions of terms. All changes went back to the contributors to assure the accuracy of their work. We think the reader will find the final result to be an authoritative source of concise, accurate, and complete definitions of marketing terms. The reader will find it as authoritative as the impressive list of contributors would indicate.

Now that this version of the *Dictionary of Marketing Terms* is complete, it is time for the ongoing language of the discipline and profession to be in the hands of those who practice either or both. We hope our readers will contribute to the next version of this dictionary through their comments, criticism, and suggestions. These can be suggestions for additional terms which should be included, changes in definitions, or others. Such suggestions should be addressed to:

Peter D. Bennett, Editor
Dictionary of Marketing Terms
707J Business Administration Bldg.
Pennsylvania State University
University Park, PA. 16802

As editor of the volume, I am pleased to be able to publicly thank the people who contributed to this work. All members of the marketing discipline/profession owe them a debt of gratitude. My appreciation also to Francesca Van Gorp, AMA's Supervisor of Publishing, for her efforts in putting this volume together.

Peter D. Bennett

abandonment: The discontinuance of a marketed product. Also called product deletion or product elimination. Abandonment may occur at any time from shortly after launch (a new product failure) to many years later. The criterion for this decision is the same as for a new product: net present value of the product's estimated stream of future earnings, both direct and indirect. Simplified heuristics (e.g. number of years without a profit) may be substituted for this criterion. [CMC]

ABC inventory classification: Classification scheme used to implement inventory management strategies. Products are segmented into groups based upon unit sales or some other criterion. (Class A items highest frequency of sales, etc.) Inventory management is then guided by segmentation. [DJB/BJL]

acceptable price range: Those prices that buyers are willing to pay for a good or service (See also **price thresholds**.) [KM]

accessories: Items that are offered in women's apparel stores and department and specialty stores carrying goods for women and include gloves, hosiery, handbags, jewelry, handkerchiefs, scarves, etc. [WRD]

accessory equipment: Portable factory equipment and tools that are used in the production process and do not become part of the finished product. They are generally inexpensive, short-lived, and relatively standardized. Examples are hand tools, lift trucks, office equipment (typewriters, desks). [GLL/DTW]

accommodation desk: A service area in a department store for customer accommodation on such things as wrapping, exchanges or refunds, gift certificates, or stamping parking permits. [WRD]

account: A customer, usually an institution or another organization, that purchases a company's products or services. [BAW]

account classification: The categorization of a salesperson's customers into groups, based on criteria such as potential sales, for the purpose of developing a call plan. Comment: The classification scheme reflects the relative attractiveness of the various customers and is used to direct sales effort. [BAW]

account executive: 1. The person in an advertising agency who acts as the liaison officer and coordinates the activities of the agency as well as maintaining contact with the client (the advertiser). [AMB] **2.** A salesperson who has responsibility for the overall relationship between his or her firm and a few major accounts Comment: Account executives coordinate financial, production, and technical capabilities of their firm to satisfy the needs of their account. [BAW]

account openers: A premium or special promotion item offered to induce the opening of a new account, especially in financial institutions and stores operating on an installment credit basis. [WRD]

account representative: (See **account executive**.) [BAW]

accumulation: A sorting process that brings similar stocks from a number of sources together into a larger homogeneous supply. [JRN]

acquisition: The acquiring by one firm of other technology (process, facility, or material), product rights (trade marks), or entire businesses in order to increase its total sales. The acquisition may be related to the firm's current business (e.g., the acquisition of a competitor, a supplier or a buyer) or may be the unrelated (e.g., the acquisition of an entirely new business). Acquisition is a method of expanding one's product offering by means other than internal development. Any combination that forms one company from two or more previously existing companies is known as a merger. [GSD and CMC]

action program: (See **implementation**).

activity quota: A quota which focuses on the activities in which sales representatives are supposed to engage. Activity quotas attempt to recognize the investment nature of a salesperson's efforts rather than the sales volume outcomes of these activities. Examples of activity quotas include number of letters to potential accounts, number of product demonstrations, number of calls on new accounts, and number of proposals submitted. [OCW]

adaptation pricing policy: A pricing for the rest of the world (row) of adapting home country prices to local competitive and market circumstances. Also known as polycentric pricing policy. [WJK]

adaptive product: Also called adapted product, this market entry acquires its uniqueness by variation on another, morepioneering product. The degree of adaptation is more than trivial (to avoid being an emulative or me-too product) but it varies greatly in significance. [CMC]

adaptive experimentation: An approach (and philosophy) for management decisions, calling for continuous experimentation to establish empirically the market response functions. Most common in direct marketing, it can and has been applied to advertising and other marketing variables. The experiment should reflect the needed variation in stimuli, cost of measuring the results, lost opportunity cost in the non-optimal cells, and management confidence in the base strategy. [DCS/YJW]

ADBUDG: A decision calculus model for the advertising budgeting decision. The model assumes that there is a fixed upper limit of response to saturation advertising, and also assumes that there is a fixed lower limit to response under no advertising for an extended period. Within this range, increases in ad spending increase response and reductions in ad spending lead to a decay in response over time. The model's parameters are calculated using subjective responses to a series of point-estimate questions concerning the likely impact of various advertising spending decisions (Little 1970). The effectiveness of the model's use has been discussed by Chakravarthi, Mitchell and Staelin (1981) and Little and Lodish (1981). For other advertising decision support systems see ADMOD and MEDIAC. [DCS/YJW]

add-ons: In charge accounts, purchasing additional merchandise without paying in full for previous purchases, especially in installment credit selling. [WRD]

additional markdown: An increase of a previous markdown to further lower the selling price. [WRD]

additional markup cancellation: A downward adjustment in price that is offset against an additional markup. [WRD]

additional markup: The adding of another markup to the original markup; the amount of a price increase, especially in stores operating under the retail inventory method of accounting. [WRD]

administered vertical marketing system: A form of vertical marketing system designed to control a line or classification of merchandise as opposed to an entire store's operation. Such systems involve the development of comprehensive programs for specified lines of merchandise. The vertically aligned companies, even though in a non-ownership position, may work together to reduce the total systems cost of such activities as advertising,transportation, and data processing. (See also **corporate vertical marketing system** and **contractual vertical marketing system**.) [WRD]

administrative control: Term applied to studies relying on questionnaires and referring to the speed, cost, and control of the replies, afforded by the mode of administration. [GAC]

ADMOD: A model providing a decision support system for making advertising budget, copy, and media allocation decisions. The model assumes that an advertising campaign of given duration has as its objective specific changes in the cognitions and/or decisions in various consumer market segments. It evaluates the value of any potential media insertion schedule by aggregating over all segments (and individuals within each segment) the projected impact of the schedule for each individual (Aaker 1975). For other advertising decision support systems see ADBUDG and MEDIAC. [DCS/YJW]

adopter categories: Persons or firms which adopt an innovation are often classified into five groups according to the sequence of their adoption of it: (1) Innovators (the first 2-5%); (2) Early adopters (the next 10-15%); Early majority (the next 35%); Late majority (the next 35%); Laggards (the final 5-10%). The numbers are percents of the total number of actual adopters, not of the total adopter categories: number of persons or firms in the market place. There is wide disagreement on the exact portion in each category. [CMC]

adoption process: An ambiguous term sometimes used to refer to a model of stages in the purchase process ranging from awareness to knowledge, evaluation, trial, and adoption. In other cases, it is used as a synonym for the diffusion process. [JPP/JCO]

advalorem duties: A duty or tax that is levied as a percentage of the value of the imported goods. Also known as a tarrif. (See also **tarrif**.) [WJK]

advance dating: Arrangement by which the seller sets a specific future date when the terms of sale become applicable. For example, the order may be placed on January 5, and the goods shipped on January 10 but under the terms "2/10, net 30 as of May 1." In this case, the discount and net periods are calculated from May 1. 'Season Dating' is another name for terms of this kind. [WRD]

advance order: An order placed well in advance of the desired time of shipment. By placing orders in advance of the actual buying season, a buyer is enabled often to get a lower price because he gives the supplier business when the latter would normally be receiving little. [WRD]

advertised brand: Brand that is owned by an organization (usually a manufacturer) that uses a marketing strategy usually involving substantial advertising. An advertised brand is a consumer product, though it need not be, and is contrasted with a private brand, which is not normally advertised heavily. (See also **private brand**.) [CMC]

advertising: Paid, nonpersonal communication through various media by business firms, nonprofit organizations, and individuals who are in some way identified in the advertising message and who hope to inform and/or persuade members of a particular audience; include communication of products, services, institutions, and ideas. [AMB]

advertising agency: An organization that provides a variety of advertising services on behalf of the advertiser. A "full-service" agency typically is engaged in the planning of an advertising campaign —including the setting of objectives and strategies, the research on which the advertising is based, creative services (copy, art, and production), media strategy and tactics, and the overall coordination of advertising with other marketing activities (such as sales promotion); a "limited-service" agency concentrates on one of the major advertising functions (See also **limited-service advertising agency**). [AMB]

advertising appropriation: The strategic decisions involved in deciding how much money should be spent for advertising in order to accomplish a particular task or set of tasks; once an appropriation is established, the advertising "budget" describes how appropriated funds are allocated to various advertising functions, such as by various media, creative approaches, time of year, and the like. [AMB]

advertising budget: (See **advertising appropriation**.)

advertising campaign: The process of analyzing the marketing and communication situations in order to establish objectives and the making of sound strategic decisions that can be carried out by designing a series of advertisements and commercials and placing them in the various advertising media; includes advertising that is run over a particular period of time (e.g., one year) in which there is a similarity of appeals and/or executions. [AMB]

Advertising Council: A nonprofit organization composed of advertisers, advertising agencies, and advertising media whose purpose is to organize and carry out public service advertising campaigns. The council decides which public service programs will be supported; volunteer agencies create the advertising campaign and media donate space and time in which the advertising is run. [AMB]

advertising effectiveness: The process of determining whether or not advertising campaigns and individual advertisements have accomplished stated objectives; a variety of test measures are used that attempt to determine audience reaction in terms of communication and sales effects. (See also **inquiry tests**, **readership tests**, and **recall tests**). [AMB]

advertising exposure: (See **exposure**.)

advertising manager: Participates in the development of marketing plans; acts as the principal contact with the advertising agency; provides the agency with market and product data and budget guidelines; and critiques the agency's creative and media recommendations at the time of (or prior to) their submission to marketing management. The advertising manager normally reports to the corporate or Division marketing manager. Comment: Many consumer packaged goods companies with product manager setups do not have an advertising manager; rather the functions listed above are performed by product or brand managers for their assigned products. If, in such setups, there is an advertising manager, this executive usually is limited to providing expert counsel and services to the product managers. [VPB]

advertising media: The channels through which the advertising message is carried to the audience. Media "types" include newspapers, magazines, direct mail, radio, television, outdoor, and transit; a "vehicle" is the specific publication or program in which the advertisement/commercial appears (such as *The New York Times* newspaper). [AMB]

advertising messages: The visual and verbal communication aspects of advertising; often referred to as the "creative" facet of advertising. [AMB]

advertising models: Large numbers of models have been used to assist in making advertising decisions. Econometric and other market models, as well as decision calculus models such as ADBUDG, have been used in the determination of advertising budgets. Media selection and scheduling models have included linear and nonlinear programming-type models, such as MEDIAC, and decision calculus models. Few models, such as Aaker's ADMOD (1975), have been designed to deal simultaneously with budget, copy, and media allocation decisions. [DCS/YJW]

advertising objectives: Statement of what the advertising program is to accomplish, either at a particular point in time or over a designated time period. Objectives can be stated, for example, in terms of sales (or the equivalent of sales for nonprofit advertisers), but also can be stated on a nonsales basis, such as communication (e.g., want an audience to have a certain level of "awareness" of the advertised product, service, or idea). Objectives, or "goals," are also established for the various functions of advertising, such as message (or "creative") objectives and media objectives. [AMB]

advertising, regulation of: Under the Wheeler Lea Amendment to the Federal Trade Commission Act, unfair or deceptive acts or practices (which include advertising) are prohibited. Besides the FTC, the Alcohol Tobacco and Tax Division of the Internal Revenue Service, the FCC, the FDA, the SEC, and the U.S. Postal Service are involved in regulating advertising. [DC]

ADVISOR: A descriptive model explaining the level of marketing communication expenditures for industrial products. Two of the more important explanatory variables are the size of the product (i.e., dollar sales in the previous year) and the number of potential customers that the marketing effort is to reach (Lilien 1979). [DCS/YJW]

advocacy advertising: A type of nonproduct advertising that communicates a controversial viewpoint. [AMB]

affiliated store: A store operated as a unit of a voluntary chain or franchise group. Also, a store controlled by another store but operated under a separate name. [WRD]

affinities: Retail stores that naturally have a tendency to be located in close proximity to one another. For example, furniture stores in a city may be located in close proximity to one another in order to facilitate consumer comparison shopping. [WRD]

after sales support: Services offered by the selling firm after the sale has been made to promote goodwill, ensure customer satisfaction, and develop customer loyalty. Comment: This requires a salesperson to monitor order processing, to ensure proper installation and initial use of products, to provide maintenance, repair services and information on the care and use of products. [BAW]

after-market: Potential future sales generated by owners of equipment for repair and replacement parts. [DLS]

agency costs: The dollar reduction in welfare experienced by the principal due to the inherent nature of the agency relationship with management. [PFA]

agency theory: A theory of the firm which seeks to explain corporate activities as arising out of the natural conflicts between the principals (stockholders) and agents (managers) of a firm. [PFA]

agent: 1. A business unit which negotiates purchases, sales, or both but does not take title to the goods in which it deals. 2. A person agent: who represents his principal (who, in the case of retailing, is the store or merchant) and who acts under authority, whether in buying or in bringing his principal into business relations with third parties. (See also **sales agent**.) [WRD]

agents and brokers: Independent middlemen (intermediaries) who do not take title to the goods they handle, but do actively negotiate the purchase or sale of their goods for their clients. [JRN]

aggregation: A concept of market segmentation that assumes that all consumers are alike. Retailers adhering to the concept focus on common dimensions of the market rather than uniqueness and the strategy is to focus on the broadest possible number of buyers by an appeal to universal product themes. Reliance is on mass distribution, mass advertising, and a universal theme of low price. [WRD]

aging: 1. In retailing, aging is the length of time merchandise has been in stock. 2. The aging of certain products is part of the curing— tobacco, liquor, cheese. [WRD]

agricultural advertising: (See **business advertising**.)

AIDA: An approach to understanding how advertising and selling supposedly works. The assumption is that the consumer passes through several steps in the influence process. First Attention must be developed, to be followed by Interest, Desire, and finally Action as called for in the message. Another, but similar scheme, was developed by Lavidge and Steiner in 1961, later to be dubbed the AIDA: Hierarchy of Effects Model by Palda in 1966. This approach involves the hierarchy of effects: Awareness, Knowledge, Liking, Preference, Conviction, and final Purchase in that order. Note the similarity to the adoption process. (See also **formula selling**.) [HHK]

AIO: An acronym standing for activities, interest, and opinions. AIO measures are the primary method for investigating consumer lifestyles and forming psychographic segments. (See also **psychographic analysis**.) [JPP/JCO]

Airline Deregulation Act (1978):   Ended classical economic regulation of the airline industry by gradually phasing out price and entry controls and eventually abolishing the Civil Aeronautics Board. [DC]

aisle table: A table in a major store aisle, between departments, used to feature special promotional values. [WRD]

all-purpose revolving account: A regular 30-day charge account which if paid in full within 30 days from date of statement has no service charge. But when installment payments are made, a service charge is made on the balance at the time of the next billing. [WRD]

all-you-can-afford budgeting: Advertising appropriation method that establishes the amount to be spent for advertising by first allocating all other unavoidable investments and expenditures. [AMB]

alliances: The pooling of complementary resources by two firms in an arrangement that falls short of a full merger or acquisition. They typically involve coordinated activity from very early in the process of new technology development. [GSD]

allocation: A sorting process which consists of breaking a homogeneous supply down into smaller and smaller lots. [JRN]

alteration cost: Net cost of altering goods for customers and stock repair. Includes labor, supplies, and all expenses including costs for this service when purchased outside the store. [WRD]

alteration room (department):   A section, run in conjunction with one or more selling departments, that alters merchandise to customers' wishes, especially for men's and women's apparel. [WRD]

analysis of variance (ANOVA):   Statistical test employed with interval data to determine if $k(k>2)$ samples came from populations with equal means. [GAC]

analytic hierarchy process (AHP):   A three-step process for making resource allocation decisions. First, the organization's objectives, subobjectives and strategies are organized hierarchically. Next, the decision maker evaluates, in a pairwise fashion, each of the elements in a particular stratum of the hierarchy with respect to its importance in accomplishing each of the elements of the next-higher stratum. Finally a model is applied to these pairwise judgments, which produces a set of importance (or priority) weights for each element of each stratum in the hierarchy (Wind and Saaty 1980). Areas of application in marketing include the product portfolio decision, selection of new products to develop, and generation and evaluation of various marketing mix strategies. [DCS/YJW]

anchor store: Usually a large and well known retail operation located in a shopping center and serving as an attracting force for consumers to the center. [WRD]

ancillary services: Such include layaway, gift wrap, credit, and any service that is not directly related to the actual sale of a specific product within the store. Some of these services are charged for and some are not. [WRD]

Anti-Merger Act (1950): Commonly called the Celler-Kefauver Act, this act amends the Clayton Act to prohibit mergers and acquisitions in restraint of competition by the purchase of assets as well as stocks. [DC]

anticipation: A discount in addition to the cash discount if a bill is paid prior to the expiration of the cash discount period, usually at the rate of 6% per annum—e.g., at this rate, for 60 days prepayment which is 1/6 of an interest year, the anticipation ratio would be 1% of the face amount. [WRD]

antitrust laws: Federal antitrust policy is set forth in four laws: the Sherman Act, the Clayton Act, the Federal Trade Commission Act and the Robinson Patman Act. These laws are negative in character and outlaw restraints of trade, monopolizing, attempting to monopolize, unfair methods of competition, and, where they may substantially lessen competition or tend to create a monopoly, price discrimination, exclusive dealing and mergers. [DC]

AOG: An acronym for arrival of goods. Applicable to the cash discount period indicating that the discount will be granted if payment is made within the number of days specified, calculated from the time the goods arrive at the destination; used for the purpose of accommodating distantly located customers. Net payment period, however, is computed from the time of shipment. [WRD]

apothecary: In America, until recent times, the word referred to a compounder of drugs; predecessor of pharmacy or pharmacist. [WRD]

approach, sales: The initial stage in a sales interaction. Comment: The objectives of the approach are to secure approval for the sales call and build rapport with the customer. [BAW]

approval sale: A sale subject to later approval or selection; the customer having unlimited return privileges. [WRD]

apron: A form attached to invoice or copy of purchase order in retail stores, containing details to check before payment; sometimes called "rider". [WRD]

arbitrage: The simultaneous purchase and sale of the same commodity or security in two different markets in an attempt to profit from price differences in the two markets. [DLS]

arbitrage pricing theory (APT): A theory which states that the expected return on any asset or security is given by the following formula:

$$E_a = E_0 + (E_{p1} - E_0)\beta_{a1} + E_{(p2} - E_0)\beta_{a2} + \ldots + (E_{pk} - E_0)\beta_{ak}$$

where

$$E_a = \text{the expected return on an asset a,}$$

$$E_0 = \text{the expected return on a riskless asset,}$$

$$\beta_{a1} \ldots \beta_{ak} = \text{the beta coefficients for each of the k factors, and}$$

$$E_{p1} \ldots E_{pk} = \text{the expected returns on portfolios of securities which have a beta}$$
coefficient of 1 when regressed on the kth factor and a beta of zero on all others.

The APT is designed as a replacement for the untestable CAPM. In essence, the APT says that asset returns are a linear function of various macroeconomic factors (e.g., industrial production, the spread between long and short interest rates, expected and unexpected inflation, the spread between high- and low-grade bonds, etc.). At the present time the model's empirical validity, testability, and the number and identity of its return generating factors are controversial issues in financial economics. [PFA]

arcade shopping center: Enclosed shopping area with a number of stores in lanes under archways, with lanes, and one roof overhead. [WRD]

area of dominant influence (ADI): Arbitron Ratings Company geographic area comprising those counties in which broadcast stations of the originating market account for a greater share of the viewing households than those from any other market [similar to A. C. Nielsen's Designated Market Area (DMA)]; each county in the U.S. is assigned exclusively to a particular television market. [AMB]

area sampling: Form of cluster sampling in which areas (for example, census tracts, blocks) serve as the primary sampling units. The population is divided into mutually exclusive and exhaustive areas using maps, and a random sample of areas is selected. If all the households in the selected areas are used in the study, it is one-stage area sampling, while if the areas themselves are subsampled with respect to households, the procedure is two-stage area sampling. [GAC]

artificial intelligence (AI): Area of computer science concerned with designing smart computer systems. AI systems exhibit the characteristics generally associated with intelligence in human learning, reasoning, and solving problems. [DJB/BJL]

as is: Merchandise offered for sale without recourse to an adjustment or a refund. The goods may be "irregulars," shop-worn, or damaged, but that is understood. [WRD]

aspirational group: A reference group that an individual consumer wants to join or be similar to. [JPP/JCO]

assemblers: Establishments engaged primarily in purchasing farm products or seafoods in growers' markets or producing regions. They usually purchase in relatively small quantities, concentrate large supplies, and thus assemble economical shipments for movement into major wholesale market centers. [WRD]

ASSESSOR: A model for predicting the market share of a new frequently purchased product using pre-test market information. Perceptions and preferences of potential customers are measured via interview and a simulated shopping experience conducted at a central location. The prediction is based on the sample participants' reaction to advertising (exposure to ads for several brands), estimated level of product trial (based on the simulated shopping experience), estimated repeat purchase level (via follow-up interview) and brand preference judgments (Silk and Urban 1978). Evidence on the model's predictive validity has been reported by Urban and Katz (1983). For other models predicting sales of new products see LITMUS, NEWS, SPRINTER MOD III and TRACKER. [DCS/YJW]

assignment: Formal transfer of property, as for benefit of creditors, especially accounts receivable as collateral for a loan. [WRD]

associated buying office: A type of resident buying office that is cooperatively maintained in a central market by a group of non-competing independent stores. It is controlled and financed by the stores, each store paying its prorated share of the office expenses. (See also **resident buying office**.) [WRD]

Association of South East Asian Nations (A.S.E.A.N.):   An association of countries established in 1967 at Bankok, Thailand, to accelerate economic progress and to increase the stability in the South East Asian region. [WJK]

assorting: A sorting process which consists of building an assortment of products for use in association with each other. [JRN]

assortment: 1. (Retailing) The range of choice offered to the consumer within a particular classification of merchandise. In terms of men's shirts, for example, the range of prices, styles, colors, patterns, and materials that is available for customer selection. The range of choice among substitute characteristics of a given type of article. [WRD] 2. (Other) A combination of similar and/or complementary products that, taken together, have some definite purpose for providing benefits to specific markets. [JRN]

atmospherics: Store architecture, layout, lighting, color scheme, temperature, access, noise, assortment, prices, special events, etc., that serve as stimuli and attention attractors of consumers to a retail store. [WRD]

attention: The point at which a consumer becomes aware or conscious of particular stimuli in the environment. [JPP/JCO]

attitude: A cognitive process involving positive or negative valences, feelings or emotion. An attitude toward an object always involves a stirred-up state—a positive or negative feeling or motivational component. It is an interrelated system of cognition, feelings, and action tendencies. [HHK]

attitude models: (See **multiattribute attitude models**.)

attraction model: A market share model that predicts a particular brand's market share as the quotient of that brand's "attraction" divided by the sum of the "attraction" level for all brands in the market. The attraction level for a brand is often in turn expressed as a function of customer characteristics, the marketing mix, and the competitive environment. Conditions under which an attraction model can be expected to hold have been described by Bell, Keeney and Little (1975). [DCS/YJW]

attribute: (See **product attributes**.)

auction company: Business establishment engaged in selling merchandise on an agency basis by the auction method. [WRD]

auction: A market in which goods are sold to the highest bidder; usually well publicized in advance or held at specific times well-known in the trade. Exchange is effected in accordance with definite rules, with sales made to the highest bidder. [WRD]

audience: The total number of persons or households who are exposed to an advertising medium or medium vehicle. [AMB]

audience accumulation: The total number of different persons or households exposed to an advertising media vehicle over a given period of time; used primarily to measure audience delivery in the same media vehicle over time, in contrast to the delivery obtained from insertions in different media vehicles. [AMB]

audience duplication: The total number of persons or households who are exposed more than once to the same advertising media vehicle over time or to different media vehicles. [AMB]

audimeter: An electronic metering device of the A. C. Nielsen Company used to measure when a television set is on, to what channel it is tuned, and how long the set is tuned to a specific channel. [AMB]

Audit Bureau of Circulations (ABC):   An organization sponsored by advertisers, advertising agencies, and print media publishers that audits and verifies circulation figures claimed by newspapers and magazines; auditing is limited to publications that meet prescribed ABC standards, in particular a requirement of a certain percentage of "paid" circulation. ABC also develops standards for reporting various aspects of a publication's circulation. [AMB]

audited sales: Reconciliation of daily cash and charge sales against the recorded total on cash register. Accomplished in a back office procedure at the end of the day. [WRD]

auditing (post and pre):   Transportation freight bills are checked to assure billing accuracy. A preaudit determines the proper rate and charges prior to payment of a freight bill. Postaudits make the same determination after payment. [DJB/BJL]

augmented product: The view of a product which includes not only its core benefit and its physical being, but adds other sources of benefits such as service, warranty, and image. The augmented aspects are added to the physical product by action of the seller, e.g. with company reputation or with service. [CMC]

authorized dealer: A dealer who has a franchise to sell a manufacturer's product. He is usually the only dealer or one of a few selected dealers in a trading area. [WRD]

authorizing: The process by which credit sales are approved either through a telephone system from the selling floor to the credit office or by an automated system tied into a point-of-sale system. [WRD]

automated guided vehicle system (AGVS):   A material handling system that does not require a driver. The AGVS is automatically routed and positioned at destination by an optical or magnetic guidance system. [DJB/BJL]

automated storage and retrieval equipment (ASAR):   Automated unit-load handling system using high-rise, structured steel vertical racks. Material-handling productivity is improved and provides maximum storage density per square foot of floor space and minimizes the direct labor required for handling. [DJB/BJL]

automated teller machine: The use of special cards by consumers to make deposits, withdraw cash or transfer funds via electronic funds transfer. [WL]

automatic reorder:　The reorder of staple merchandise on the basis of predetermined minimum stock and specified reorder quantities without the intervention of the buyer except for periodic revision of items to be carried and the minimum and reorder quantities; can be handled manually by reorder clerks or automatically by computer methods. [WRD]

automatic selling:　The retail sale of goods or services through coin-or-currency-operated machines activated by the ultimate consumer-buyer. [WRD]

Automobile Information Disclosures Act (1958):　Mandates the display of various kinds of information on every new automobile including the suggested price of the car and of all optional equipment, and transportation costs. [DC]

autonomic decision making:　A pattern of decision making within a family in which an equal number of decisions are made individually by each spouse. [JPP/JCO]

average fixed cost:　Total fixed cost divided by the number of units produced and sold. [KM]

average revenue (AR):　Total revenue divided by the number of units marketed. [DLS]

average total cost:　Total cost divided by the number of units produced and sold. [KM]

average variable cost:　Total variable cost divided by the number of units produced and sold. [KM]

awareness-trial-repeat (A-T-R):　A paradigm consisting of three key steps by the intended user; the steps take the person or firm from a state of ignorance about a new product to the point of product adoption. Awareness (cognition) may be of the product generally, its brand, and one or more of its attributes. Trial means some form of test purchase or use, following upon favorable affect stemming from knowledge regarding the attributes. Repeat means the trial was sufficiently successful to warrant one or more repeat purchases. There are other, similar, paradigms, for example "attention, interest, desire, action", but these are not new product specific, and do not cover the entire product adoption process. (See also **product adoption process** and **AIDA**.) [CMC]

back haul: 1. Rerouting a freight shipment back over a route that it has completed. 2. Using a firm's empty delivery equipment to haul back purchases of merchandise from suppliers who are located near customer destinations. [WRD]

back order: A part of an order that the vendor has not filled on time and that he intends to ship as soon as the goods in question are received, manufactured, or procured. [WRD]

back-haul provision: Current transportation regulation authorizes a freight allowance for customer pick up of specific commodities rather than delivered pricing. This provision often increases utilization of transportation capacity. [DJB/BJL]

back-order: An order not filled or shipped at time originally requested and "kept on the books" to be shipped later. [DJB/BJL]

backdoor selling: 1. Sales to ultimate consumers by wholesalers who hold themselves out to be sellers only to retailers. 2. A salesperson's practice of avoiding a purchasing agent by visiting departments in plants to obtain orders without authorization from the purchasing agent. [WRD]

backward integration: (See **integration**).

bait advertising: An alluring but insincere offer to sell; part of a plan or scheme whereby the advertiser does not intend to sell the advertised product at the advertised price; purpose is to increase customer traffic. Also called "Bait and Switch Advertising". [WRD]

bait (and switch) advertising: Offering a product at an unusually low price to entice buyers to the store, where they may find it difficult or impossible to buy the product at the advertised price (and will instead be switched to a higher priced item). [AMB]

bait and switch: A deceptive sales practice whereby a low- priced product is advertised to lure customers to a store, who are then induced to buy higher priced models by disparaging the less-expensive product. [DC]

balance of payments: A record of all the economic transactions between a country and the rest of the world. For the world as a whole, theoretically, imports must equal exports. The balance of payments can be divided into the so called "current" and "capital" accounts. The current account is for goods and services, the capital account is for money and investments. [WJK]

balanced stock: The offering of merchandise in the colors, sizes, styles, and other assortment characteristics that will satisfy customer wants. [WRD]

barriers to competition: Economic, legal, technical, psychological, or other factors that reduce competitive rivalry below the level that would otherwise occur naturally. Included are branding, advertising, patents, entry restrictions, tariffs and quotas. Product differentiation is a barrier to competition. [WL]

barriers to entry: Economic, legal, psychological, technical and other forces which limit access to markets and hence, reduce the threat of new competition. (See also **barriers to competition.**) [WL]

barter: 1. (advertising) The practice of selling time or space in an advertising medium in return for merchandise or other nonmonetary returns. "Syndicated" barter involves a national advertiser providing a local television station with a program in which a certain number of the advertiser's commercials are included; the local station can then sell the remaining commercial positions to other advertisers. [AMB] 2. (international) A type of trade transaction where there is a direct exchange of goods or services between two parties. Although no money is involved, both partners construct an approximate shadow price for products flowing in each direction, without the use of money; e.g., A West German company sells a $60 million steel making complex to Indonesia and is paid in 3,000,000 barrels of Indonesian oil. (The shadow price of the oil would thus be $20 per barrel. [WJK]

basement store: A department store division which is organized separately from the main store departments (not necessarily located in a basement), handles merchandise in lower price lines, features frequent bargain sales, purchases and offers considerable distress or job-lot merchandise, and usually offers a much more limited range of services and breadth of assortment than main store departments. [WRD]

basic low stock: The lowest level of stock judged permissible for an item; indicates a conception of the smallest number of units that could be on hand without losing sales at the lowest sales period of the year or season. [WRD]

basic stock lists: An assortment plan for staple items which are continuously maintained in stock; usually for a period of a year or more. [WRD]

basing-point pricing: A variation of delivered pricing. The delivered price is the product's list price plus transportation from a basing point to the buyer. The basing point is a city where the product is produced. But, in basing-point pricing the product may be shipped from a city other than the basing point. [KM]

BCG matrix: (See **growth-share matrix**).

behavioral analysis: A Sales Management evaluation and control method for monitoring sales force performance. A behavioral analysis involves evaluating the actual behavior of salespeople as well as their ultimate performance in terms of sales volume. Examples of behavioral analysis techniques include self-rating scales, supervisor ratings and field observations. [OCW]

behavioral intention: A cognitive plan created through a choice/decision process that focuses on performing an action, e.g., "I intend to go shopping later." [JPP/JCO]

belief: A cognition or cognitive organization about some aspect of the individual's world. Unlike an attitude, a belief is always emotionally or motivationally neutral. Krech and Crutchfield define belief as a generic term that encompasses Knowledge, Opinion, and Faith - an enduring organization of perceptions and cognition about some aspect of the individual's world. It is the pattern of the meanings of a thing, the cognition about that thing. [HHK]

benefit segmentation: The process of grouping consumers into markets on the basis of different benefits sought from the product. For example, the toothpaste market may include one segment seeking cosmetic benefits such as white teeth and another seeking health benefits such as decay prevention. [JPP/JCO]

benefit, product: The value provided to a customer by a product feature. [BAW]

Bernoulli process: A probabilistic process in which the probability p that an event of interest occurs remains the same over repeated observations. That is, p stays the same over time, and does not depend on the outcome of past observations. This stationary, zero order process has been used to represent brand choice behavior or media viewing behavior by individuals (Greene 1982; Lilien and Kotler 1983). [DCS/YJW]

Beta binomial model: A probability mixture model commonly used to represent patterns of brand choice behavior or media exposure patterns. The model assumes that each individual's behavior follows a Bernoulli process. That is, an individual performs some behavior of interest (e.g., buying a brand of interest) with probability p on each possible opportunity (e.g., occasion on which a purchase is made from the product category of interest). The number of times that the behavior of interest is exhibited, out of a given number of opportunities, has the binomial distribution for any individual. The model further assumes that the probability values p vary across individuals according to a beta distribution (Greene 1982; Massy, Montgomery and Morrison 1970). A generalization of this model to represent choice among more than two items is termed the Dirichlet multinomial model. These models are used to predict future brand choice or media exposure patterns based on individuals' past behavior. [DCS/YJW]

beta coefficient: A measure of the systematic risk (the risk that cannot be diversified away by holding a diversified portfolio) of an asset or security—where the variance of the return distribution is used as the risk surrogate. Beta is generally estimated as the slope coefficient of a linear regression of the asset or security's return on the market's return for some "representative" number of periods:

$$R_{ij} = \alpha_j + \beta_j R_{im}$$

where:

R_{ij} = the return on security j during period i,

α_j = the intercept coefficient for security j,

β_j = the beta coefficient for security j, and

R_{im} = the return on all market securities during period i. [PFA]

better business bureaus: Non-profit organizations sponsored by local businesses. They currently number 150 and offer a variety of consumer education programs and materials, handle consumer inquiries, mediate and arbitrate complaints and maintain records of consumer satisfaction and dissatisfaction with individual companies. [DC]

bid: A legal document in which a seller agrees to provide products and/or services to a potential buyer at specific price under specified conditions. [BAW]

bidding: An invitation to potential suppliers to submit their offers and a price for a particular opportunity. A closed bid is formal, written and sealed, and usually all closed bids are opened and reviewed at the same time, with the contract being awarded to the lowest bidder who meets the specifications. Open bidding is usually more informal and is used when specific requirements are hard to rigidly define or when products vary substantially. [GLL/DTW]

bill of exchange: An unconditional order in writing addressed by one person (the drawer) to another (the drawee), signed by the person giving it, requiring the person to whom it is addressed to pay on demand, or at a fixed or determinable future time, a sum certain in money to, or to the order of, a specified person or to bearer. [WJK]

bill of lading: 1. (physical distribution) The basic document in the purchase of transport services. It describes commodities and quantities shipped as well as the terms and conditions of carrier liability. Current law allows the bill of lading to be electronically generated and transmitted. [DJB/BJL] 2. (international) A vital document in international trade which is required to establish legal ownership and facilitate financial transactions. The Bill of Lading serves the following purposes: (1) as a contract for shipment between the carrier and the shipper; (2) as a receipt from the carrier for shipment; and (3) as a certificate of ownership or title to the goods. [WJK]

bill of materials (BOM): An assessment of the combination of assemblies, subassemblies, parts, and materials needed to support planned production as detailed in the materials requirement plan. [DJB/BJL]

billed cost: The price appearing on a vendor's bill before deducting cash discounts, but after deducting any trade and quantity discounts, from the list price. [WRD]

black market: The availability of merchandise at a higher price when difficult or impossible to purchase it under normal market circumstances; commonly involves illegal transactions. [WRD]

blanket order: A general order placed with a manufacturer without specifying detailed instructions, such as sizes, styles, and shipping dates, all of which are to be furnished later, often in several orders for specific shipments. [WRD]

bleed advertisement: The area of an advertisement that extends beyond the trim mark of the printed page, allowing the background to extend to the edge of the page; no margins or border; generally sold at a premium price. [AMB]

blocked currency: Currency regulated by a government in a manner that precludes it being taken out of the country or converted to other currencies. [DLS]

blunder: Error that arises when editing, coding, key- punching, or tabulating the data. [GAC]

bonded warehouse: A warehouse that is bonded to insure the owners of the stored goods against loss. [WRD]

bonus: A special compensation option which is a payment made at the discretion of management for achieving or surpassing some set level of performance. Whereas commissions are typically paid for each sale that is made, a bonus is typically not paid until the salesperson surpasses some level of total sales or other aspect of performance. When the salesperson reaches the minimum level of performance required to earn a bonus, however, the size of the bonus might be determined by the degree to which he/she exceeds that minimum. Thus, bonuses are usually additional incentives to motivate salespeople to reach high levels of performance rather than as part of the basic compensation plan. [OCW]

bonus pack: A special container, package, carton, or other holder in which the consumer is given more of the product for the same or perhaps even lower price than in the regular container. [DES]

book inventory: An inventory which is compiled by adding units and/or the cost or retail value of incoming goods to previous inventory figures and deducting them from the units and/or cost or retail value of outgoing goods; or the units and/or cost or retail value of goods on hand at any time per the perpetual inventory records. [WRD]

booking: Order-taking, especially for delivery at a later date; frequently the amount of production is based on the booking of advance orders. [WRD]

Boston Consulting Group matrix: (See **growth-share matrix**).

bounce back offer (coupon): A coupon or other selling device included in a customer ordered product, premium, refund or other package which attempts to sell more of the same or another product to the recipient. [DES]

boutique: Actually in French the word means "little shop," but in American retailing the term has come to mean a carefully selected group of merchandise with unusual displays and fixtures; informal and attractive decor; and an atmosphere of individualized attention in the personalized manner of the image created in the operation. (See also **boutique store layout**.) [WRD]

boutique store layout: A form of retail store layout pattern that brings together complete offerings from one vendor or for one use in one section as opposed to having the items in separate departments. For example, a tennis boutique in a department store will feature rackets, balls, shoes, and tennis outfits. [WRD]

Box-Jenkins method: A method for forecasting sales that relies on procedures for identifying models that best fit a set of time series data and statistical tests to examine the adequacy of the fitted models where the models consist of a combination of autoregressive and moving average terms. [GAC]

boycott: A refusal to deal with, or cooperate with a firm or nation to signal extreme disapproval of its policies and actions. Boycotts induce change, as for example, when consumers boycott a retail chain to gain redress for perceived inequities. [WL]

bracket creep: The movement of consumers to higher and higher income tax brackets during periods of inflation regardless of the lack of any real increase in income. This phenomenon is less serious after the 1986 tax reform which greatly reduced the number of tax brackets. [WL]

brainstorming: A group method of problem solving, used in product concept generation. It is sometimes thought to be an open, free-wheeling, idea session, but more correctly is a specific procedure developed by Alex Osborn, with precise rules of session conduct. Now has many modifications in format of use, each variation with its own name. [CMC]

branch house (manufacturer's): An establishment maintained by a manufacturer, separate from the headquarters establishment, and used primarily for the purpose of stocking, selling, delivering, and servicing his product. [WRD]

branch house wholesaler: A national, regional, or sectional wholesaler who operates a number of branches to provide better customer service in all parts of the territory covered; differs from a chain wholesaler in that each branch is closely supervised as an extension of the main wholesale house. [WRD]

branch store: Satellites of a large store, usually administered by the operating executives of the so-called main or parent store. [WRD]

branching question: A technique used to direct respondents to different places in a questionnaire based on their response to the question at hand. [GAC]

brand: A name, term, design, symbol, or any other feature that identifies one seller's good or service as distinct from those of other sellers. The legal term for brand is trademark. A brand may identify one item, a family of items, or all items of that seller. If used for the firm as a whole, the preferred term is trade name. (See also **trademark**, **family brand**, and **individual brand**.) [CMC]

brand choice: The selection of one brand from a set of alternative brands. [JPP/JCO]

brand choice models: Stochastic models of individual brand choice focus on the brand that will be purchased on a particular purchase occasion, given that a purchase event will occur. This type of model includes Bernoulli models and Markov models. Models in this category vary in their treatment of population heterogeneity, purchase event feedback, and exogenous market factors (Lilien and Kotler 1983). [DCS/YJW]

brand development index: A measure of the extent to which the sales of products in a market category have captured the total potential in a geographical area, based on the population of that area and the average consumption per user nationally. The brand development index is usually calculated for separate metropolitan areas, and is used to determine high-potential (under-developed) areas for new product entries or for primary demand promotions. [CMC]

brand extension: A product line extension marketed under the same general brand as a previous item or items. To distinguish the brand extension from the other item(s) under the primary brand, one can either add a secondary brand identification or add a generic. Thus an Epson FX-85 printer is an extension of Epson that used the secondary brand of FX-85, while Jello Instant Pudding is an extension of the Jello brand that uses a generic. A brand extension is usually aimed at another segment of the general market for the overall brand. (See also **family brand** and **individual brand**.) [CMC]

brand generic: The second half of a product's identifying title. Brand is the first half, and identifies one seller's version, while the generic is the second half and identifies the general class of item. [Example: Jello (brand) gelatin dessert (generic).] Not to be confused with generic brands (such as on some low-price items in supermarkets) where there is no individual brand. (See also **generic brands**.) [CMC]

brand image: The perception of a brand in the minds of persons. The image is a mirror reflection (though perhaps inaccurate) of the brand personality or product being. It is what people believe about a brand—their thoughts, feelings, expectations. [CMC]

brand indifference: A purchasing pattern characterized by a low degree of brand loyalty. [JPP/JCO]

brand label: (See **label**.)

brand loyalty: The degree to which a consumer consistently purchases the same brand within a product class. [JPP/JCO]

brand manager: (See **product manager**.)

brand mark: That part of a brand name which cannot be spoken. It most commonly is a symbol, picture, design, distinctive lettering, color, or a combination of these. [CNC]

brand name: That part of a brand which can be spoken. Letters, numbers, or words. The term trademark covers all forms of brand (name, mark, etc.), but brand name is the form most often meant when trademark is used. (See also **brand** and **trademark**.) [CMC]

brand personality: The psychological nature of a particular brand, as intended by its sellers, though persons in the marketplace may see the brand otherwise (called brand image). These two perspectives compare to the personalities of individual humans: what we intend or desire, and what others see or believe. [CMC]

brand positioning: (See **product positioning**.)

brand switching: A purchasing pattern characterized by a change from one brand to another. [JPP/JCO]

brand-switching matrix: Two-way table that indicates which brands a sample of people purchased in one period and which brands they purchased in a subsequent period, thus highlighting the switches occurring among and between brands as well as the number of persons who purchased the same brand in both periods. [GAC]

BRANDAID: A decision support system for determining the marketing mix for a particular brand. The model has submodels dealing with advertising spending level, price, and salesperson effort (i.e., dollars per customer per year). Its parameters can be calibrated by combining historical data (e.g., on sales, market share, advertising spending, etc.) with structured subjective judgments (Little 1975). [DCS/YJW]

branded merchandise: Goods which are identified by brands. Contrasts with generic goods, which are identified only by commodity type. [CNC]

branding, family: (See **family brand**.)

branding, generic: (See **generic brands**.)

branding, individual: Using separate brands for each product, without a family brand to tie them to other brands of that firm. Individual brands are used when the products are different physically, are of different quality levels, are targeted for different users or uses, or vary in some other way that might cause confusion or loss of sales if brought together under a family brand umbrella. (see also **family brand**) [CMC]

branding, line family: Using a family brand to cover only some of a firm's products, in those cases where the term family brand is used only to designate the firm's entire product line. [CMC]

break-bulk: The process of dividing larger quantities into smaller quantities in the transportation-warehousing system as goods get closer to the final market. [DJB/BJL]

break-even analysis: A method of examining the relationships between fixed costs, variable costs, volume, and price. The objective of the analysis is to determine the break-even point at alternative prices and a given cost structure. [KM]

break-even point: The sales volume where total revenues are equal to total costs. [KM]

breaking bulk: (See **allocation**.)

Bretton Woods Agreement: An agreed statement of aims for post-war monetary policy which resulted from an international monetary and financial conference held at Bretton Wood, New Hampshire, in July 1944. Its aims were: (a) to make all currencies freely convertible and thereby encourage multilateral trade; (b) to keep exchange rates stable; (c) to provide some means of assisting a country with temporary difficulties with its balance of payments; and (d) to encourage economic growth and development. [WJK]

broken case lot selling: To accommodate retailers who cannot afford to buy in full shipping case lots, many wholesalers break cases and sell smaller quantities. [WRD]

broken lot: Less than some understood standard unit of sale. [WRD]

broker: A middleman that serves as a "go-between" for the buyer or seller; assumes no title risks, does not usually have physical custody of products, and is not looked upon as a permanent representative of either the buyer or seller. [WRD]

brown goods: Merchandise in the consumer electronic audio- visual field, such as television, radio, stereo sets, etc. Name came from the brown (furniture color) cases in which such merchandise is frequently manufactured. At one time the term also included all furniture. [CMC]

budgets: The detailed financial component of the strategic plan which guides the allocation of resources and provides a mechanism for identifying deviations of actual from desired performance so corrective action can be taken. Budgets assign a dollar figure to each revenue and expense related activity. They are usually prepared for a period of one year by each component of an organization. Like the action program, budgets provide both a guide for action as well as a means of assessing performance. [GSD]

bulk marking: The practice of placing the price only on the original shipping containers or at least bulk packages; individual units are not marked until the merchandise is transferred from reserve to forward stock; also referred to as "deferred marking". [WRD]

bushelman: A repairer of garments, especially in the alteration room for men's clothing. [WRD]

business advertising: The kind of advertising that is directed to individuals who are interested in products or services related to their business function, rather than that which applies to persons seeking to satisfy personal or household needs and wants. Business advertising includes: (1) industrial advertising, which involves the advertising of goods and services that are used in the production of further goods and services; (2) trade advertising, which is directed to wholesalers and retailers who buy products and services for resale; (3) professional advertising, which encourages professional people to recommend a particular product or service to their clients/patients, or to use such items in their own practice; and (4) agricultural advertising, which addresses the farmer as a business consumer. [AMB]

business analysis: A term of many meanings, and in marketing is usually associated in some way with the evaluation of new product proposals. In format, it may consist of a five-year, discounted cash flow, net present value type of financial analysis, or it may be a more comprehensive analysis of the entire situation surrounding the proposed product. Chronologically, it may come early in the development process (when it is used to decide whether expensive R&D should be undertaken), and/or late in the product development cycle when the commercialization decision is being made. [CMC]

Business Conditions Digest: The U.S. Department of Commerce's monthly publication of economic time series covering such data as business and consumer expectations, cyclical indicators, national income, foreign trade and price movements. [WL]

business cycle: A rhythmic wave-like pattern of changes in business conditions over a period of time. (See also **depression, recovery, prosperity,** and **recession.**) [DLS]

business definition: Specifies the present and/or prospective scope of a strategic business unit's activities in terms of the boundaries of the arena in which the business elects to compete. The definition also serves to direct attention to the true function of the business—that is, the way that the business meets the needs of its target customers. A complete definition requires choices about the business position along four dimensions: (1) **customer functions,** addressing the benefits being provided; (2) **customer segments,** specifying the customer groups seeking similar benefits and sharing characteristics that are strategically relevant; (3) **technology,** specifying the alternative ways in which a particular function can be performed; and (4) **vertical business system,** specifies where the business chooses to participate in the sequence of stages in the vertical business system (or value-added system). [GSD]

business goals: (See **goals**).

business planning process: (See **strategic planning**).

business portfolio matrices: (See **portfolio analyses**).

business services: Intangible products (services), such as banking and maintenance, that are purchased by organizations who produce other products. A type of industrial product. (See also **industrial products and services.**) [CMC]

business strengths: (See **distinctive competences**).

business system: (See **value chain**).

buyclasses: Buying situations that are distinguished on four characteristics; newness to decision makers, numbers of alternatives to be considered, uncertainty inherent in the buying
situation, and the amount of information needed for making a buying decision. There are
three buyclasses; new task, modified rebuy, and straight rebuy. A new task is a problem or
requirement that has not arisen before such that the buying center does not have any relevant
experience with the product or service. **A modified rebuy** is a situation such that the buying
center has some relevant experience to draw upon. The alternatives considered, however, are
different, or changed from the ones considered the last time a similar problem arose.   **A
straight rebuy** is the purchase of standard parts, MRO items or any recurring need that is
handled on a routine basis. (See also **buygrid framework**.) [GLL/DTW]

buyer: The organizational member that carries out the purchase procedures of a product. A
buyer may or may not make the buying decision. The buyer will manage the buying process
e.g. place the order and process the paperwork. (See also **buying center** and **procurement**.)
[GLL/DTW]

buyer behavior: This term is often used as an alternative to consumer behavior, but also used
when the purchaser is not the ultimate consumer but rather an industrial buyer, a buying
center, or other middlemen between the seller and the ultimate user. Defined by some as the
more general term with consumer behavior and organizational buyer behavior as subsets.
(See also **consumer behavior**.) [HHK]

buyer Intention: A measure of a buyer's intention to buy a product or service. It can be
measured as the subjective probability that a buyers' beliefs and attitudes will be acted upon in
a purchasing framework. [GLL/DTW]

buyer readiness stage: The stage in which the buyer is regarding his readiness to buy a
certain product or service. At any time, people are in different stages: unaware, aware,
informed, interested, predisposed to buying, and intending to buy. [GLL/DTW]

buyer's intentions method: (See **users' expectations method**.)

buyers intention survey: A survey of buyers to measure their purchase intentions. Best
results are obtained if the buyers have clearly formulated intentions. (See also **buyer intention**.) [GLL/DTW]

buyers market: Such economic conditions that favor the position of the retail buyer (or
merchandiser) rather than the vendor; in other words, economic conditions are such that the
retailer can demand and usually get concessions from suppliers in terms of price, delivery,
and other market advantages. Just the opposite of a sellers market. (See also **sellers market**)
[WRD]

buyflow: Communication network between all individuals involved in a buying decision and
the actions that take place during the course of making the purchase decision. (See also
buying center and **buyphases**.) [GLL/DTW]

buygrid framework: A conceptual model that describes the organizational buying process. It
consists of two dimensions; buyclasses and buyphases. The buyclasses are new task, modified

rebuy, and straight rebuy. The buyphases are need recognition, need definition, need description, seller identification, proposal solicitation, proposal evaluation and selection, ordering procedures, and performance review. (See also **buying center** and **buyphases**.) [GLL/DTW]

buying calender: A plan of a store buyer's market activities, generally covering a six-month merchandising season based on a selling calender that indicates planned promotional events. [WRD]

buying center: The group of individuals that consists of all organizational members who are involved in any way, to any extent, in any phase of a specific buying decision. [GLL/DTW]

buying committee: 1. (industrial) An officially appointed group that is responsible for purchasing goods and services. (See also **buying center**.) [GLL/DTW] 2. (retailing) A committee that has the authority for final judgment and decision on such matters as adding or eliminating new products; especially common in supermarket companies and resident buying offices. [WRD]

buying criteria: The factors considered by buyers in their evaluation of alternative suppliers such as: dependability, product quality, cost, vendor production capacity, after- sale service, vendor reliability and integrity, reciprocity, and emotional factors. They can be categorized as product- related, e.g., technical specifications; company related e.g., reputation; and salesperson-related, e.g., expertise and trustworthiness. [GLL/DTW]

buying decisions: The different buying situations a buyer would face in the course of purchasing a product/service to satisfy a need. Three buying decisions can be distinguished: (1) **product decision**, deciding on which product(s) will be purchased with available resources; (2) **brand decision**, deciding on which brand(s) will be purchased among competing products; and (3) **supplier decision**, deciding on which supplier(s) will be patronized among competing brands. [GLL/DTW]

buying habits: (See **routinized response behavior**.) [HHK]

buying influences: The buying center members or their sources of information who have influence upon the other buying center members such that these other individuals can change in their behavior and/or attitudes in the process of making a specific buying decision. (See also **influence**.) [GLL/DTW]

buying motives: The forces that have been activated into a state of tension causing the buyer to seek a specific need. Organizational buyers are influenced by both rational motivations (e.g., economic factors such as cost, quality and service) and emotional motivations (e.g., status, security and fear). (see also motivation.) [GLL/DTW]

buying period: The sum of the reorder period and the delivery period, under periodic stock counting methods of unit control. [WRD]

buying plan: A breakdown of the dollar open-to-buy figure of a department or merchandise classification to indicate the number or value of units to purchase in different classifications and subclassifications. [WRD]

buying policy index: A leading indicator of business activity, published monthly by NBER, based on the proportion of purchasing agents reporting their buying commitments for the months ahead. [WL]

buying power: 1. (consumer) A term found in Economic Psychology implying the income available for discretionary spending among segments in the population. A measure of the ability and willingness to buy goods or services. [HHK] 2. (industrial) Refers to the relative influence an individual or a job function (engineering, purchasing, production) has in a purchase decision. Power may be based on reward abilities (granting monetary or perceptual benefits), coercion (imposing punishment), legitimacy (formal authority), personality (based on individual characteristics or status) or expertise (special knowledge or expertise). [GLL/DTW]

buying power index: A weighted index that converts three basic elements—population, effective buying income, and retail sales—into a measurement of a market's is ability to buy. The index is expressed as a percentage of total U.S. potential, and is published annually by **Sales and Marketing Management** magazine. [GLL/DTW]

buying roles: The activities that one or more person(s) might play in a buying decision. Six roles can be distinguished: (1) **initiator**, the person who first suggests or thinks of the idea of buying the particular product or service; (2) **influencer**, a person whose views influence other members of the buying center in making the final decision; (3) **decider**, a person who ultimately determines any part of, or the entire buying decision—whether to buy, what to buy, how to buy, or where to buy; (4) **buyer**, the person who handles the paper work of the actual purchase; (5) **user**, the person(s) who consumes or uses the product or service; and (6) **gatekeeper**, the person(s) who controls information or access, or both, to decision makers and influencers. (See also **buying center**.) [GLL/DTW]

buying signal: A verbal or visual cue that indicates a potential customer is interested in purchasing a product or service. Comment: A buying signal indicates that a salesperson should begin to close the sale. [BAW]

buying styles: The way a customer buys a given product/service. Styles range from deliberate buying to impulsive buying. [GLL/DTW]

buyphases: (See **buygrid framework**.)

cable television: System whereby television signals are distributed to subscriber homes by coaxial cable; contrasts with signals received from over-the-air broadcast stations. [AMB]

call frequency: The number of sales calls per time period made on a particular customer. Comment: The call frequencies assigned to customers are used by salespeople to plan their own route and call schedules. [BAW]

call report: A salesperson's report of a sales call made on a customer. [BAW]

call system: A system of equalizing sales among salespersons—e.g., some stores rotate salespeople, giving each an equal opportunity to meet customers. [WRD]

CALLPLAN: A decision calculus model providing a decision support system for determining the amount of time that a salesperson should spend with current customers and sales prospects. The model's parameters are calculated using subjective responses to a series of point-estimate questions concerning the likely impact of various numbers of customer visits on sales from each customer (Lodish 1971). Evidence regarding the model's effectiveness has been reported by Fudge and Lodish (1977). For other salesforce planning decision support systems see **DETAILER and GEOLINE.** [DCS/YJW]

cancellation: A notification to a vendor that a buyer does not wish to accept ordered merchandise; also, merchandise declared surplus by retailers, often sold in broken lots to discount houses. (Out-of-style or slightly damaged shoes are frequently sold as "cancellation shoes".) [WRD]

canned sales presentation: A standardized sales presentation that includes all the key selling points arranged in the order designed to elicit the best response from the customer. [BAW]

canned sales talk: A prepared sales talk repeated from memory. [WRD]

cannibalization: The loss of sales in established products experienced by a firm resulting from its own introduction of new products that are partial or complete substitutes. That is, the new product "steals" some of the sales of the established product. [GSD]

canvasser: (See house-to-house salesperson.) [WRD]

capacity requirements planning (CRP): Evaluation of planned production to determine if it can be accomplished within the capacity limitations of manufacturing facilities. A capacity load projection is completed for each item in the master production schedule. The calculated load requirement is compared to available capacity thus determining underutilization or overutilization of facilities. [DJB/BJL]

capital: 1. Produced goods used for further production instead of consumption. 2. The owner's investment in a business. 3. All economic goods in existence at a given period of time used by society for production. [DLS]

capital asset pricing model (CAPM): A theory which states that the expected return on any asset or security is given by the following formula:

$$E(R_j) = R_f + [E(R_m) - R_f]\beta_j$$

where:

$$E(R_j) = \text{the expected return on any security j,}$$

$$R_f = \text{the risk-free rate of interest (often estimated by the return on U.S. Treasury bills),}$$

$$E(R_m) = \text{the expected return on all securities in the market (often estimated by the return on the Standard \& Poor's 500- stock index), and}$$

$$\beta_j = \text{the beta coefficient for security j.}$$

It is generally conceded in finance that the CAPM is effectively untestable. [PFA]

capital goods: Instruments of production that make up an organization's plant and operating capacity. [DLS]

capital intensive: A term applied to a product or an industry where plant and equipment requirements are large relative to labor. [DLS]

capital turnover: The number of times total capital investment is divisible into sales—the greater this figure, the smaller the net profit on sales required to meet a given return on investment. [WRD]

CAPM approach to investment analysis: A technique that employs the CAPM equation to calculate the risk-adjusted, after-tax required rate of return in the NPV equation. This approach replaces the use of the traditional weighted average cost of capital. Beta is usually estimated as the average of the betas for firms already operating (exclusively) in the market in which the investment will be made. [PFA]

captive market: The potential clientele of retail or service businesses located in hotels, airports, railroad stations, etc., where consumers do not have reasonable alternative sources of supply. [WRD]

carload: Shipment by rail of a full load. Usually qualifies for lower freight rate than smaller shipments. [DJB/BJL]

carousel: Material handling equipment that delivers the desired item to the order picker. Typically a carousel consists of a series of bins mounted on an oval track. The entire carousel rotates bringing the bin to the operator. [DJB/BJL]

carriage trade: An old expression that refers to a wealthy class of patrons accorded special services. [WRD]

carrier: In transportation, a car, truck, vessel, plane, helicopter, train. [WRD]

carry over (lag effect) models: Models in which the effect of a marketing variable is assumed to last beyond a single time period. A transformation often applied in modelling the effect of lagged marketing expenditures (e.g., advertising expenditures in previous periods) on the current period's sales is the Koyck transformation. When it is assumed that the effect of the marketing expenditure decays geometrically over time (i.e., loses a constant proportion of its remaining impact in each subsequent period), then the Koyck transformation allows the analyst to estimate all of those lagged marketing expenditure effects using a single one-period-lagged-sales term to predict current sales. The transformation thus greatly simplifies the task of estimating lagged effects in sales response models. The validity of the assumptions required for the transformation to be appropriate has, however, been challenged. For reviews see Parsons and Schultz (1976 Chapter 8) or Lilien and Kotler (1983 Chapter 4). [DCS/YJW]

carrying charge: The sum paid for credit service on certain charge accounts; an interest usually charged on the unpaid balance. [WRD]

cartel: A combination of separate firms who collusively set prices and control output with the intent of maximizing mutual profits. [DLS]

cash cow: (See growth-share matrix).

cash discount: A premium for advance payment at a rate which is usually higher than the prevailing rate of interest; a reduction in price allowed the buyer for prompt payment. [WRD]

cash flow: The cash generated by after-tax earnings plus depreciation minus cash used within the business. Or more simply, the movement of cash into and out of the business. Where the "in-flows" (receipts) have exceeded the "out flows" (disbursements) in a specified period of time, the cash flow is said to be positive and provides additional net cash. When the disbursements exceed the receipts in a specified period of time, the cash flow is said to be negative and reduces net cash. [GSD]

cash on delivery: Commonly referred to as C.O.D. Refers to the practice of collecting for the price of the merchandise plus the relevant transportation charges. [KM]

cash register bank: An assortment of change for the use of the salesperson or transaction station operator. It is prepared at the end of the day by the person operating a cash register or prepared by a cashier for the cash register operator. [WRD]

cash terms: The payment of cash for the purchase of goods, usually within a certain time period—e.g., 10 to 14 days. [WRD]

catalog: A publication containing the descriptions or details of a number or range of products used to increase mail order sales, phone sales, and in-store traffic of the sender. [DES]

catalog showroom: A retail outlet that consumers visit to make actual purchases of articles described in catalogs mailed to their homes. [WRD]

categorization: A cognitive process by which objects, events, and persons are grouped together and responded to in terms of their class membership rather than their uniqueness. [JPP/JCO]

causal research: Research design in which the major emphasis is on determining a cause-and-effect relationship. [GAC]

cease and desist order: An order from an administrative agency or court prohibiting the continuation of a particular course of conduct. [DC]

Celler-Kefauver Act (1950): (See **Anti-Merger Act of 1950.**)

census: A complete canvass of a population. [GAC]

census block: A census block is a well defined rectangular area bounded by streets or roads. However, it may be irregular in shape and may be bounded by physical features such as railroads or streams. Blocks do not cross boundaries of countries, tracts, or block numbering areas. [DLH]

census tract: Census tracts are small, relatively permanent areas into which metropolitan statistical areas (MSAs) and certain other areas are divided for the purpose of providing statistics for small areas. When census tracts are established, they are designed to be homogeneous with respect to population characteristics, economic status, and living conditions. Tracts generally have between 2,500 and 8,000 residents. [DLH]

central business district (CBD): For statistical purposes, this area is specifically defined for individual cities. Because there are not generally accepted rules for determining what a CBD area should include or exclude, the U. S. Bureau of the Census did not provide rigid specifications for defining the CBD but provided a general characterization of the CBD, describing it as an area of very high land valuation, an area characterized by a high concentration of retail businesses, offices, theaters, hotels, service businesses, and an area of high traffic flow, and required that the CBD ordinarily should be defined to follow existing tract lines—i.e., to consist of one or more whole Census tracts. [WRD]

central buying: A type of central market representation in which the authority and responsibility for merchandise selection and purchase are vested in the central market office, rather than in the individual store units represented by the central office. Also referred to as consolidated buying. [WRD]

central market: A place where a large number of suppliers are concentrated. The locations may be a simple area, such as a merchandise mart, or they may be located in the same general section of a city. For example, New York is still the primary central market for many types of merchandise, especially women's wear. [WRD]

central office edit: Thorough and exacting scrutiny and correction of completed data collection forms, including a decision about what to do with the data. [GAC]

central place theory: A normative theory that explains the size, number, and spacing of distribution centers to serve a dispersed population. [DLH]

central route to persuasion: One of two types of cognitive processes by which persuasion occurs. In the central route, consumers focus on the product messages in the ad, interpret them, form beliefs about product attributes and consequences, and integrate these meanings to form brand attitudes and intentions. (See also **peripheral route to persuasion.**) [JPP/JCO]

centralized adjustment system: A centralized office that handles complaints, whether placed by telephone, mail, or a personal visit to the store. Would not apply to routine matters, as the return of merchandise in good condition and within the limits of the store's policy governing "approval" sales, exchanges, and so on. [WRD]

centralized management: The practice of referring matters for decision to higher levels of management, particularly to corporate management. [VPB]

centralized sales organization: A sales force, reporting to corporate or group management, may sell the products of two or more divisions. This may be appropriate when the products of the divisions are distributed through the same channels. [VPB]

cents-off offer: A sales promotion technique offering a certificate good for a discount off the posted purchase price of a particular product. (See also **coupon.**) [DES]

chain discount: A series of trade-discount percentages or their total— e.g., if a list (catalog) price denotes $100 and is subject to a 40-15-15 discount to dealers, the total or chain discount is $56.65— i.e., $100 - .40 = 60, $60 - .15 = $51, $51, - .15 = $43.35. [WRD]

chain store system: A group of retail stores of essentially the same type, centrally owned and with some degree of centralized control of operation. The term **chain store** may also refer to a single store as a unit of such a group. [WRD]

chain store warehouses: Establishments that are operated by retail multiunit organizations primarily for the purpose of assembling and distributing goods and performing other whole-sale functions for the stores of such organizations. [WRD]

channel captain: (See **channel leader.**)

channel conflict: A situation in which one channel member perceives another channel member(s) to be engaged in behavior that is preventing or impeding the attainment of its goals. [JRN]

channel control: (See **channel power.**)

channel cooperation: Willingness of channel members to work together to accomplish inter-organizational goals. [JRN]

channel effectiveness: A channel performance dimension based on how well the channel satisfies the demands placed on it by the consumption sector in terms of lot size, delivery time, location convenience and assortment breadth. [JRN]

channel equity: A channel performance dimension based on the extent to which the channels serve problem-ridden and disadvantaged market segments. [JRN]

channel flows (functions):   Marketing functions performed by manufacturers, wholesalers, retailers and other channel members within the channel. Eight universal marketing flows that have been identified include physical possession, ownership, promotion, negotiation, financing, risking, ordering, and payment. [JRN]

channel leader: A channel member who uses power bases like reward, expert, legitimate, referent, information or coercion to influence the decisions and behavior of other channel members. Channel leadership may be assumed by manufacturers, wholesalers or retailers. [JRN]

channel of distribution: An organized network [system] of agencies and institutions which, in combination, perform all the activities required to link producers with users to accomplish the marketing task. [JRN]

channel performance: An outcome measure of channels of distribution. The performance of marketing channels or institutions can be assessed by considering a number of performance dimensions including effectiveness, equity, productivity (efficiency) and profitability. [JRN]

channel power: The capacity of a particular channel member to control or influence the behavior of another channel member(s). The level and effectiveness of control is a function of leadership quality, magnitude of power sources deployed and the tolerance of power by other channel members. [JRN]

channel productivity (efficiency): A channel performance dimension based on the degree to which the channels' total investment in the various inputs necessary to achieve a given distribution objective can be optimized in terms of outputs. [JRN]

channel profitability: A channel performance dimension based on the financial performance of channel members in terms of ROI, liquidity, leverage, growth in sales and profits, etc. [JRN]

channel specialization: Channel members choice of unique positions in the channel based on their capacities, interests, goals, expectations, values and frames of references. Hence, each performs those tasks (participates in those flows) which they can perform at a comparative advantage. [JRN]

checklist: A memory-jogger list of items, used to remind an analyst to think of all relevant aspects. It finds frequent use as a tool of creativity in concept generation and as a factor-consideration list in concept screening. [CMC]

cherry picking: Buyer selection of only a few numbers from one vendor's line, other numbers from another line, failing to purchase a complete line or classification of merchandise from one resource. [WRD]

Child Protection Act (1966): Amended the Hazardous Substances Act by stating toys and other children's articles which contained hazardous substances were banned. [DC]

child protection: A term covering the totality of measures necessary for a child's physical, moral and mental well- being. [DC]

choice criteria: The specific attributes or consequences used by consumers to evaluate and choose from a set of alternatives. [JPP/JCO]

C.I.A. (cash in advance): Used interchangeably with cash before delivery, and applies in the same instance as the latter. [WRD]

CIP: An acronym standing for consumer information processing. [JPP/JCO]

circulation: The number of copies of a print advertising medium that are distributed (not typically applied to broadcast media); for outdoor and transit, the number of people who have a reasonable opportunity to see. "Paid" circulation refers to publications for which a certain percentage of distributed copies are purchased; "controlled" circulation is the distribution of publicatioins, usually free, to selected individuals. [AMB]

class rate: All products transported by common carriers are classified for purposes of transportation pricing. The price in dollars and cents per hundredweight to move a specific product classification between two locations is the class rate. [DJB/BJL]

classic merchandise: Merchandise not influenced by style changes, for which a demand virtually always exists. [WRD]

classical conditioning: A process through which a previously neutral stimulus, by being paired with an unconditioned stimulus, comes to elicit a response very similar to the response originally elicited by the unconditioned stimulus. [JPP/JCO]

classification: A grouping of merchandise into a homogeneous category usually smaller than a department and is useful for control purposes particularly. (See also **dissection control.**) [WRD]

classification control: A form of dollar inventory control where the dollar value of each classification of goods is smaller than the total stock of the department—e.g., the sporting goods department may be divided into several classifications or dissections, such as golf, fishing, active sport, etc. [WRD]

Clayton Act (1914): Specifically outlaws discrimination in prices, exclusive and tying contracts, intercorporate stockholdings, and interlocking directorates "where the effect...may be to substantially lessen competition or tend to create a monopoly." [DC]

Clean Air Act 1970: Requires the Environmental Protection Agency to establish air-quality standards based on considerations of public health. [DC]

clearance sale: An end-of-season sale to make room for new goods; also "pushing" the sale of slow moving, shop-worn, and demonstration model goods. [WRD]

clearinghouse: Central processing location where coupons or other sales promotion offers are collected, analyzed and sorted for payment or fulfillment. [DES]

close (or closing): The culmination of a sales presentation in which a sales person attempts to get a customer to commit to buying a product or service. [BAW]

close-out: Offer at reduced price to clear slow-moving or incomplete stock; also, an incomplete assortment, the remainder of a line of merchandise that is to be discontinued, offered at a low price to ensure immediate sale. [WRD]

closed stock: Items sold only in sets with no assurance to the customer that the same pattern and quality can be bought at any later time. The merchandise is generally sold only in sets with no provision for replacing broken pieces. [WRD]

closed-door discount houses: A discount store that sells only to consumers who purchase a membership card. [WRD]

club plan selling: An arrangement in which a consumer is awarded prizes or granted discount buying privileges by getting new customers to join the "club." The "club" is the group of customers served by the selling organization, and one joins by making purchases. [WRD]

cluster analysis: Body of techniques concerned with developing natural groupings of objects based on the relationships of the p variables describing the objects. [GAC]

cluster sample: A probability sample distinguished by a two-step procedure in which (1) the parent population is divided into mutually exclusive and exhaustive subsets, and (2) a random sample of subsets is selected. If the investigator then uses all of the population elements in the selected subsets for the sample, the procedure is one-stage cluster sampling; if a sample of elements is selected probabilistically from the subsets, the procedure is two- stage cluster sampling. [GAC]

co-op coupons: Offers from a group of non-competitive or mutually enhancing group of sellers who have either joined or been gathered together to offer a greater value than any could alone. [DES]

co-op mailings: Distribution of coupons or other sales promotion offers for a variety of products through a single mailing piece. [DES]

coalitions: (See **alliances**).

C.O.D. (collect on delivery):   The buyer must make payment for purchase at time of delivery of goods; considered a poor substitute for cash before delivery (C.B.D.) or cash in advance (C.I.A.), because if the purchaser refuses, the seller incurs return freight charges and any deterioration of the products in the process. [WRD]

coding: Technical procedure by which data are categorized; it involves specifying the alternative categories or classes into which the responses are to be placed and assigning code numbers to the classes. [GAC]

coefficient of income sensitivity: The average percent that sales of a product vary over a period of time relative to a one percent change in personal disposable income. [DLS]

cognition: 1. The sum total of an individual's beliefs, attitudes, perceptions, needs, goals, and learned reactions about some aspect of the individual's world. A cognition is the pattern of meaning of a thing. [HHK] 2. The total complex of mental structures and processes including rational, emotional, and subconscious events. [JPP/JCO]

cognitive dissonance: A term coined by Leon Festinger to describe the feeling of discomfort or imbalance that is presumed to be evident when various cognitions about a thing are not in agreement with each other. For example, knowledge that smoking leads to serious physical ailments is dissonant with the belief that smoking is pleasurable and the psychophysiological need to smoke. Cognitive Dissonance is similar to Heider's work on Balance Theory and Osgood and Tannenbaum's Congruity Theory. Dissonance is presumed to be an uncomfortable state that the individual strives to reduce. [HHK]

cognitive processing: The mental activities by which external information in the environment is transformed into meanings or patterns of thought and combined to form judgments about behavior. [JPP/JCO]

cognitive response: A mental reaction to a message such as to accept or counterargue it. [JPP/JCO]

cold-canvassing: A method of prospecting under which a salesperson calls on every potential customer that might have need for a product or service. [BAW]

collect rate shipment: A freight bill is a carrier's method of charging for transportation services. If it is collect, the buyer is responsible and must pay transport costs upon arrival of the shipment. [DJB/BJL]

column inch: A unit of print advertising space, one column wide by one inch deep. [AMB]

combination compensation plan: 1. A compensation plan for salespeople which combines a base salary with commissions and/or a bonus. [BAW]2. A compensation plan that offers a base salary plus some proportion of incentive pay. Combination plans combine a base salary with commissions, bonuses, or both. When salary plus commission is used, the commissions are tied to sales volume or profitability, just as with a straight commission plan. The only difference is that the commissions are smaller in a combination plan than when the salesperson is compensated solely by commission. [OCW]

commercial auction: An agent business unit which effects the sale of goods through an auctioneer, who, under specified rules, solicits bids or offers from buyers and has power to accept the highest bids of responsible bidders and, thereby, consummates the sale. [WRD]

commercialization: A stage (usually the last) in the development cycle for a new product. Commonly thought to begin when the product is introduced into the marketplace, but actually starts when a management commits to marketing the item. Subsequent activity during commercialization includes manufacturing and distribution, as well as promotion. May precede the product announcement date by months. (See also **new product development.**)

commissary store: Retail outlet owned and operated by one of the armed forces to sell food and related products to military personnel at special prices. [WRD]

commission: Compensation paid to salespeople based on a fixed formula related to the salesperson's activity or performance. Comment: The basis for calculating commissions is frequently a fixed percentage of sales or gross margin generated. Salespeople may have to achieve a pre-specified level of performance before they are eligible to receive commissions. [BAW]

commission buyers of farm products: Wholesale establishments primarily engaged in buying farm products on a commission basis from farmers for others. [WRD]

commission buying office: One that receives its remuneration in the form of commissions on orders placed from manufacturers rather than from retailers. [WRD]

commission house (commission merchant): An agent who usually exercises physical control over and negotiates the sale of the goods he handles. He generally enjoys broader powers as to prices, methods, and terms of the sale than does the broker although he must obey instructions issued by the principal. He often arranges delivery, extends necessary credit, collects, deducts fees, and remits the balance to the principal. [WRD]

commission system: The method whereby advertising agencies receive a commission (usually 15 percent) from the advertising media for advertising which is bought on behalf of the advertiser client; contrasts with the "fee" system, in which the agency is compensated by the advertiser for all services rendered. [AMB]

commissioners: A specialized type of buying agency that brings the buyer in contact with proper vendors in foreign markets and acts as an interpreter; also, they facilitate the procedures of foreign exchange and shipping. [WRD]

committee buying: Whenever the buying decision is made by a group of people rather than a single buyer. A multiunit operation is usually the type of firm that uses this procedure. [WRD]

commodity exchange: An organization usually owned by the member-traders which provides facilities for bringing together buyers and sellers, or their agents, of specified standard commodities for promoting trades in accordance with prescribed rules—either spot or future, or both—in these commodities. [WRD]

commodity rate: A transportation rate published for specific commodities without regard to classification. Carriers commonly publish commodity rates when a large quantity of product moves between the two locations on a regular basis. When a commodity rate exists, it supercedes the corresponding class or exception rate. [DJB/BJL]

common carrier: A company that offers to transport property for revenue at any time and any place within its operating authority without discrimination. A common carrier is authorized to conduct for-hire transportation after receiving certification as Fit, Able, and Willing. [DJB/BJL]

common costs: Common or general costs support a number of activities or profit segments. These costs cannot be traced to a product or segment. [KM]

communication: Method of data collection involving questioning of respondents to secure the desired information using a data collection instrument called a questionnaire. [GAC]

community shopping center: A type of shopping center usually having a gross floor area of 100,000 to 300,000 square feet, and whose trading area normally does not extend beyond the community in which it is located. [WRD]

company potential: (See **sales potential**.)

comparative advertising: Advertising that compares explicitly or implicitly two or more actual brands, or the comparison of the advertised brand with a hypothetical "Brand X" or "other leading brands." [AMB]

comparative prices: Statements in advertisements or signs comparing specific prices with previous prices, other prices, or prices goods are estimated to be worth. [WRD]

comparative scale: Scale requiring subjects to make their ratings as a series of relative judgments or comparisons rather than as independent assessments. [GAC]

comparison shopping: Two major types of activity, namely merchandise shopping and service shopping are involved. 1. Merchandise shopping activities rendered by an organized shopping bureau include checks of new items being offered by competing stores; reports on advertised promotions of competitors; comparison price shopping, etc. 2. Service shopping is normally performed by shoppers who pose as customers and report the quality of selling service on standard forms. [WRD]

compensatory rule: In evaluating alternatives, the compensatory rule suggests that a consumer will select the alternative with the highest overall evaluation on a set of criteria. Criteria evaluations are done separately and combined arithmetically such that positive evaluations can offset (compensate for) negative evaluations. This term is also called compensatory process, compensatory integration procedure, and compensatory model. (See also **noncompensatory rules**.) [JPP/JCO]

competences of firm: (See **distinctive competences**).

competition: Refers to rivalry among sellers trying to achieve such goals as increasing profits, market share, and sales volume by varying the elements of the marketing mix: price, product, distribution and promotion. The product of vying for customers by the pursuit of differential advantage, i.e., changing to better meet consumer wants and needs. In economic theory various competitive states such as monopolistic competition, oligopoly, perfect competition and monopoly are delineated based on the degree of control that sellers have over price. [WL]

competitive advantage: A competitive advantage exists where there is a match between the distinctive competences of a firm and the factors critical for success within the industry that permits the firm to outperform its competitors. Advantages can be gained by having the lowest delivered costs and/or differentiation in terms of providing superior or unique performance on attributes that are important to customers. (See also **differential advantage**.) [GSD]

competitive analysis: The analysis of factors designed to answer the question, "how well is a firm is doing compared to its competitors." The analysis goes well beyond sales and profit figures in assessing the firm's ratings on such factors as price, product, technical capabilities, quality, service, delivery, and other important factors compared to each of the major competitors. [WL]

competitive bidding: The practice of competition where firms submit offers or bids that detail the services and product specifications to be offered at a stated price. [KM]

competitive brands: Brands which are considered as alternatives by buyers in a particular market segment; sometimes called the evoked set. Occasionally is used to mean a (smaller) set of products which a particular seller wishes to be competing with; more rarely, it means the full set of competitors in fact competing in a given market. [CMC]

competitive intelligence: Refers to the gathering of data and information about all aspects of competitors' marketing and business activities for the purposes of formulating plans and strategies and making decisions. [WL]

competitive parity budgeting: Advertising appropriation method whereby an advertiser determines advertising expenditures by assessing competitors' spending. [AMB]

competitive position: The position of one business relative to others in the same industry. There are a multitude of factors contributing to (and which can be used to measure) competition. The major categories are (1) **market position,** relative share of market, rate of change of share, variability of share across segments, perceived differentiation of quality/service/price, breadth of product and company images; (2) **economic and technological position,** relative cost position, capacity utilization, technological position, and patented technology, product or process; and (3) **capabilities,** management strength and depth, marketing strength, distribution system, labor relations, relationships with regulators. [GSD]

competitive strategy: A plan that attempts to define a position for the business that utilizes the competitive advantages that the business has over its competitors. [GSD]

complement of markup percentages: One hundred percent less markup percentage on retail. [WRD]

complementary products: 1. Products that are manufactured together, sold together, bought together, or used together. One aids or enhances the other. (See also **substitute products.**) [CMC] 2. Products whose demands are positively related, i.e., an increase in quantity demanded by the market of Product A results in an increase in the quantity demanded for Product B. [DLS] 3. Products that are used jointly with other products, such as razors and blades, or toothbrushes and toothpaste. [WL]

completed fertility: The average number of births for all women in a society. [WL]

completely randomized design: Experimental design in which the experimental treatments are assigned to the test units completely at random. [GAC]

component parts: The industrial products that either are ready for direct assembly into the finished product or require only a minor amount of further processing. Examples are switches, transistors, motors, gears, nuts, bolts, and screws. (See also **parts.**) [GLL/DTW]

comprehension: The cognitive processes involved in understanding and knowing about concepts, events, objects, and persons in the environment. [JPP/JCO]

computer integrated manufacturing (CIM):   An approach to managerial control that focuses on the automated flow of information among participants in the stages of manufacturing. [DJB/BJL]

computerized buying: The use of computers in managing the purchasing process. Such tasks as calculating current inventory figures, computing economic order quantities, preparing purchase orders, developing requests for vendor quotations, expediting of orders, and generating printouts of dollars spent on vendors and products can be part of the system. Some systems may have decision support models to assist in analysis of purchase alternatives. [GLL/DTW]

concentration: The process of bringing goods from various places together in one place. It includes the sorting processes of accumulation and assorting. [JRN]

concentration (economic):   A measure of the dominance of a market exercised by the top few firms in an industry. [DLS]

concentration ratio: 1. Refers to a number of statistical measures, such as the percentage of a total industry's sales accounted for by the largest three firms, representing the degree of concentration of a market. [WL] 2. The proportion of industry shipments accounted for by the four largest firms in that industry, expressed as a percentage. This measure describes the structure of competition and yields insights into the intensity of rivalry in an industry. [GSD]

concentration strategy: Where a company chooses to pursue a large share of one or more submarkets rather than chasing a small share of a large market. The strategy can be somewhat risky if the demand in the submarket falls away or if one or more competitors enter the submarket. [GSD]

concentric diversification: (See **diversification**).

concentric zone theory: A theory of urban land-use patterns, developed by William Burgess, which states that a city will assume the form of five concentric urban zones: the central business district, the zone in transition, the zone of working persons' homes, the zone of better residences, and the commuters' zone. Growth is accomplished by the expansion of each zone into the next zone. [WRD]

concept: (See **product concept.**)

concept statement: A verbal and/or pictorial statement of a concept (for a product or for advertising) that is prepared for presentation to potential buyers or users to get their reaction prior to its being implemented. Product concepts are followed by prototypes, advertising concepts by one of several forms of semi-finished production. [CMC]

concept statement commercialized: A term used in distinguishing two types of product concept statements. A commercialized product concept statement is prepared in an advertising format, as a persuasive statement. A non- commercialized product concept statement is prepared in neutral, non-persuasive format. [CMC]

concept testing and development: The process in which a concept statement is presented to potential buyers or users, for their reactions. These reactions permit the developer to estimate the sales value of the concept (whether product or advertising) and to make changes in it so as to enhance its sales value. [CMC]

conditional sale contract: Agreement under which the title does not pass to the buyer until he has fulfilled his contract obligations. The buyer assumes complete responsibility upon delivery, must maintain the article purchased, and must make regular payments. If he defaults, the seller may repossess, use the proceeds of a sale of the item to satisfy the remaining obligation, and refund the excess, if any, above the cost of repossession and sale, to the buyer. If the proceeds of a sale are insufficient, the buyer is still technically liable to the seller for the remainder. [WRD]

confirmation: In consumer satisfaction theory, confirmation refers to a situation in which a product performs exactly as it was expected to, ie., prepurchase expectations are confirmed. [JPP/JCO]

confirmation (of order): From the store's standpoint, the official order of a store for goods made out on the store order form and countersigned by the buyer and merchandise manager.

It is distinguished from the memoranda that buyers often make out on vendors' order blank that are not official orders and are not binding on the store. From the vendor's standpoint the acknowledgment of a buyer's order by the vendor; his legal acceptance of the offer made by the buyer generally in writing. [WRD]

conglomerate: A firm with large diversified holdings acquired through acquisitions and mergers. Also known as multi-market firms. [WL]

conglomerate diversification: (See **diversification**).

conglomerate mergers: Mergers of companies in unrelated businesses, such as the merger of automobile manufacturers with electronics products manufacturers, or the airlines with hotels and rental cars. [WL]

conjoint analysis: Technique in which respondents' utilities or valuations of attributes are inferred from the preferences they express for various combinations of these attributes. [GAC]

conjunctive rule: A decision making rule of thumb or heuristic in which the consumer is assumed to set up minimum cutoffs for each of several attributes or dimensions of a product or thing. If the brand or item does not meet all of the minimum criteria, it is rejected. The evaluation rule leads to an acceptable or nonacceptable decision. For example, a conjunctive rule may be that a slice of bread must have at least 3 grams of protein, minimum percentages of specific vitamins, less than 100 mg sodium and less than 75 calories per slice to be acceptable. A brand must meet all of these minimum attributes or it is unacceptable. A shortfall in one attribute is not offset by excessive endowment in another attribute. (See also **disjunctive rule, lexicographic rule,** and **noncompensatory rules.**) [HHK]

conscious parallelism: 1. Evidence of concert of action implied from business behavior, such as setting parallel prices, without proof of an express agreement. [DC] 2. The pattern within an industry where firms prefer to "follow" other firms (typically the market leader) rather than pursue a different course. The reason for behaving in this manner is that there is little opportunity and/or little gain to be made by adopting a different strategy from the others in the industry. It is most often observed as similarity in pricing actions. [GSD]

consent order: An order issued after a defendant agrees to discontinue a complained of practice without admitting any violation of the law. [DC]

consideration: Something of value received or given at the request of the promiser in reliance on and in return for his promise. It may be a payment of money, or merely an exchange of promises, as when a buyer orders goods and the vendor confirms the order. The buyer promised to buy and take the goods, and the vendor promises to sell and ship them. [WRD]

consideration set: The group of alternatives that a consumer evaluates in making a decision. [JPP/JCO]

consignee: Person or firm to whom shipments are made. [DJB/BJL]

consignment sale: Title remains with the vendor until the goods are resold by the retailer; however, any unsold portion of the goods may be returned to the vendor without payment. [WRD]

consignment: 1. A method of selling whereby a manufacturer provides an intermediary with the merchandise while retaining title to the goods. The intermediary is free to sell the product and to pay only for goods actually sold. [JRN] 2. Products shipped for future sale or other purpose, title remaining with the shipper (consignor), for which the receiver (consignee), upon his acceptance, is accountable. The consignee may be the eventual purchaser, may act as the agent through whom the sale is effected, or may otherwise dispose of the products in accordance with his agreement with the consignor. [WRD]

consolidated delivery service: A private business organized to deliver products for retailers. A fee is charged for every package delivered. [WRD]

consolidated metropolitan statistical area (CMSA): An area that contains two or more overlapping and/or interlocking primary metropolitan statistical areas. (See **primary metropolitan statistical area (PMSA)**). [DLS]

consolidation: 1. [logistics] Small shipments combined or consolidated into larger shipments to reduce transportation expenditures. Larger volume shipments typically qualify for quantity discounts. Generally the larger the shipment the lower the freight rate per hundredweight. [DJB/BJL] 2. [finance] The joining of two or more independent business firms into a new firm. Unlike a merger, the acquired company does not maintain its identity. [WL]

consolidator: Person or firm providing the service of combining small shipments into larger shipments to reduce transportation expenditures. [DJB/BJL]

constant dollars: Dollars that have been adjusted statistically to a base period in an attempt to remove the effects of inflation and deflation. [DLS]

constant dollar value: The adjustment of dollar values by purchasing power to eliminate or allow for the effects of price changes on data in dollars reported over time. This is sometimes referred to as real dollars. [WL]

constant sum method: A type of comparative rating scale in which an individual is instructed to divide some given sum among two or more attributes on the basis of their importance to him or her, or by using some other criterion. [GAC]

constitutive (conceptual) definition: Definition in which a given construct is defined in terms of other constructs in the set, sometimes in the form of an equation that expresses the relationship among them. [GAC]

construct validation: Approach to validating a measure by determining what construct, concept, or trait the instrument is in fact measuring. [GAC]

consultative selling: A low-pressure selling approach in which the salesperson is viewed as an expert and serves as a consultant to the customer. Comment: This sales approach is consistent with the marketing concept since it emphasizes identifying and satisfying customer needs. [BAW]

consumable supplies: The products that are used up or consumed in the operation of the business. Examples are cleaning compounds, business forms, soaps, and small tools. [GLL/DTW]

consumer: Traditionally the ultimate user or consumer of goods, ideas and services. However the term is also used to imply the buyer or decision maker as well as the ultimate consumer. A mother buying cereal for consumption by a small child is often called the consumer although she may not be the ultimate user. [HHK]

consumer behavior: 1. The dynamic interaction of cognition, behavior, and environmental events by which human beings conduct the exchange aspects of their lives. 2. The overt actions of consumers. [JPP/JCO] 3. The behavior of the consumer or decision maker in the market place of products and services. Often used to describe the interdisciplinary field of scientific study that attempts to understand and describe such behavior. [HHK]

consumer "bill of rights":   President John F. Kennedy's directive to the Consumer Advisory Council in 1962 setting forth the federal government's role in consumerism in aiding consumers to exercise their rights: to safety, to be informed, to choose and to be heard. [DC]

consumer buying behavior: (See **consumer behavior.**) [HHK]

consumer cooperative: A marketing organization owned and operated for the mutual benefit of consumer-owners who have voluntarily associated themselves for the purpose. [WRD]

consumer credit: Credit used by individuals or families for the satisfaction of their own wants; also, the granting of credit by retailers, banks, and finance companies for this purpose. [WRD]

Consumer Credit Protection Act (1968):   Also known as the "truth-in-lending" act, requires full disclosure of terms and conditions of finance charges, and restricts the garnishment of wages. [DC]

consumer decision making: (See **decision making, consumer.**)

consumer decision making unit: The decision maker in the family, organization, or group. The decision making unit need not necessarily be a single individual but may be a committee or informal set of individuals that make the final choices. Often the decision reflects not only the attributes of the products being considered but also the influence patterns found in formal and informal groups. [HHK]

consumer education: Formalized teaching efforts to provide consumers with skills and knowledge to allocate their resources wisely in the marketplace. [DC]

consumer expenditure survey: A survey of a representative sample of the U.S. population conducted by the U.S. Bureau of the Census for the Bureau of Labor Statistics to provide a continuous flow of data on the buying habits of American consumers. The survey consists of two components: an interview panel survey of 5 interviews every 3 months and a diary or record keeping survey of households for 2 consecutive 1-week periods. [WL]

consumer (or personal) finance companies: lending agencies licensed under state laws to engage in the business of lending money to consumers. [WRD]

Consumer Goods Pricing Act (1975):   Repealed the Miller Tydings Amendment and the McGuire Act, thereby removing federal antitrust exemption for resale price maintenance agreements. [DC]

consumer information: Policies aimed at providing consumers with marketplace information and fostering effective utilization leading to improved consumer choice. [DC]

consumer information processing: The mental processes by which consumers interpret and integrate information from the environment and make it meaningful. [JPP/JCO]

consumer motivation: The needs, wants, drives and desires of an individual that lead him or her toward the purchase of products or ideas. The motivations may be physiologically, psychologically or environmentally driven. [HHK]

consumer movement: A mix of people, ideas, or organizations representing previously unrepresented groups or concerns and having change or reform as common ends. [DC]

consumer price index (CPI):   A statistical measure maintained by the U.S. government that shows the trend of prices of goods and services (a "market basket") purchased by consumers. [DLS]

Consumer Product Safety Act (1972):   Established the Consumer Product Safety Commission and transferred a number of product safety functions previously assigned to other agencies to this commission. [DC]

Consumer Product Safety Commission: A federal regulatory agency which conducts investigations on consumer product safety, tests consumer products, provides training in product safety, promulgates product safety standards, and collects data relating to causes and prevention of injury associated with consumer products. [DC]

consumer products: Products produced for, and purchased by, households for their use. (See also **convenience products, shopping products,** and **specialty products.**) [CMC]

consumer protection: The body of federal, state and local government legislation designed to assure safety, purity, quality and efficacy of many products and services and the reliability of statements in advertising about them. [DC]

consumer protection legislation: The basic consumer protection legislation enacted by the federal government is the Federal Trade Commission Act which prohibits unfair or deceptive acts or practices. Others include the Consumer Product Safety Act, the National Highway Traffic Safety Act, the Food and Drug Acts and the Magnuson-Moss Act, and consumer credit protection and environmental protection acts. [DC]

consumer relations: Communications efforts used to support the marketing mix for a product or service. Generally includes product publicity, company image support, interaction with consumer groups, and customer inquiry response systems. [DES]

consumer sales promotion: Externally directed selling offers to the ultimate consumer. These usually consist of offers such as coupons, rebates, premiums, etc., designed to gain one or more of the following: product trial, repeat usage of product, more frequent or multiple product purchases, introduce a new/improved product, introduce new packaging or different size packages, neutralize competitive advertising or sales promotions, capitalize on seasonal, geographic, or special events, encourage consumers to "trade up" to a larger size, more profitable line, or another product in the line. [DES]

consumer satisfaction: The post-purchase evaluation of a consumer action by the ultimate consumer or the decision maker. The beliefs, attitudes and future purchase patterns, word-of-mouth communication, and legal and informal complaints have been related to the post-purchase satisfaction-dissatisfaction process. (See also **post purchase evaluation.**) [HHK]

Consumer Sentiment Index: The Index of Consumer Sentiment was developed at the University of Michigan Survey Research Center to measure the confidence or optimism (pessimism) of consumers in their future well-being and coming economic conditions. The index measures short- and long-term expectations of business conditions and the individual's perceived economic well-being. Evidence indicates that the ICS is a leading indicator of economic activity as consumer confidence seems to precede major spending decisions. [HHK]

consumer sovereignty: Refers to the dominant role of the consumer in dictating the type and quality of goods produced in an economic system. [DC]

consumer's surplus: Gap between total utility a given consumer gets and total market value. Consumer's surplus is created by the fact that the last consumer buys at a price where the amount of utility of the good and market price are equal; consumers who would have paid more for earlier units have to pay only the market price and receive a surplus. [DLS]

consumerism: The widening range of activities of government, business and independent organizations that are designed to protect individuals from practices that infringe upon their rights as consumers. Or, the organized efforts of consumers seeking redress, restitution and remedy for dissatisfaction they have accumulated in the acquisition of their standard of living. [DC]

consumption: Direct and final use of goods or services in satisfying the wants of free human beings. [DLS]

consumption function: Relation of personal expenditures to income at different levels of income. (See also **propensity to consume.**) [DLS]

containerization: The physical grouping of master cartons into one unit load for material handling or transport. The basic objective is to increase material-handling efficiency. [DJB/BJL]

containerizing: The practice in transportation of consolidating a number of packages into one container which is sealed at point of origin and remains sealed until it reaches the point of destination. [WRD]

content analysis: Analysis of articles and news stories in various media as a method of identifying positive and negative mentions about an organization, product, service, or issue. It is a method used to measure impact of publicity. [DES]

content validity: Approach to validating a measure by determining the adequacy with which the domain of the characteristic is captured by the measure; it is sometimes called face validity. [GAC]

contests: A sales promotion technique requiring the participant to use specific skills or ability to solve or complete a specified problem to qualify for a prize or award. [DES]

contests, sales: Short-term incentive programs designed to motivate sales personnel to accomplish specific sales objectives. Comment: In general, contests are used by firms to stimulate extra effort for obtaining new customers, promoting the sales of specific items, generating larger orders per sales call, etc. [BAW]

contingency planning: The development of plans to provide an alternative to the main plan in the event of threats or opportunities that were thought to have a low probability of occurring at the time of the preparation of the main plan. The contingency plan deals not with unforeseen events, but with events that were foreseen but considered unlikely to occur. [GSD]

continuity: The timing pattern of advertising message deliveries in various advertising media over the planning period. [AMB]

continuity plans: Any type of sales promotion technique that encourages customers to purchase products on a continuing basis or over time. Often based on some sort of saving or accumulation scheme such as trading stamps, points, coupons, or the like. [DES]

continuous demand: Demand for products that have a long, relatively stable history of sales. [DLS]

contract carrier: Performs transport services on a selected basis after receiving authorization in the form of a permit. The contract refers to the agreement between the shipper and a contract carrier. [DJB/BJL]

contract carriers: Transportation companies that provide shipping service to one or various shippers on a contract basis. They do not maintain regularly scheduled service and their rates are more easily adapted to specific situations than those of the common carrier. [WRD]

contract department: Unit in a department store set up to sell in quantity to institutions such supplies as food, bedding, floor coverings; a department that arranges for the sale of goods in quantity to large buyers at special prices. [WRD]

contract manufacturing: A joint venture method by which work is contracted to a qualified manufacturer to produce the product(s) that the firm wishes to market. Contract manufacturing offers a chance to enter a market faster with less risk, but has the drawback of less control over the manufacturing process. [GLL/DTW]

contracts: Agreements between two or more persons which create an obligation to do or not to do a particular thing. Its essentials are competent parties, subject matter, legal consideration, mutuality of agreement and mutuality of obligation. [DC]

contracts, tying: Exists when a person agrees to sell one product, the "tying product," only on the condition that the vendee also purchase another product, the "tied product." It is also called a tie-in arrangement and is generally illegal under the Sherman Act or Clayton Act. [DC]

contractual vertical marketing system: 1. A marketing channel that achieves vertical coordination between independent firms at different channel levels through the use of contractual agreements. The three principal types of contractual systems are wholesaler-sponsered voluntary groups, retailer- owned cooperative groups and franchise systems. [JRN] 2. A form of vertical marketing system in which independent firms at different levels in the channel operate contractually to obtain the economies and market impacts that could not be obtained by unilateral action. Under this system, the identity of the individual firm and its autonomy of operation remain intact. [WRD]

contribution: The amount of revenue left over from the sale of a product after the direct and indirect costs related to the product have been subtracted out. [KM]

contribution pricing: A method of determining the price of a product or service that uses the direct or indirect traceable costs related to the production and sale of the product or service as the relevant costs. [KM]

control group: A group of subjects in an experiment who are not exposed to any of the experimental treatments or alternatives whose effects are to be measured; the control group is used to assess what part of the total observed effect was due to things other than the experimental variables(s). [GAC]

controllable costs: Costs which vary in volume, efficiency, choice of alternatives, and management determination; any cost an organizational unit has authority to incur and/or ability to change. [WRD]

controlled circulation: (See **circulation.**)

convenience products: Consumer goods and services (such as soap, candy bars, and shoe shines) that are bought frequently, often on impulse, with little time and effort spent on the buying process. They usually are low-priced, and are widely available. (See also **staples, impulse products,** and **emergency products.**) [CMC]

convenience sample: Nonprobability sample that is sometimes called an accidental sample because those included in the sample enter by accident in that they just happen to be where the study is being conducted when it is being conducted. [GAC]

convenience store: A retail institution whose primary advantage to consumers is locational convenience. These are high-margin, high-turnover retail institutions. [WRD]

convergent validity: Confirmation of the existence of a construct determined by the correlations exhibited by independent measures of the construct. [GAC]

converters: In the textile and paper trades, wholesaling firms engaged in manufacturing activities to a significant degree; also, a firm or merchant who purchases grey cotton cloth (woven but not finished) and has it bleached, dyed, printed, or mercerized before sale. [WRD]

conveyor: A material handling device widely used in shipping and receiving operations. Conveyors are classified as power or gravity with roller or belt movement. [DJB/BJL]

cooperative: An establishment owned by an association of customers of the establishment whether or not they are incorporated. In general, the distinguishing features of a cooperative are patronage dividends based on the volume of expenditures by the members and a limitation of one vote pre member regardless of the amount of stock owned. [WRD]

cooperative advertising (co-op): Retail (local) advertising partly or fully paid for by a manufacturer; also, an advertisement sponsored by two or more manufacturers or retailers. [AMB]

cooperative buying: Any and all consolidations of orders by a number of stores or store buyers in separate stores. Also, affiliated buying. [WRD]

cooperative chain: A group of retailers who on their own initiative have banded together for the purpose of buying, merchandising, or promoting. [WRD]

cooperative delivery: Cooperative ownership and management of a single delivery system serving several retailers. [WRD]

cooperative exporting: Cooperation of domestic firms for the purpose of international exports. Firms that compete domestically may collaborate internationally. [WJK]

cooperative group or chain: A contractual marketing system where retailers combine to form a wholesale warehouse operation. Services to retailer members are primarily large-scale buying and warehousing operations. [JRN]

cooperative marketing: The process by which independent producers, wholesalers, retailers, consumers, or combinations of them act collectively in buying or selling or both. [WRD]

cooperative wholesaler: A wholesale business owned by retail merchants. Typically, the wholesale establishment buys in its own name. Examples exist in the food, drug, and hardware lines. [WRD]

copyright: 1. Offers the owner of original works which can be printed, recorded or "fixed" in any manner the sole right to reproduce and distribute the work, display or perform it, and authorize others to do so during the author's lifetime and for fifty years thereafter. [DC] 2. An exclusive right to the production or sale of literary, musical, or other artistic work, or to the use of a print or label. Occasionally applied to a brand, but brands are usually protected by registration in the Patent and Copyright Office as a trademark. [CMC]

core product: The central benefit or purpose for which a consumer buys a product. Varies from purchaser to purchaser. The core product or core benefit may come either from the physical good or service performance, or it may come from the augmented dimensions of the product. (See also **augmented product.**) [CMC]

corporate advertising: (See **institutional advertising.**)

corporate culture: The patterns and norms that govern the behavior of a corporation and its employees, particularly, the shared values, beliefs and customs. [WL]

corporate marketing system: A marketing channel that achieves vertical coordination through the joint ownership and operation of two or more channel members on different levels of distribution. [JRN]

corporate purpose (or mission):   The "raison d'etre" of the firm that describes the scope of the firm, and the dominant emphasis and values. The purpose (or mission) of an organization is a function of five elements: (1) the history of the organization; (2) the current preferences of the management and/or owners; (3) environmental considerations; (4) the resources of the organization; and (5) the distinctive competences of the organization. [GSD]

corporate relations: The use of communication and public relations techniques to build favorable attitudes toward a particular company with competitors, consumers, the financial community, stockholders, and other publics. [DES]

corporate strategy: The overall plan that integrates the strategies of all the businesses within the corporation. It usually describes the overall mission (see **corporate purpose**), the financial and human resource strategies and policies that affect all businesses within the corporation, the organization structure, the management of the interdependencies among businesses and major initiatives to change the scope of the firm such as acquisitions and divestments. [GSD]

corporate vertical marketing system: A form of vertical marketing system in which all of the functions from production to distribution are at least partially owned and controlled by a single enterprise. Corporate systems typically operate manufacturing plants, warehouse facilities, and retail outlets. (See also **contractual vertical marketing system** and **administered vertical marketing system.**) [WRD]

corrective advertising: Messages that correct earlier claims a company has made in advertising; typically used when the Federal Trade Commission (FTC) has determined that an advertising claim is false or misleading and the FTC thus requires the advertiser to run messages that correct earlier deception. [AMB]

correlation analysis: Statistical technique used to measure the closeness of the linear relationship between two or more intervally scaled variables. [GAC]

cost analysis: A sales management evaluation and control method for monitoring sales force performance. A cost analysis involves monitoring the costs of various selling functions across individual salespeople, districts, products, and customer types. When put together with the data from sales analysis, this procedure allows a firm to judge the profitability of various products and customer types. [OCW]

cost center: A division, department, or subdivision thereof, a group of machines, men, or both, a single machine, operator, or any other unit of activity into which a business is divided for cost assignment and allocation. [WRD]

cost codes: Item cost information indicated on price tickets in code. A common method of coding is the use of letters from an easily remembered word or expression with nonrepeating letters corresponding to numerals. The following is illustrative:

y o u n g b l a d e
1 2 3 4 5 6 7 8 9 0   [WRD]

cost department: A manufacturing or processing department within a retail store that is operated on the cost method of accounting; also, one of the independent departments selling merchandise or service (principally service) but carrying no inventories at retail value— e.g., restaurant, barber shop, fur storage, and beauty parlor. [WRD]

cost inventory: The actual cost or market value, whichever is lower, of the inventory on hand at any time. The term seldom refers to the original price paid for the merchandise, but rather the present depreciated worth. If original price is to be designated, the term generally used is "billed cost of inventory". [WRD]

cost method of inventory: The determination of the cost of inventory on hand by marking the actual cost on each price ticket in code and computing inventory value using these unit cost prices. [WRD]

cost multiplier: The complement of the markon percent. This figure indicates the average relationship of cost to retail value of goods handled in the accounting period. Also referred to as the cost complement or cost percent. [WRD]

cost of industrial sales call: Includes the salaries, commissions, bonuses, travel expenses, and entertainment expenses that a company encounters each time a salesperson makes a face-to-face presentation to one or more persons. [GLL/DTW]

cost of living: The money required to maintain a particular standard of living expressed in terms of the purchase of specified goods and services. [WL]

cost oriented strategies: An approach to improving performance by reducing the costs per unit. The cost advantage can be used to improve profit margins or increase market share by cutting prices. (See also **experience curve analysis**). [GSD]

cost-of-living allowance (COLA):   An adjustment to wages and earnings, particularly during periods of rapid increases in prices, to keep them in line with the cost of living. [WL]

cost-per-rating (point) [CPR or CPRP]:   A method of comparing two or more alternative media vehicles; the cost of an advertising unit (e.g., 30-second television commercial) divided by the rating of the media vehicle. [AMB]

cost-per-thousand (CPM):   A method of comparing two or more alternative media vehicles; the cost to deliver 1,000 people or homes or circulated copies of an advertising media vehicle. CPM is computed by dividing the cost of an advertising unit by the media delivery (e.g., number of circulated copies, readers, viewers) and multiplying the quotient by 1,000. [AMB]

cost-plus: Method of determining the selling price of goods or services whereby cost is increased in an amount equal to an agreed increment to cost. [WRD]

cost-plus pricing: A method of determining the price of a product or service that uses direct, indirect, and fixed costs whether related to the production and sale of the product or service or not. These costs are converted to per unit costs for the product and then a predetermined percentage of these costs is added to provide a profit margin. The resulting price is cost per unit plus the percentage markup. [KM]

Council for Mutual Economic Assistance (COMECON):   A council founded in 1949 to assist the economic development of its member states through joint utilization and coordination of efforts. Members include the U.S.S.R. and its East European border countries. [WJK]

count and recount promotion: A trade sales promotion technique where inventory is counted at the beginning of the promotion and recounted at the end of the promotion period. Discounts are then allowed based on the total quantity of product moved during the promotion period. [DES]

counterpurchase: Also termed parallel trading or parallel barter. A transaction where each delivery is paid for in cash. In most counterpurchase transactions, two seperate contracts are signed, one in which the supplier sells products for a cash settlement (the original sales contract), the other in which the supplier agrees to purchase and market unrelated products from the buyer (a seperate, parallel contract). [WJK]

countertrade: A broad term incorporating a real distinction from barter, since money or credit is involved in the transaction. Countertrade broadly defines an arrangement in which firms both sell to and buy from their overseas customers. It is a sale of goods and services tied to an offsetting transaction, spelled out in a countertrade agreement. For example, a company sells jet engines to country X and agrees as a condition of the sale to purchase goods or services of a designated value or quantity as a full or partial offset. [WJK]

countervailing power: 1. Power exercised by large organizations with diverse and conflicting interests in the marketplace. [DLS]2. The ability of individuals, companies or groups to offset the power of large enterprises or large purchasers. [WL]

coupon: Usually a printed certificate entitling the bearer to a stated price reduction or special value on a specific product, generally for a specific period of time. The value of the coupon is set and redeemed by the seller. [DES]

coupon fraud: A planned misredemption of coupon offers designed to illegally obtain the value of a coupon without adhering to the published rules for redemption. [DES]

coupon redemption: The use of a seller's value certificate at the time of purchase to obtain either a lower price or greater value than normal. Also, used to describe the act of accepting a seller's certificate by a retailer or other intermediary. [DES]

courtesy days: Days on which stores extend to credit customers the privilege of making purchases at sale prices in advance of public sale. [WRD]

coverage: A term used to describe the degree to which a particular advertising medium delivers audiences within a specified geographical or target market area; the calculation of coverage varies by individual media type. [AMB]

credit: The method of purchasing wherein the product or service is acquired for the promise of paying money for the acquisition at a later time. [KM]

credit bureau: An organization that collects, maintains and provides credit information to members or subscribers; sometimes cooperatively owned by users of the service. Maintains an up-to-date file containing a so-called "master card" (of credit information) for each consumer who has asked for credit from local merchants who use the service of the bureau. [WRD]

credit limits: The quantitative limit that indicates the maximum amount of credit that may be allowed to be outstanding on each individual customer account. [WRD]

credit unions: Cooperative savings and loan organizations formed for the purpose of encouraging thrift among members and making loans to them at relatively low rates of interest. [WRD]

crisis management: An attempt by an organization to reduce, minimize or control the impact of a calamitous event through various communication techniques. [DES]

critical success factors: (See **key success factors**).

cross impact analysis: A forecasting technique often used in futures research that logically studies the effects of the interaction of specified events with each other. The wide variety of impacts that can occur are analyzed and assessed to determine the overall effect. It has been used to assess market and product opportunities. [WL]

cross ruff: A sales promotion technique in which a noncompetitive product is used as the vehicle to distribute a coupon, sample, or other sales promotion offer for another product. [DES]

cross selling: The process of selling between and among departments to facilitate larger transactions and to make it more convenient for the customer to accessorize. (See also interselling. [WRD]

cross tabulation: Count of the number of cases that fall into each of several categories when the categories are based on two or more variables considered simultaneously. [GAC]

cross-elasticity of demand: A measure of the extent that a change in the price of one product affects the sale of another, e.g., a small percentage change in the price of Product A may result in a large change in the sales of Product B. [DLS]

cross-sectional study: Investigation involving a sample of elements selected from the population of interest which are measured at a single point in time. [GAC]

crude birth rate: The number of live births per year per thousand population. [WL]

cue: A technical term from psychological learning theory for the stimulus that impels some sort of action. An advertisement may be the cue leading to desire or purchase of a product. [HHK]

cultural ecology: The study of the process by which a society adapts to its environment by social transformations and evolutionary changes. [WL]

cultural environment: Refers to the aggregate of patterns and norms that regulate a society's behavior including the values, beliefs and customs that are shared and transmitted by the society. [WL]

cultural lag: Refers to the differences in the rates of change in various parts of the same culture, such as the relatively slow rate of acceptance of products or ideas by some market segments compared to others. Also used to indicate the failure of a society to keep up with technological and environmental changes in its economic, social, legal and political policies. [WL]

culture: 1. The complex of learned values and behaviors that are shared by a society and are designed to increase the probability of the society's survival. [JPP/JCO] 2. The institutionalized ways or modes of appropriate behavior. The modal or distinctive patterns of behavior of a people including implicit cultural beliefs, norms, values, and premises which govern conduct. The shared superstitions, myths, folkways, mores, and behavior patterns that are rewarded or punished. [HHK]

cumulative audience: (See **reach.**)

cumulative markon: The total of markon on the beginning inventory in any accounting period plus the aggregate purchase markon during the period, including additional markups, before any markdowns; the difference between the total cost and the total original retail value of all goods handled to date; commonly expressed as Percentage of Cumulative Original Retail. [WRD]

cumulative quantity discount: A reduction in the price to be paid for purchases that exceed a given level of volume over a specified period of time. (This form of discount is also referred to as a deferred discount, or a patronage discount.) [KM]

cumulative reach: (See **reach.**)

currency devaluation: The reduction in the value of one currency vis-a-vis other currencies. Devaluation takes place when currency values adjust in foreign exchange markets in response to supply and demand pressure, or in the case of regulated currency rates, when the government decides to change the rate. [WJK]

currency revaluation: An increase in the value of one currency vis-a-vis other currencies. Revaluation takes place when currency values adjust in the foreign exchange markets in response to supply and demand pressures. [WJK]

Current Population Reports: (See **current population surveys.**) [WL]

current population surveys (CPS): A monthly nationwide survey of scientifically selected sample of about 71,000 housing units in 729 areas, covering about 1,200 counties and cities in every state and the District of Columbia. The U. S. Bureau of the Census issues a series of publications on the results under the title of Current Population Reports. [WL]

custom union: A market which is created when countries agree to eliminate trade and tarrif barriers among the participating countries. The custom union is an important element in a broader framework of economic intregration. [WJK]

customer: Actual or prospective purchaser of products or services. [BAW]

customer satisfaction: The degree to which there is match between the customer's expectations of the product and the actual performance of the product. Expectations are formed based on information consumers receive from sales people, friends, family, opinion leaders, etc., as well as past experience with the product. This is an important measure of the ability of a firm to successfully meet the needs of its customer. [GSD]

customer service: A customer oriented corporate philosophy which integrates and manages all of the elements of the customer interface within a pre-determined cost-service mix. [DJB/BJL]

customer service: Identifiable, but essentially intangible, activities that are offered by a seller in conjunction with a product, such as delivery and repair. May be priced separately, but usually are not, and are provided only with a product that is being sold. Not to be confused with intangible products (services), types of products for which the activity is the primary purpose of a sale. The sale of service products may be accompanied by the provision of customer services, an example being the courteous treatment a bank client receives when entering the lobby for the purchase of any of several service products such as check cashing or a loan. (See also **marketing services.**) [CMC]

customization: Tailoring the product to the special and unique needs of the customer. Each buyer is potentially a unique segment. [GLL/DTW]

cutthroat competition: The temporary reduction of prices, often to unreasonable levels, such as below costs, for the purpose of eliminating competitors so as to be able to control a product's or service's price. [WL]

cycles (business, or economic): (See **business cycles.**) [DLS]

C.W.O. (cash with order): The seller demands that cash covering the cost of merchandise and delivery accompany the customer's order; cash before delivery (C.B.D.) and cash in advance (C.I.A.) apply similarly. [WRD]

cyclical business: A business where sales and profits are determined largely by the fluctuations of business conditions or the business cycle. [WL]

data system: The part of a decision support system that includes the processes used to capture and the methods used to store data coming from a number of external and internal sources. [GAC]

day-after-recall (DAR): A test of advertising effectiveness to determine how many persons recall a message one day after possible exposure; often seeks to determine the extent of brand name recognition as well as the communication of various selling points made in the advertisement/commercial. [AMB]

deal: An inducement such as a price reduction, free goods offer or other special offering made by a seller to a channel member or the ultimate consumer, generally for a limited period of time. [DES]

deal merchandise: Products which a seller may offer at a reduced price or which may have been specially bundled, processed, or manufactured for a limited period of time. [DES]

deal proneness: A consumer's general inclination to use promotional deals such as buying on sale or using coupons. [JPP/JCO]

dealer loader: A premium or other reward which is used to encourage a retailer to develop a special display or product offering. Commonly, the item is a reusable product which forms the basis for the display. When the event is over, the retailer is allowed to keep the premium. [DES]

dealer tie-in: Local support by a retailer for a national advertiser's promotional program through use of in-store display materials, cooperative advertising, local contests, identification in media advertisements and so on. [DES]

decennial census: The complete count of the population every 10 years by the U.S. Bureau of the Census, as is provided by the U.S. Constitution. This enumeration and compilation of information about the characteristics of the U.S. population is a rich source of information for marketing. [WL]

decentralized adjustment system: Customers take their complaints directly to the selling department involved. Sales people may make most of the adjustments, although the final approval of the department head or floor manager is often a requirement. [WRD]

decentralized management: The practice of delegating decision-making authority to lower levels of management. Comment: This is particularly important in marketing so that decisions are made by managers who are close to their markets. [VPB]

decentralized sales organization: Each division has its own sales force. This is appropriate when company divisions sell different products to different markets through different channels, and when the divisions are large enough to afford their own sales forces. [VPB]

deceptive advertising: Advertising intended to mislead consumers by falsely making claims, by failure to make full disclosure, or by both. [DLS]

deceptive pricing: Savings claims, price comparisons, "special" sales, "two-for-one" sales, "factory" prices, or "wholesale" prices are unlawful if false or deceptive. When these terms are used, the terms and conditions of the sale must be made clear at the outset. False preticketing—the practice of marking merchandise with a price higher than that for which it is intended—is unlawful. [DC]

decision calculus models: Quantitative models of a process that are calibrated by examining subjective judgments about outcomes of the process (e.g., market share or sales of a firm) under a variety of hypothetical scenarios (e.g., advertising spending level, promotion expenditures). Once the model linking process outcomes to marketing decision variables has been calibrated, it is possible to derive an optimal marketing recommendation (Little 1970; Chakravarthi, Mitchell and Staelin 1981; Little and Lodish 1981). Examples for advertising decisions include ADBUDG, ADMOD and MEDIAC. For overall brand/product decisions see BRANDAID and STRATPORT. For salesforce decisions see CALLPLAN and DETAILER. [DCS/YJW]

decision making, consumer: 1. The process of selecting from several choices, products, brands or ideas. The decision process may involve complex cognitive or mental activity, a simple learned response, or an uninvolved and uninformed choice that may even appear to be stochastic or probabilistic, occurring by chance. [HHK] 2. The process by which consumers collect and analyze information and make choices among alternatives. [JPP/JCO]

decision support system (DSS): 1. A coordinated collection of data, system tools, and techniques with supporting software and hardware by which an organization gathers and interprets relevant information from business and the environment and turns it into a basis for making management decisions. [GAC]2. A system, usually based on a model and computer software package, that describes the implications of specific marketing decisions and/or recommends specific marketing actions, using a set of input information. This information may either reside permanently in the DSS or be input for the particular scenario of interest (or both). The information can consist of primary information (e.g., sales and cost information from company records, or subjective judgments by managers about the likely impact of increased ad spending) and/or secondary information (e.g., sales of competitors' products from a syndicated database constructed via store audits). An important aspect of many decision support systems is the facilitation of "what if" analyses; i.e., the sensitivity of optimal marketing strategy to the assumptions in the input information. For examples see CALLPLAN, decision calculus models, POSSE and STRATPORT. [DCS/YJW]

decision variables, marketing: These correspond to the major marketing functions that influence revenue and profit. They are summarized in the well known four P's: product, price, promotion and place (distribution). Other marketing decision variables may include service policies, credit and so forth. [GSD]

decision-making unit: (See **buying center.**)

decline stage of the product life cycle: The fourth stage of a product life cycle, in which sales of the product fall off from their levels during the maturity (third) stage. May lead to abandonment or efforts at rejuvenation of the product. [CMC]

DEFENDER: A model representing customers' brand choice decisions as a function of brand attributes. Key features include the incorporation of heterogeneous customer preferences and the representation of attribute levels in a "per dollar" multiattribute space. Based on the model, several qualitative normative implications hold regarding the optimal competitive response by "defending" brands against a new market entrant (Hauser and Gaskin 1984; Hauser and Shugan 1983). [DCS/YJW]

deflation: An economic condition characterized by continually declining prices. [DLS]

delivered price: A quoted or invoice price that includes delivery costs to the F.O.B. point the latter being a freight terminal, warehouse, or another location commonly accepted in the particular trade or specifically agreed upon between buyer and seller. [WRD]

delivered pricing: A form of geographical pricing in which the price quoted by the manufacturer includes both the list price and the transportation costs. In such cases, the prices are quoted as f.o.b. destination, meaning the manufacturer bears the responsibility of selecting and paying for the method of transporting the product. [KM]

delivery period: The normal time between the placing of an order and the receipt of stock. [WRD]

delivery reliability: The degree to which a seller delivers a product according to the schedule promised at the time of sale. [CMC]

Delphi technique: 1. A method of forecasting that relies on repeated measurement and controlled feedback among those participating along the following lines: (1) each individual prepares a forecast; (2) the forecasts are collected, and an anonymous summary is prepared by the person supervising the process; (3) the summary is distributed to each person who prepared a forecast; and (4) those participating in the process are asked to study the summary and submit a revised forecast. The process is repeated until the forecasts converge. [GAC] 2. A frequently used method in futures research to obtain the consensus opinion of a group of experts about likely future developments. A series of questionnaires is used with controlled feedback given to participants between rounds of questions. [WL]

demand: 1. (economic definition) A schedule of the amounts that buyers would be willing to purchase at all possible prices at any one instant of time. 2. (business executive definition) the number of units of a product sold by a market over a period of time. [DLS]

demand analysis: A study of the reasons underlying the demand for a product with the intent of forecasting and anticipating sales. [DLS]

demand creation: The use of price reductions and/or other incentives, such as premiums, rebates, etc. to create or increase immediate sales response for the product or service. (See also **sales promotion.**) [DES]

demand curve: A graph of the quantity of products expected to be sold at various prices, given that other factors are held constant. [DLS]

demand factors: Elements that determine the consumers' willingness and ability to pay for products. [DLS]

demand, industrial: Includes the goods and services that are required by all individuals and organizations that are engaged in the production of other goods and services. [GLL/DTW]

demand-backward pricing: The act of setting a price by starting with the estimated price consumers will pay and working backwards with retail and wholesale margins. [DLS]

demand-oriented pricing: A method of pricing where the seller attempts to set price at the level that the intended buyers are willing to pay. Also called value-oriented or value-in-use pricing. [KM]

demand-pulled innovation: Innovation that is caused or at least stimulated by the needs, wants, or desires of customers. Contrasts with supply-pushed innovation. Other terms for these two ideas are market- or customer-driven innovation and technology-driven innovation.

demographic environment: The human population conditions that surround a firm or nation and that greatly affect markets. Included are such factors as age distributions, births, deaths, immigration, marital status, sex, education, religious affiliations and geographic dispersion, characteristics which are often used for segmentation purposes. [WL]

demographics: The study of total size, sex, and territorial distribution, age, composition and other characteristics of human populations; the analysis of changes in the make up of a population. [WL]

demography: The study of people in the aggregate, including population size, age, sex, income, occupation, and family life-cycle. [DLS]

demonstration, sales: An aspect of the sales presentation which provides a sensory appeal to show how the product works and what benefits it offers the customer. [BAW]

demonstrations, as retailer sales promotion: An exhibition of a product in use or in its ultimate form as an inducement to prospective purchasers. Examples are: preparation and dispensing of food products in supermarkets, sampling of beverages in liquor stores, or demonstration of cooking equipment in department stores, all intended to call additional attention to the product or service. [DES]

demurrage: A carrier charge incurred when freight cars are retained beyond the specified time allowed for loading or unloading. Railroads charge demurrage for delays in excess of 48 hours in returning a car to service. [DJB/BJL]

department store: A retail establishment which carries several lines of merchandise, such as women's ready-to-wear and accessories, mens' and boys' clothing, piece goods, small wares, and home furnishing, all of which are organized into separate departments for the purpose of promotion, service, accounting, and control. For census purposes, establishments normally employing 25 or more people and engaged in selling some items in each of the following lines of merchandise: furniture, home furnishings, appliances, radio and TV sets; a general line of apparel for the family; household linen and dry goods. An establishment with total sales of less than $5,000,000 in which sales of any one of these groupings is greater than 80 percent of total sales is not classified as a department store. [WRD]

department store ownership groups: Aggregations of centrally owned stores in which each store continues to be merchandised and operated primarily as an individual concern with central guidance rather than central management or direction. [WRD]

developing countries: Countries with semi-developed markets whose 1987 GNP ranged from $1,001 to $2,500. The characteristics of this category of countries are: (1) more than 33% of the population is engaged in agriculture and less than 30% of the population is urban; (2) at least 50% of the population is literate; and (3) there are often highly developed industrial sectors and consumer markets are also of significant size on a per capita basis. (See also pre-industrial countries, underdeveloped countries, industrialized countries, and post-industrial countries.) [WJK]

departmentized specialty store: A term used to designate a concern organized in the same way as a department store but handling a narrower range of merchandise. [WRD]

departmentizing: The process of classifying merchandise into somewhat homogeneous groups known as departments. [WRD]

depression: A phase of the business cycle characterized by a rapid decline in gross national product and employment. [DLS]

depth interview: Unstructured personal interview in which the interviewer attempts to get subjects to talk freely and to express their true feelings. [GAC]

derived demand: Demand for one product that is derived from the purchase of another. The demand for industrial products is created by the purchase of consumer products which use or incorporate industrial products in them or in their manufacture. [CMC]

descriptive billing: A type of charge statement prepared for the customer in which a print out of the period's (usually a month) purchases appear on one statement with a description of the item purchased, the date, and the price but the original sales check is not included in the statement; only the description. [WRD]

descriptive labeling: The use of descriptive information (e.g. size, ingredients, or use) on labels. Contrasts with grade labeling, in which code letters or numbers are used to describe the relative quality of goods. [CMC]

descriptive research: Research design in which the major emphasis is on determining the frequency with which something occurs or the extent to which two variables covary. [GAC]

designated market area (DMA):   Term used by the A. C. Nielsen Company to define a geographic area based on those counties in which television stations of the originating market account for a greater share of the viewing audience than those from any other area [similar to Arbitron Ratings Company's area of dominant influence (ADI)]. [AMB]

detail salespeople: Missionary salespeople employed by pharmaceutical companies to call on physicians and attempt to get them to prescribe their firm's products. [BAW]

DETAILER: A decision calculus model providing a decision support system for allocating a salesforce's selling effort across the items in a firm's product line. The model's parameters are calibrated using subjective responses to a series of questions concerning projected sales under various levels of detailing effort and over various time periods (Montgomery, Silk and Zaragoza 1971). For other salesforce planning decision support systems, see CALLPLAN and GEOLINE. [DCS/YJW]

detailing: Personal sampling and other promotional work among doctors, dentists, and other professional persons done for pharmaceutical concerns, in order to secure goodwill and possible distribution or prescription of the product. [WRD]

detention: A carrier charge incurred when trailers of motor carriers are retained beyond the specified loading or unloading time. The permitted time is specified in the tariff and normally is limited to a few hours. [DJB/BJL]

dialog system: The part of a decision support system that permits users to explore the data bases by employing the system models to produce reports that satisfy their particular information needs. Also called "language systems." [GAC]

dichotomous question: Fixed-alternative question in which respondents are asked to indicate which of two alternative responses most closely corresponds to their position on a subject. [GAC]

differential advantage: 1. A property of any product which is able to claim a uniqueness over other products in its category. To be a differential advantage, the uniqueness must be communicable to customers and have value for them. The differential advantage of a firm is often called its distinctive competency. [CMC]2. An advantage unique to an organization; an advantage extremely difficult to match by a competitor. [DLS](See also **competitive advantage.**)

differentiated oligopoly: An oligopoly that produces and markets products that consumers consider close, but less than perfect, substitutes, e.g., automobiles. [DLS]

diffusion model: A model representing the contagion or spread of something through a population. Diffusion models in marketing often are applied to the adoption of a new product, or the exposure of potential customers to some information about a product (e.g., an advertising message). Numerous specific mathematical formulations have been applied to diffusion processes, and these are reviewed by Lilien and Kotler (1983 Chapter 19) and Mahajan and Wind (1986). The most widely cited of these models was introduced to Marketing by Bass (1969). It incorporates explicitly an innovation effect and an imitation effect. When both effects are present, the time path of adoption follows an S-shaped curve. [DCS/YJW]

diffusion of innovation: The process by which the use of an innovation is spread within a market group, over time, and over various categories of adopters. (See also **adopter categories.**) [CMC]

diffusion process: The process by which new ideas and products become accepted by a society. (See also **adopter categories** and **adoption process.**) [JPP/JCO]

diminishing marginal utility: A situation where the marginal utility, i.e., the extra utility added by consumption of a last unit, tends to decrease. [DLS]

diminishing returns: A situation where after a point the extra output resulting from an increase in some inputs relative to other fixed inputs tends to become less and less. [DLS]

diminishing utility: A situation where consumption of successive new units of a good causes total utility to grow at an increasingly slower rate, i.e., psychological factors cause a consumer to give a lesser appreciation to the later units. [DLS]

direct advertising: Mass or quantity promotion, not in an advertising medium, but issued from the advertiser by mail or personal distribution to individual customers or prospects; also, advertising literature appearing in folders, leaflets, throw-aways, letters, and delivered to prospective customers by mail, salespersons, dealers, or tucked into mailboxes. [WRD]

direct channels: A channel whereby goods and services are sold directly from producer to final user without involvement of other independent middlemen. [JRN]

direct cost method of inventory: A system under which the cost value of each item sold is recorded along with the selling price so an accurate costing of sales may be obtained. [WRD]

direct costs: Direct costs (also called traceable or attributable costs) are those costs incurred by and solely for a particular product, department, program, sales territory, or customer account. These costs may be fixed or variable. [KM]

direct exporting: The type of exporting where firms enter foreign markets directly and do their own export marketing. It means that the firm itself undertakes the complete export marketing task, which is extensive. Direct exprorting includes: choosing appropriate foreign markets, selecting agents or distributors to represent the firm in those markets, motivating and controlling those distributors choosing the product line for the target markets, setting prices and determining promotional strategies for those markets, handling international shipping and fianance, and preparing export documentation. [WJK]

direct fixed costs: Costs that are incurred by and solely for a particular product or segment but which do not vary with an activity level. [KM]

direct marketing: The total of activities by which the seller, in effecting the exchange of goods and services with the buyer, directs efforts to a target audience using one or more media (direct selling, direct mail, telemarketing, direct-action advertising, catalogue selling, cable selling, etc.) for the purpose of soliciting a response by phone, mail or personal visit, from a prospect or customer. [JRN]

direct product profitability (DPP): Managerial accounting practice of allocating costs to specific products. Method of evaluating distribution alternative such as direct store delivery. [DJB/BJL]

direct response advertising: Advertising that seeks an immediate action or response and which allows the consumer to respond directly to the advertiser, such as by mail or telephone, rather than going to a retail store or other distribution channel. [AMB]

direct sales force: A sales force consisting of salespeople employed by the company for whom they sell products or services. [BAW]

direct selling: 1. A marketing approach which involves direct sales of goods and services to consumers through personal explanation and demonstrations, primarily in their homes.

[BAW]2. Process whereby the firm responsible for production sells to the user, ultimate consumer, or retailer without intervening middlemen. [WRD]

direct selling organizations: Nonstore retailing establishments which solicit orders and distribute their products direct to consumers. [WRD]

direct store delivery (DSD): A system whereby goods are delivered to the buyer's store instead of going through a warehouse or distribution center. This can result in less handling and faster deliveries, but does not necessarily result in lower costs. [DJB/BJL]

direct variable costs: Costs that vary directly with an activity level. [KM]

Dirichlet multinomial model: A probability mixture model commonly used to represent patterns of brand choice behavior. Over repeated occasions on which purchases are made from the product category, the set of brands chosen are assumed to follow the multinomial distribution for any given individual. The model also assumes that individuals differ from each other in their set of brand choice probabilities. These probabilities are taken to have a Dirichlet distribution across individuals. The Dirichlet is a parsimonious distribution for the set of brand choice probabilities: for n brands there are n Dirichlet distribution parameters; n-1 of which indicate the average share of choices for each brand, and the n'th indicating the amount of heterogeneity in preference across individuals. The model thus can be used to predict brand choice patterns exhibited over time by a set of individuals (Jeuland, Bass and Wright 1980; Goodhardt, Ehrenberg and Chatfield 1984). [DCS/YJW]

disconfirmation: In consumer satisfaction theory, disconfirmation refers to a situation in which a product performs differently than expected prior to purchase. Positive disconfirmation occurs when the product performs better than expected; negative disconfirmation occurs when the product performs worse than expected. [JPP/JCO]

discount: A reduction in price. [KM]

discount house: A retailing business unit, featuring consumer durable items, competing on a basis of price appeal, and operating on a relatively low markup and with a minimum of customer service. [WRD]

discount store: Generally a large retail store open to the public which incorporates aspects of supermarket merchandising strategy to a high degree, attempts to price merchandise at a relatively low markup, carries stocks, renders only limited types of consumer services and usually on the basis of a specific extra charge. Can be distinguished from regular retailers only by its consistent emphasis upon "discount prices" and its self-designation as a discount store. [WRD]

discrete-lot-sizing: An inventory management technique to help determine order quantities. The procurement objective is to obtain a quantity of components that equals the net requirement needed at a specific time. Purchase quantities will vary from order to order because of fluctuations in component requirements. [DJB/BJL]

discretionary buying power: Money in the hands of consumers after the payment of taxes and the purchase of necessities; popularly called "hot money" or "loose money." [DLS]

discretionary income: (see **discretionary buying power**). [DLS]

discriminant analysis: Statistical technique employed to model the relationship between a dichotomous or multichotomous criterion variable and a set of p continuous predictor variables. [GAC]

discriminant consequences: Consequences that differ across a set of alternatives that may be used as choice criteria. [JPP/JCO]

discriminant validity: Criterion imposed on a measure of a construct requiring that it not correlate too highly with measures from which it is supposed to differ. [GAC]

discriminative stimulus: A stimulus that by its mere presence or absence changes the probability of a behavior. For example, a 50 percent off sign in a store window could be a discriminative stimulus. [JPP/JCO]

diseconomies of scale: Losses that stem from producing a larger amount rather than a small amount, i.e., higher per unit costs for a product are incurred as the scale of operations is increased. [DLS]

disjunctive rule: As compared with the conjunctive or lexicographic rule, the disjunctive heuristic (or rule of thumb) assumes that the consumer develops acceptable standards for each dimension (which may be higher than the minimum cutoff levels for the conjunctive heuristic). According to Bettman, if a product, brand, or alternative passes that standard for any attribute, it is accepted. The evaluation process yields groups of acceptable and unacceptable alternatives and hence the evaluation is derived rather than direct. (See also **conjunctive rule , lexicographic rule,** and **noncompensatory rules.**) [HHK]

dispersion: The process of breaking down a supply of goods into smaller lots. It includes the sorting processes of allocation and sorting out. [JRN]

displays: Special exhibits of products at the point of sale, generally over and above standard shelf stockings. [DES]

disposable personal income (DPI):   1. Personal income less federal, state, and local taxes. 2. A consumer's total money income less taxes paid to all government agencies; popularly shortened to "disposable income". [DLS]

disproportionate stratified sampling: Stratified sample in which the individual strata or subsets are sampled in relation to both their size and their variability; strata exhibiting more variability are sampled more than proportionately to their relative size, while those that are very homogeneous are sampled less than proportionately. [GAC]

dissatisfaction: (See **consumer satisfaction** and **post purchase evaluation.**) [HHK]

dissection control: The subdividing of existing departments into relatively narrow groupings, then the establishing of dollar stock control records for each grouping. (See also **classification.**) [WRD]

dissociative group: A reference group that an individual does not want to join or be similar to. [JPP/JCO]

dissonance reduction: (See **cognitive dissonance.**) [HHK]

distinctive competences: The strengths of the firm. That is, the particular characteristics of the firm which make it uniquely adapted to carry out its task(s) and to fulfill its purpose(s) in the industry within which it participates. The converse to the firm's distinctive advantages are its weaknesses which inhibit and limit the ability of the firm to fulfill its purpose. [GSD]

distinctiveness: A uniqueness that one product or one firm has over others. May exist in any attribute, and may only be perceived, not real. (See also **differential advantage.**) [CMC]

distress merchandise: Goods that are (or soon will be) past the point where they can be sold at anything close to normal prices. Includes perishable, unfashionable, damaged, and unseasonal items which still have some market value. [CMC]

distribution: 1. (economic definition) A study of how factors of production are priced in the market place, i.e., the determination of rents, wages, interest, and profits. 2. (marketing definition) The marketing and carrying of products to consumers. 3. (business definition) The extent of market coverage. [DLS]

distribution manager: (See **physical distribution manager.**) [VPB]

distribution models: In modeling the key decisions of which channel of distribution to choose, management can use any of the general models for option generation and evaluation. Specialized models have been developed, however, for specific distribution decisions such as site selection and logistics. Most of the gravitational site selection models follow Huff(1964), who developed a model in which the attraction of a site is proportional to the size of the retail center and inversely proportional to the customers' distance from the site. This model has been extended to incorporate not only size of retail site, but also image. These models are extensions of the Multiple Competitive Interaction Model (MCI). Logistics-related optimization models have also been developed for warehouse locations and inventory management. Most of the models are based on mathematical programming or simulations. [DCS/YJW]

distribution of income: The manner in which income is received among various groups of consumers. [DLS]

distribution requirements planning (DRP): A planning technique that seeks to time-phase movement of products from manufacturing through the distribution channel. The objective is to forward allocate as little inventory as practical while satisfying customer service goals. [DJB/BJL]

distributive education: A federally assisted program of education for workers in the distributive occupations at the high school and adult training level augmented by state and local support. Classwork in school facilities is combined with concurrent work experience. [WRD]

distributive trades: Establishments that are engaged principally in marketing (wholesale trade, retail trade, and service industries). [WRD]

distributor: Wholesale middlemen, especially in lines where selection or exclusive agency distribution is common at the wholesale level and the manufacturer expects strong promotional support; often a synonym for wholesaler. [WRD]

distributor's brand: A brand that is owned and controlled by a reseller (distributor) such as a retailer or a wholesaler, as opposed to a brand owned by the manufacturer. The term applies only to the brand itself, not to the product or to its content. Often called a private brand or private label, and (with exceptions such as Sears' brands) is usually not advertised heavily. (See also **private brand.**) [CMC]

distributorship: A type of franchise system wherein franchisees maintain warehouse stock to supply other franchises. The distributor takes title to the goods and provides services to other customers. [WRD]

diversification: A means whereby a business builds its total sales by identifying opportunities to build or acquire businesses that are not directly related to the company's current businesses. The major classes of diversification are concentric, horizontal and conglomerate. **Concentric diversification** results in new product lines or services that have technological and/or marketing synergies with existing product lines, even though the products may appeal to a new customer group. **Horizontal diversification** is where the company acquires or develops new products that could appeal to its current customer groups even though those new products may be technologically unrelated to the existing product lines. **Conglomerate diversification** occurs when there is neither technological nor marketing synergies and requires reaching new customer groups. [GSD]

diversion-in-transit: A change of direction from original destination while freight is in transit. [WRD]

diversion: Changing the destination of a shipment while it is enroute and prior to arrival at the originally planned destination. [DJB/BJL]

divest strategy: The sale or liquidation of businesses or product lines in order to limit losses or in order to avoid predicted losses and/or because the resources freed up can be better used in other businesses. [GSD]

divisional organization: A form of organization which breaks the company into two or more business units (commonly called divisions). A division is a profit center and the division manager is responsible for attaining profit goals. A division may be responsible for a share of the company's existing product lines or for a separate business. The division manager reports to a top corporate executive. A division may be organized functionally or (as it expands) with the assistance of product or market managers. (See also: **integrated division, partially integrated division,** and **marketing (only) division**). [VPB]

dog: (See **growth-share matrix**).

dollar control: Control of sales, stocks, markdowns and markups in terms of dollars rather than in terms of pieces or items. [WRD]

domesticated markets: Markets that once were competitive that have been restructured as a result of voluntary, long term binding agreements. A significant proportion of all transactions in these markets are planned and administered on the basis of negotiated rules of exchange. The benefits are reduced certainty, reduced transactions costs and access to economies of scale. [GSD]

domestics: A subdivision of the "piece goods" classification of merchandise, including muslins, sheets, pillowcases, tubing, cotton, outing flannel, etc. [WRD]

donor market: A target audience asked to give money, goods, body organs or blood to an organization or individual without expecting a tangible benefit in return. Comment: Donor marketing can be carried out by for-profit organizations. For-profit organizations can also be the recipients of the donations (although this is rare). [ARA]

door-to-door selling: (See **direct selling.**) [BAW]

double-barreled question: A question that calls for two responses and thereby creates confusion for the respondent. [GAC]

downturn: (See **recession.**) [DLS]

draw: Money paid to salespeople against future commissions, usually in a period when commissions are low, in order to ensure that they may take home a specified minimum level of pay each month. [BAW]

drive: (See **motivation.**) [HHK]

drop shipment: Limited-function wholesalers known as drop shippers seldom take physical possession of the goods. They often specialize in heavy or bulky commodities that require the economies of volume shipment. The drop shipper buys the carload, but does not take physical possession. The order, or drop shipment, is shipped direct from the supplier to the customer. [DJB/BJL]

drop shipper (desk jobber): A special type of wholesaler who deals in large lots shipped direct from the factory to the customer of the drop shipper, takes title to the goods, assumes responsibility for the shipment after it leaves the factory, extends credit, collects the account, and incurs all the sales costs necessary to secure orders. [WRD]

dual career path, sales: The provision of a choice made available to junior salespeople in an organization to receive more pay and recognition through promotions to managerial positions or through promotions within the sales rank with compensation being similar at similar levels along each path. [BAW]

dual distribution: 1. Describes a wide variety of marketing arrangements by which a manufacturer or a wholesaler reaches its final markets by employing two or more different types of channels for the same basic product. [JRN] 2. Under this type of distribution program, manufacturers sell directly to contractors and other large accounts at prices equal to or less than those available to retailers in the same market and who are reselling the manufacturers' products. [WRD]

dumping: The practice of selling a product at a lower price overseas than at home. [DLS]

duplication: (See **audience duplication.**)

durable goods: Consumer goods that are used over an extended rather than a brief period of time. Usually, but not necessarily, of more substantial manufacture. Examples are automobiles and furniture. [CMC]

dwelling unit: A single home, apartment, townhouse or other unit in which a single person, family, or cohesive set of unrelated individuals reside. Typically, many goods are purchased in common. [HHK]

early adopters: The second identifiable sub-group within a population that begins use of an innovation. They follow innovators and precede the early majority. Their role is to be opinion leaders and have influence over the early majority. (See also **adoption process, adopter categories,** and **product adoption process.**) [CMC]

early majority: The third identifiable sub-group within a population that adopts an innovation. Preceded by early adopters and innovators. The early majority like to await the outcome of product trial by the two earlier groups, yet are not as slow to adopt as the next two groups, late majority and laggards. (See also **adoption process, adopter categories,** and **product adoption process.**) [CMC]

early markdown: A markdown taken early in the season or while the demand for the merchandise is still relatively active. [WRD]

earned income: Income resulting from work or services performed as contrasted with income from such sources as investments or rent. [WL]

EBA model: See Elimination-By-Aspects model. [DCS/YJW]

ecology: The study of the relations among living species and their physical and biotic environments, particularly adaptations to environments through the mechanisms of various systems. Consideration is given to environmental impact on development, behavior and spatio-temporal and demographic relations. [WL]

economic concept of rent: A term reflecting the maximum amount that can be spent by a retail store for yearly rent expenses. It is calculated by subtracting from planned sales all projected nonrent costs including a projected or planned profit figure. [WRD]

economic determinism: A philosophy, perspective or belief that economic forces ultimately are determinants of social and political change. [WL]

economic environment: Encompasses such factors as productivity, income, wealth, inflation, balance of payments, pricing, poverty, interest rates, credit, transportation, and employment; the totality of the economic surroundings that affect a company's markets and its opportunities. [WL]

economic goods: Goods that are so scarce relative to human wants that human effort is required to obtain them. [DLS]

economic indicator: Data collected over time that reflect economic activity and general business conditions. [DLS]

economic infrastructure: Internal facilities of a country available for conducting business activities, especially the communication, transportation, distribution, and financial systems. [DLS]

economic man: A model of human behavior assumed by economists in analyzing market behavior. The economic person is a rational person who attempts to maximize the utility received from his/her monetary outflows and sacrifices. [DLS]

economic organization: The way in which the means of production and distribution of goods are organized, such as capitalism or socialism. [WL]

economic shoppers: Shoppers who try to maximize the ratio of total utility and dollars of expenditure. [DLS]

economic-lot-sizing: An inventory management technique used to determine order quantity or order period which minimizes the total cost of inventory maintenance and ordering. Requires continuous demand. [DJB/BJL]

economics: The science that deals with human wants and satisfaction. [DLS]

economies of scale: The savings derived from producing a large number of units, e.g., in a situation where all inputs are doubled, output may be more than doubled. [DLS]

economy pack: A merchandising phrase pointing out savings by including several products in one wrapping. [WRD]

ecosystem: The complex of interactions of all the organisms with their environments and with each other. Technically, a subunit of the biosphere or a unit of a landscape. The interactions of members of a distribution channel, or the interaction of a company and its products with consumer environments are examples of marketing applications. [WL]

editing: Inspection and correction, if necessary, of each questionnaire or observation form. [GAC]

effective demand: People with money and the inclination to buy. [DLS]

effective frequency: (See **frequency**.)

efficient market hypothesis: In its so-called "semi-strong" form, this hypothesis states that in setting security prices at any time, the market correctly uses all publicly available information about the underlying corporations whose stock is traded in the market. In the absence of inside information, this implies that investors cannot consistently achieve performance in excess of the market "average" for any given level of risk. The "semi-strong" hypothesis enjoys wide acceptance in financial economics. [PFA]

ego: According to Freudian Theory, one prong of the three parts of the personality. The ego is the executive, or the planner, compromising between the demands for immediate gratification of the id and the pristine rigidity of the super-ego (conscience or moral self). (See also **id, superego** and **ego defenses**). [HHK]

ego defenses: The tools the ego has available to defend the individual from psychological stresses such as the forces of the id (libido) and the super-ego. Ego defenses are psychological constructs such as repression, rationalization, sublimation, reaction formation, identifications, etc. [HHK]

ego defensive drives: (See **ego defenses**.) [HHK]

elastic demand: 1. A situation where a cut in price increases the quantity taken in the market enough that total revenue is increased. 2. A situation where the percentage of quantity taken "stretches" more than the percentage drop in price. [DLS]

elasticity: A term used to indicate the degree that an economic variable changes in response to a change in another economic variable. [KM]

elasticity coefficient: 1. A measure of the responsiveness of the quantity of a product taken in the market to price changes. 2. (technical) E is the limit as the change in price tends to zero of a ratio composed of two ratios: the change in quantity/quantity divided by change in price/price. E is always negative: if the absolute value of E is greater than one, demand is said to be elastic; if exactly equal to one, unit elasticity prevails; if less than one, demand is said to be inelastic. [DLS]

elasticity of demand: (See **price elasticity of demand**). [DLS]

elasticity of expectation: A measure of the changes in prices of goods and changes in the quantity taken by the market stemming from expectations by consumers. [DLS]

elasticon: A conjoint analysis-based model for estimating self- and cross-price elasticity. Respondents are asked to indicate their likelihood of buying each brand (when each brand is priced at some experimental level). A first order Markov model represents the price induced brand switching. The price-demand model is fitted by generalized least-squares to the share of choices (Mahajan, Green, and Goldberg 1982). [DCS/YJW]

electronic data interchange (EDI): Communication system which allows direct electronic transfer of information between two enterprises. [DJB/BJL]

electronic fund transfer: The use of electronic means, such as computers, telephones, magnetic tape and so on, rather than checks, to transfer funds, or authorize or complete a transaction. This development has given rise to the concept of the cashless economy. [WL]

Elimination-By-Aspects (EBA) model: A choice model that represents the ultimate selection decision as a series of eliminations. Each alternative available for choice is viewed as having some set of aspects (e.g., product features). At each stage of the choice process an aspect is selected (with probability proportional to that aspect's importance for this consumer), and all alternatives still being considered that do not possess the selected aspect are eliminated. The process continues until only one alternative remains, and that remaining item is assumed to be the one chosen by the consumer (Tversky 1972). Although more difficult to calibrate and apply than the Luce model for choices, it does avoid the Independence from Irrelevant Alternatives property of the latter model, which is often seen as an appealing feature of the EBA model. It has led to the development of other hierarchical/sequential choice models, including the Hierarchical Elimination Model (HEM) (Tversky and Sattath 1979) and Generalized Elimination Model (GEM) (Hauser 1986). [DCS/YJW]

emergency products: Goods (such as portable generators) and services (such as ambulance delivery) where an essentially non-deliberative purchase decision is based on critical and timely need. [CMC]

employee discount: Most general merchandise retailers offer employees a certain discount from retail price. It is a kind of retail reduction from the point of view of accounting. Usually stores grant a larger percentage on personal wearing apparel than on gifts purchased by the employee. [WRD]

emulative product: A new product that imitates another product already on the market. Is somewhat different from previous products (not a pure me-too), but the difference is not substantial or significant. (See also **adaptive product and innovative imitation.**) [CMC]

end sizes (outsizes): Those usually large, small, or extraordinary in some respect. [WRD]

end user: A person or organization that consumes a good or service that may consist of the input of numerous firms. For example, an insurance company may be the end user' for a keyboard for a personal computer, originally produced for and sold to the personal computer manufacturer. [GLL/DTW]

end-aisle display: Exhibits of products set up at the end of the aisle in retail stores to call attention to special offerings or prices. [DES]

endless chain method: A method of prospecting in which a salesperson asks customers to suggest other customers who might be interested in the salesperson's offerings. [BAW]

enduring involvement: The general, personal relevance of a product or activity. [JPP/JCO]

Engels Law: The observation that the proportion of income spent on food declines as income rises with given tastes or preferences. This law or tendency was formulated by Ernst Engel (1821-1896) in a paper published by him in 1857. [WJK]

environment: The complex of physical and social stimuli in the external world of consumers. [JPP/JCO]

environmental analysis: Gathering and analyzing data about a company's or nation's external environment to identify trends and their impact upon an organization or country. Included among the environmental forces considered are the political, cultural, social, demographic, economic, legal and international and ecological factors. [WL]

environmental monitoring: Activities aimed at keeping track of changes in external factors that are likely to affect the markets and demand for a firm's products and services. Among the external factors usually considered are the economic, social, demographic, political, legal, cultural, and technological forces. [WL]

Environmental Protection Agency (1970): A federal agency which regulates the amount of pollutants manufacturers can emit. [DC]

environmental scanning: (See **environmental monitoring.**) [WL]

environmental stimuli: (See **external stimulus.**) [HHK]

environmentalism: 1. Refers to public concern over protecting, enhancing and improving the environment which includes conserving natural resources, eliminating pollution and hazardous substances, historic preservation, and preventing the extinction of plant and animal species. [DC] 2. That part of consumerism that concentrates on ecology issues such as air, water, and noise pollution and the depletion of natural resources. Marketing decisions and action, such as new product offerings can impact directly on physical environments. [WL]

E.O.M. (end of month) dating: The cash discount and the net credit periods begin on the first day of the following month rather than on the invoice date. E.O.M. terms are frequently stated in this manner: "2/10, net 30, E.O.M.". Suppose an order is filled and shipped on June 16 under these terms. In such a case, the cash discount may be taken any time through July 10 and the net amount is due on July 30. [WRD]

episodic knowledge: Mental representations of the specific events in a person's life. (See also **semantic knowledge.**) [JPP/JCO]

Equal Credit Opportunity Act (1974):   Prohibits discrimination by a creditor against any applicant for credit on the basis of sex or marital status. [DC]

equal time: Section 315 of the Federal Communication Commission Act provides that if a broadcaster permits a legally qualified candidate for any public office to use a broadcasting station, he shall afford equal opportunity to use the broadcasting station to all other candidates for that office. (See also **fairness doctine.**) [DC]

equalized workload method: A method of determining sales force size which is based on the premise that all sales personnel should shoulder an equal amount of work. The method requires that management estimate the work required to serve the entire market. The total work calculation is typically treated as a function of number of accounts, how often each should be called on, and for how long. This estimate is then divided by the amount of work an individual salesperson should be able to handle to determine the total number of salespeople required. [OCW]

erratic demand: A pattern of demand for a product that is varied and unpredictable, e.g., the demand for large automobiles. [DLS]

esteem needs: (See **hierarchy of needs.**) [HHK]

ethnocentric: A home country orientation or an unconscious bias or belief that the home country approach to business is superior. [WJK]

ethnocentric pricing policy: (See **extension pricing policy.**)

eurocurrency: A national currency deposited outside the country of denomination. A U.S. dollar deposited in a foreign bank is a eurocurrency. [WJK]

European Community: An association of European countries, viz. Germany, France, Italy, Belgium, Luxembourg, The Netherlands, The United Kingdom, Ireland and Denmark, with uniform trade rules built upon the elimination of internal tarrif barriers and the establishment of common external barriers. Its goal is to integrate and harmonize the economic, social, and political life of members. On the economic front, the goal is the elimination all barriers and restrictions on the movement of goods and services. [WJK]

European Free Trade Association (EFTA):   An association established by the Stockholm Convention of 1959, with member countries being Austria, Finland (associate member), Iceland, Norway, Portugal, Sweden and Switzerland. EFTA's objective is to bring about free trade in industrial goods and an expansion of trade in agricultural goods. [WJK]

evaluation of alternative suppliers, in organizational buying: Formal supplier evaluation is the rating of alternative suppliers on pre-set criteria in order to evaluate their technical, financial, and managerial abilities. It is a way to substitute facts for feelings in selecting suppliers. [GLL/DTW]

event creation: The use of communication techniques such as news releases, press conferences, etc., to call attention to activities to promote a company, product, or service. [DES]

evoked set: 1. The set of alternatives that are activated directly from memory. [JPP/JCO] 2. The set of possible products or brands that the consumer may be considering in his decision process. The set of choices that has been evoked and are salient as compared with the larger number of available possible choices. For example, from the many brands of breakfast cereals on supermarket shelves, it is the half a dozen brands (or so) that the buyer may remember and be considering for purchase. [HHK]

ex-parte: A regulatory practice of pretesting proposed regulatory rules in an effort to get reactions and comments from shippers, carriers and other interested parties. [DJB/BJL]

exchange: All activities associated with receiving something from someone by giving something voluntarily in return. [DLS]

exchange control: The control of movement of funds and of purchases of currency by a government. Exchange control may be utilized in support of any of the following objectives: (a) to keep exchange rates stable, (b) to keep the currency undervalued to stimulate exports or (c) to keep the currency overvalued to handicap exports and encourage imports. [WJK]

exchange desk: A station within a store where customers take merchandise for exchange or credit depending upon company policy. Usually more functions are performed at this station than just exchange. [WRD]

exclusive agency method of distribution: The practice whereby the vendor agrees to sell his goods or services within a certain territory only through a single retailer or a limited number of retailers; may also apply to wholesalers. [WRD]

exclusive dealing: A restriction which is imposed by a supplier on a customer forbidding the customer from purchasing some type of product from any other supplier. This restriction is subject to an examination of whether it substantially lessens competition or restrains trade. Exclusive dealing should not be confused with exclusive distributorships, a term applied to arrangements in which a supplier promises not to appoint more than one dealer in each territory. [DC]

exclusive distribution: A form of market coverage in which a product is distributed through one particular wholesaler or retailer in a given market area. [JRN]

exempt carrier: Transportation provider not subject to direct regulation regarding operating rights or pricing policies. They must, however, comply with licensing and safety laws. If engaged in interstate movement, they must publish their rates. [DJB/BJL]

exhibits: Gathering and displaying products, people, or information at a central location for viewing by a diverse audience. [DES]

expansibility of demand: The degree to which the demand schedule can be shifted through the use of marketing variables such as advertising and personal selling. [DLS]

expectancy-value model: One of the major schools of motivation emerging from the work of Kurt Lewin. According to Wilkie, the major proposition is: the strength of the tendency to act in a certain way depends on the strength of the expectancy that the act will be followed by a given consequence (or goal) and the value of that goal to the individual. It assumes that the consumer behaves purposively and evaluates, say, the purchase of a particular brand in terms of how desirable the consequences of the purchase of that brand are for him or her. [HHK]

expediter: One who works to speed up shipment for delivery. [DJB/BJL]

expense account: An account maintained by salespeople, which includes travel, entertainment, telephone and other expenses which they have to incur for the purposes of business, for which they are reimbursed by their employers. [BAW]

expense center: A collection of controllable costs which are related to one particular area of work or kind of store service. [WRD]

expense center accounting: Expenses are grouped by their necessity in performing a particular kind of store service. For example, some expense centers are management, property and equipment, accounts payable, etc. Natural expenses are typically included as a part of the concept (e.g., payroll). [WRD]

experience curve analysis: Applications of the experience curve effect, to understand (1) how the components of the total cost of a company's product are affected by cumulative experience, (2) the relationship of industry experience and average industry prices and costs, and (3) how competitive cost comparisons relate to current costs of direct competitors to their cumulative experience. (See also **experience curve effect**). [GSD]

experience curve effect: A systematic decline in the cost per unit that is achieved as the cumulative volume (and therefore experience) increases. There are three sources of the experience curve effect: (1) learning—the increasing efficiency of labor that arises chiefly form practice; (2) technological improvements—including process innovations, resource mix changes and product standardization; and (3) economies of scale—the increased efficiency due to size. [GSD]

experience survey: Interviews with people knowledgeable about the general subject being investigated. [GAC]

experience-curve pricing: 1. A method of pricing where the seller sets price sufficiently low to encourage a large sales volume in anticipation that the large sales volume would lead to a reduction in average unit costs. Generally this method of pricing is used over time by periodically reducing price to induce additional sales volumes that lead to lower per unit costs. [KM] 2. A price-setting method using a markup on the average total cost as forecast by cost trends over time as sales volume accumulates. [DLS]

experiment: Scientific investigation in which an investigator manipulates and controls one or more independent variables and observes the dependent variable for variation concomitant to the manipulation of the independent variable(s). [GAC]

experimental design: Research investigation in which the investigator has direct control over at least one independent variable and manipulates at least one independent variable [GAC]

experimental group: A group of subjects in an experiment who are exposed to an experimental treatment or alternative whose effect is to be measured and compared. [GAC]

expert systems: Interactive computer systems that, by applying a variety of knowledge elements (e.g. facts, rules, models) within a specified domain, can solve a problem with an expertise comparable to that of an acknowledged human expert. As part of the development in artificial intelligence, expert systems have been developed in various fields (medicine, defense, manufacturing, etc.). In recent years, a number of marketing expert systems have been developed, including ADCAD (an expert system for the design of advertising appeals and executions—Rangaswamy, Burke, Wind, and Eliashberg (1987)). [DCS/YJW]

explicit costs: Costs, generally of a contractual or definite nature, including expenses for such items as wages, telephone bills, light bills, and supplies. They are explicitly carried on the accounting records as costs and are charges against the operation of the business because they are obvious and definite in amount. [WRD]

exploratory research: Research design in which the major emphasis is on gaining ideas and insights; it is particularly helpful in breaking broad, vague problem statements into smaller, more precise subproblem statements. [GAC]

exponential smoothing: A forecasting technique to estimate future sales using a weighted average of previous demand and forecast accuracy. The new forecast is based on the old forecast incremented by some fraction of the differential between the old forecast and sales realized. The factor used to calculate the new forecast is called an alpha factor. [DJB/BJL]

Export Import Bank (Eximbank):   The primary U.S. government agency in the business of providing funds for international trade and investment. It also plays a key role in the U.S export credit insurance program program. It is also the primarry administrator for the foreign currencies abroad which are generated by the U.S surplus farm commodities. [WJK]

export management company (EMC):   A firm which manages exports for other firms. It produces no product of its own but serves as an international marketing intermediary. It acts as the export department of the client firm and may even use its letterhead. [WJK]

export marketing: The integrated marketing of goods and services that are produced in a foreign country. Each element of the marketing mix, (product, price, promotion, and channels of distribution), is potentially variable. [WJK]

export selling: Selling to a foreign country with the focus on the product and the emphasis on selling. The key elements of marketing mix (product, price and promotion), are all the same as in the home market. Only the place or distribution is adjusted in export selling. (See also **export marketing.**) [WJK]

exposure: Opportunity for a reader, viewer, listener to see/hear the advertisements in a particular advertising media vehicle. [AMB]

expressed warranty: Spoken or written promises made by the seller of a product about what will be done if the product proves to be defective in manufacture or performance. Contrasts with promises that are only implied by common knowledge of the product or by customary practices in a trade. Expressed warranties are usually restricted to stated periods of time. (See also **implied warranty.**) [CMC]

expropriation: Government acquisition of private property without payment of prompt and full compensation to owners. [WJK]

extension pricing policy: A pricing policy which requires that the price of an item be the same around the world and that the customer absorbs freight and import duties. This is also known as ethnocentric pricing policy. [WJK]

extensive decision making: A choice involving substantial cognitive and behavioral effort. [JPP/JCO]

extensive problem solving: In the choice process, those decisions that consume considerable cognitive activity and thought, as compared to routine decisions and habitual responses. [HHK]

external data: Data that originate outside the organization for which the research is being done. [GAC]

external stimulus: A cue or stimulus or prod to action that is external to the individual such as a bright light or advertisement. Internal stimuli would be those from within the individual such as hunger pangs, the feeling of fear or glee. [HHK]

external validity: One criterion by which an experiment is evaluated; the criterion refers to the extent, to what populations and settings, to which the observed experimental effect can be generalized. [GAC]

extinction: The process by which a learned response or learned behavior pattern is extinguished or unlearned (or forgotten). Extinction is the psychological term for unlearning. It is the process of forgetting and although there is some controversy over whether or not forgetting naturally occurs over time, it is accepted that extinction can be induced. [HHK]

extra dating: A form of deferred dating. The purchaser is allowed a specified number of days before the ordinary dating begins. To illustrate, in the sale of blankets the terms "2/10-60 days extra" may be offered by the vendor. This means that the buyer has 60 days plus 10 days, or 70 days, from the invoice date in which to pay the bill with the discount deducted. [WRD]

extrinsic rewards: Rewards that are external to the individual such as money, food, or a pat on the head. Intrinsic rewards are those that are internal within the person such as "feeling good for a job well done." [HHK]

fabricating materials: All types of processed materials that are not considered component parts, and required for producing goods and services. Examples are steel plates, chemicals, glass, coke, sheet metal, plastics, and leather. [GLL/DTW]

face value: The printed financial value of a coupon (actual savings). Can be either a specific monetary amount, a percentage discount, or combination offer with another product. [DES]

facilitating agents: Business firms that assist in the performance of distribution tasks other than buying, selling and transferring title (i.e.,transportation companies, warehouses, etc.). [JRN]

factor: (1) A specialized financial institution engaged in factoring accounts receivable and lending on the security of inventory. (2) A type of commission house which often advances funds to the consigner, identified chiefly with the raw cotton and naval stores trades. [WRD]

factor analysis: Body of techniques concerned with the study of interrelationships among a set of variables, none of which is given the special status of a criterion variable. [GAC]

factoring: A specialized financial function whereby manufacturers, wholesalers, or retailers sell accounts receivable to financial institutions, including factors, banks, and sales finance companies, often on a nonrecourse basis. [WRD]

factory pack: Multiple packaging of one product, or of one product and another product of the same firm, or one product and a sample or premium. The packaging is done at the factory and arrives in the trade channel already in the promotional form. [CMC]

fads: Products (e.g., unique dolls and video arcades) whose popularity is intense but temporary. They come in fast, receive much attention and publicity, and go out fast. The time period is highly variable, and a fad can repeat at intervals of several years as the hula hoop does. (See also **fashion cycle**.) [CMC]

Fair Credit Reporting Act (1970): Designed to insure accuracy of credit reports and to allow consumers the right to learn the nature of the information and challenge and correct erroneous information. [DC]

Fair Debt Collection Practices Act (1978): A third party debt collector (i.e., one who collects debts owed to another), cannot communicate with the consumer in connection with the debt at any unusual time or place, and may not harass or abuse any person in connection with the collection of the debt. [DC]

Fair Packaging and Labeling Act (1966): Requires that labels on consumer commodities identify the type of product being sold, the name and address of the supplier, and where applicable, the quality and contents of each serving. The Act also authorizes the FTC and FDA to issue regulations concerning specific products covering items such as ingredient statements, package size standards, "slack-fill" packaging, and sales price representations. [DC]

fair trade laws: Federal and state statutes permitting suppliers of branded goods to impose resale price maintenance contracts fixing minimum retail prices. The Consumer Goods Pricing Act of 1975 outlawed such practices. [DC]

fairness doctrine: Requires broadcasters to afford reasonable opportunity for the discussion of conflicting views on issues of public importance. In 1987, the Federal Communications Commission abandoned its fairness doctrine: however, there have been efforts by legislators to place the doctrine into law. (See also **equal time**.) [DC]

family brand: A brand that is used on two or more individual products. The product group may or may not be all of that firm's product line. The individual members of the family also carry individual brands to differentiate them from other family members. In rare cases there are family brands which have as members other family brands each of which has individual brands. Automobiles fit the latter situation, as with Oldsmobile (family) Cutlass (family) Ciera (individual). (See also **branding, individual**.) [CMC]

family decision making: The processes, interactions, and roles of family members involved in making decisions. [JPP/JCO]

family life cycle: 1. A sociological concept that describes changes in families across time. Emphasis is placed on the effects of marriage, divorce, births, and deaths on families and the changes in income consumption through various family stages. [JPP/JCO] 2. Families account for a very large percentage of all consumer expenditures. Much of this spending is systematic and stems from natural needs that change as a family unit does through its natural stages of life. These range from the Young Single and the Newly Married stages to the Full Nest as the children are born and grow, to the Empty Nest and the final Solitary Survivor stage. Each transition prompts changes in values and behavior. [HHK]

family packaging: Using one design or other key packaging element to integrate the packaging of two or more individual items. The packages clearly belong to one set, but there are usually some individualizations, especially in brand name. [CMC]

family roles: (See **roles**.) [HHK]

fashion: An accepted and popular style. [WRD]

fashion coordination: The function of analyzing fashion trends in order to ensure that the merchandise offered for sale in various related apparel departments is of comparable style, quality, and appeal. [WRD]

fashion cycle: The process by which a particular design, activity, color, etc., comes into some popularity and then phases out. This cycle of adoption and rejection is quite similar to the product life cycle, but the fashion cycle uses different terms to describe its phases: (1) distinctiveness phase, when the style is eagerly sought, (2) emulation stage when its popularity grows, and (3) economic stage when it becomes available at lower prices to the mass market. [CMC]

fashion products: A sub-category of shopping products. Contains items that are wanted by consumers for their fashion aspects. [CMC]

fast food outlets: A food retailing institution featuring a very limited menu, pre-prepared or quickly prepared food, and take-out operations. [WRD]

FBI model: An acronym for the Fishbein Behavioral Intentions Model. [JPP/JCO]

FCB grid: An acronym standing for the Foote, Cone, & Belding Grid. [JPP/JCO]

fear appeals: Communications material that attempts to persuade or manipulate by using frightening message content (Not using Brand X deodorant will lead to a miserable social life). The relationship between fear and persuasibility seems to be curvilinear such that moderate levels of fear appear to be more effective than the use of either mild fear or strong fear. The difficulty is in the definitions and measurement of what is mild, moderate and extreme fear appeals. [HHK]

feature, product: Fact or technical specifications about a product. [BAW]

feature: The use of advertising, displays, or other activity to call special attention to a product, generally for a limited period of time. [DES]

Federal Cigarette and Labeling and Advertising Act (1967):   Required a warning statement on cigarette packages and prohibited the advertising of cigarettes and little cigars on electronic media under the jurisdiction of the Federal Communications Commission. In 1986, these restrictions were extended to smokeless tobacco. [DC]

Federal Communications Commission (FCC):   A federal regulatory agency responsible for supervising radio and television broadcasting. [DC]

Federal Energy Regulatory Commission (1971):   Replaced the Federal Power Commission established in 1920 and is responsible for issuing licenses for the development of water and electrical power and prohibiting operators from restricting output or restraining trade in electrical energy. [DC]

Federal Environmental Pesticide Control Act (1976):   Requires registration of a pesticide before it can be distributed, sold or offered for sale or shipped or received in any state. Responsibility for pesticide control is placed with the Environmental Protection Agency. [DC]

Federal Food, Drug and Cosmetics Act (1938):   Brought therapeutic devices and cosmetics within the regulatory authority of the FDA and strengthened the FDA's enforcement powers. [DC]

Federal Hazardous Substances Act (1960):   Requires cautionary labeling of household chemical products. [DC]

Federal Maritime Commission: Regulates foreign and offshore domestic trade. It authorizes the setting of international sea freight rates and regulates against imposition of illegal rebates and discrimination by carriers. [DC]

federal regulatory agencies: Administrative agencies which create and enforce the bulk of the laws which make up the legal environment of business. More than one hundred federal agencies exercise some degree of control over private economic activities. [DC]

Federal Trade Commission (FTC):   The FTC is responsible for enforcing the Federal Trade Commission Act which prohibits "unfair methods of competition" and "unfair or deceptive acts or practices." [DC]

Federal Trade Commission Act (1914): Placed a blanket prohibition against "unfair methods of competition" and created the FTC to enforce it. [DC]

fertility rate: The ratio of the births during a year to the total number of women, ages 15 to 49. [WL]

field edit: Preliminary edit, typically conducted by a field supervisor, which is designed to detect the most glaring omissions and inaccuracies in a completed data collection instrument. [GAC]

field experiment: Research study in a realistic situation in which one or more independent variables are manipulated by the experimenter under as carefully controlled conditions as the situation will permit. [GAC]

field sales manager: A title assigned to regional, district, branch, or unit managers in companies with large sales forces. While the lowest level of field sales management provides direct supervision of salespeople, each level has a role in the overall field sales management job of recruiting; selecting; training; compensation; motivation; assignment of territories, quotas, and expense budgets; and the measurement and control of salespeople. In companies using specialized sales forces there may be field sales management titles assigned by product lines, markets, or accounts. [VPB]

field salespeople: Salespeople who are responsible for contacting and selling goods and services to the customers in their place of business or residence. [BAW]

field study: In-depth investigation of a few cases typical of the target population, emphasizing the interrelationship of a number of factors. [GAC]

field warehouse: Warehouse facility used to store and transfer merchandise enroute from manufacturing location to other channel members. [DJB/BJL]

field warehousing: 1. A financing device whereby a field warehouse receipt is pledged as security for a loan. [DLS] 2. An arrangement by which the owner of goods leases a portion of his storage facilities to a licensed warehouseman who places a representative in charge, posts signs stating that a designated portion of the warehouse is in charge of the outside organization, and adds to or takes from stock as directed by the financial institution who has the stock as collateral. [WRD]

fighting brand: A line extension of a main brand that is marketed by one producer to compete directly with the lower-priced products of other producers in a given market. The fighting brand usually has a separate brand identity and a low price. Its quality is usually lower than that of the main brand; it may only be temporarily on the market; and its purpose is to hold customers without having to lower the price of the main brand. [CMC]

fill rate: An inventory's availability goal used when setting customer service objectives, e.g., 99 percent product fill rate or filling 99 out of 100 customer orders. [DJB/BJL]

financial analyst: A person who investigates, evaluates, and advises clients on the value and risk of investment offerings. [DES]

financial quota: A quota that examines financial criteria such as gross margin or contribution to overhead. Financial quotas are used to make salespeople conscious of the cost and profit implications of what they sell. Financial quotas are often stated in terms of direct selling expenses, gross margin, or net profit. They are most applicable when the firm's market penetration approaches saturation levels. In such instances it is hard to increase sales or market share, and an emphasis on selling efficiency and cost control becomes a logical mechanism for increasing profits. [OCW]

Fishbein Behavioral Intentions Model: An earlier name for the Fishbein Theory of Reasoned Action. [JPP/JCO]

Fishbein Theory of Reasoned Action: A theory developed by Martin Fishbein that assumes consumers consciously consider the consequences of alternative behaviors and choose the one that leads to the most desirable consequences. The theory states that behavior is closely related to behavioral intentions which are in turn the result of attitudes toward performing the behavior and social normative beliefs. [JPP/JCO]

fit, willing and able: Under current motor carrier regulations, applicants to the Interstate Commerce Commission seeking new or expanded rights must prove they are fit, willing, and able to perform the proposed service. They are no longer required to prove the service is necessary and in the public interest. [DJB/BJL]

fixed capital: That part of an investment where only a part will be recovered in the sale of a unit of the product. [DLS]

fixed cost, average: Total fixed cost divided by the number of units produced and marketed. [DLS]

fixed cost, total: The sum of costs incurred by a firm that tend to remain at the same level (fixed) no matter how many units of a product are produced and marketed. [DLS]

fixed exchange rate: Exchange rates which are fixed by government policy and which are not free to fluctuate in response to market forces. [WJK]

fixed-alternative question: Questions in which the responses are limited to stated alternatives. [GAC]

flagging: The use of special graphic techniques on the product package or store shelf to call attention to a particular offer such as a reduced price, bonus pack, etc. [DES]

flagship store: In a local department store organization, the main or downtown store, especially when large or dominant in relation to branch stores. [WRD]

Flammable Fabrics Act (1953):   Made illegal the production or distribution of any article of apparel which is "so highly flammable as to be dangerous when worn," under the FTC Act. [DC]

flanker brand: A line extension. Sometimes meant to cover only those line extensions that are not premium-priced or low-priced. [CMC]

lanking: An indirect strategy aimed at capturing market segments whose needs are not being served by competitors. Flanking can be executed by either targeting a geographical segment or a consumer segment (group) that is not being well served by competitors, where the competitor is unwilling or unable to retaliate. [GSD]

lash report: As soon as the day's sales figures have been "read" on whatever kind of register is in use, an "unaudited" report is released to give management the day's results for comparison with budget or perhaps last year's sales figure. It is tentative. [WRD]

lat rate: A print media advertising rate that does not include discounts; for example, regardless of how much advertising is purchased in a given period of time, the cost per space unit (e.g., column inch) remains the same. [AMB]

lighting: An advertising continuity or timing pattern in which advertising is scheduled for a certain amount of time, followed by a period of inactivity (called a "hiatus"), after which the advertising usually resumes; periods during which advertising is run are called "flights." [AMB]

loating exchange rate: An exchange rate which is determined by private supply and demand and which is free to respond to market forces. [WJK]

loor audit: Involves the use of floor sales registers for all transactions, both cash and credit, so as to obtain from the register readings the total sales for each salesperson, department, and type of sale. [WRD]

lying squad: Essentially in the department store field, groups of well-trained and flexible salespeople available to be placed in any and all departments within the store when needed—hence they "fly" about the store from assignment to assignment. [WRD]

.o.b. destination: A shipping term that indicates the seller pays the freight to the destination. Title does not pass until the merchandise reaches its destination, thus, the seller assumes all risks, loss, or damage while goods are in transit, except for the liability of the carrier. [WRD]

.o.b. origin pricing: A form of geographical pricing where the seller quotes prices from the point of shipment. Free on board (f.o.b.) means it is the buyer's responsibility to select the mode of transporting the goods, choose the specific carrier, handle all claims, and pay all shipping charges. [KM]

.o.b. with freight allowed: A form of delivered pricing where the buyer arranges and pays for the transportation, but deducts these transportation costs from the invoice total and remits the net amount. [KM]

ocus group interview: Personal interview conducted among a small number of individuals simultaneously; the interview relies more on group discussion than on a series of directed questions to generate data. [GAC]

ocus strategies: (See **niche strategies**).

olkways: (See **mores**.) [HHK]

Food and Drug Administration (FDA):   Created by the Pure Food and Drug Act of 1906, has the power to set standards for foods and food additives, to establish tolerances for deleterious substances and pesticides in foods, and to prohibit the sale of adulterated and misbranded foods, drugs, cosmetics and devices. All new drugs must be submitted to the FDA for approval, and applications must be supported by extensive laboratory testing indicating efficacy and safety. [DC]

Foote, Cone & Belding Grid: A two by two grid developed by the Foote, Cone, and Belding advertising agency for analyzing consumers and products. The grid divides products on the basis of whether they are higher or lower in involvement and on the basis of whether they are think or feel products. [JPP/JCO]

forecasting models: In forecasting sales, share, or other marketing objectives, a variety of models have been used, including time series models (e.g., moving averages, exponential smoothing, decompositional), econometric models (e.g., regression, input-output), and judgmental models (e.g., delphi). Most common of the econometric models are those including marketing mix variables of the firm and its competitors, thus offering diagnostic insights. A brief review of the various forecasting models is offered in Lilien and Kotler (1983, Chapter 10). [DCS/YJW]

forced sale: A sale of products at less than market price due to the urgent need for a merchant to liquidate merchandise assets, generally to meet the demand of creditors; also, the sale of goods or property under order from the court; an ordered public auction sale. [WRD]

Foreign Corrupt Practices Act (1977):   Made it illegal for members of any United States business firm to pay money or give gifts, or promise to do so, to any foreign official, foreign political party or candidates for foreign political office in order to obtain or retain business. [DC]

foreign exchange market: Buyers and a sellers of currencies which are traded for both spot and future delivery on a continuous basis. [WJK]

foreign marketing: The phenomenon of marketing in an environment different from that of the home or base environment. [WJK]

fork-lift truck: A material handling device to move unit loads. Capable of moving loads both horizontally and vertically. The most common power sources are propane gas and electricity. [DJB/BJL]

formula selling: A selling approach in which the sales presentation is designed to move the customer through stages in the decision-making process such as get customer attention, develop interest, build desire, and secure action, (AIDA). [BAW]

forward buying (order):   The practice of buying materials in a quantity exceeding current requirements in order to receive volume discounts or to ensure availability. [GLL/DTW]

forward integration: (See **integration**).

forward stock: 1. Inventory placed in the channel of distribution in advance of customer commitment. [DJB/BJL] 2. Merchandise carried on the selling floor, rather than in a reserve stockroom. [WRD]

franchise: The privilege, often exclusive, granted to a distributor or dealer by a manufacturer to sell the manufacturer's products within a specified territory. A franchise is an example of a contractual vertical marketing system. [WRD]

franchising: A contractual system of distributing goods and services whereby: one party (the franchisor) grants to another party (the franchisee) the right to distribute or sell certain goods or services; the franchisee agrees to operate his business according to a marketing plan substantially prescibed by the franchisor; and the franchisee operates his business substantially under a trade mark or trade name owned by the franchisor. [JRN]

free merchandise: A sales promotion technique in which an additional amount of the product is offered without additional cost as an incentive to purchase a minimum quantity. Typically offered for a limited period of time. [DES]

free samples: A sales promotion technique where a regular or specially sized quantity of the product is given away without cost to prospective purchasers. [DES]

free standing insert (fsi): A preprinted advertising page(s) inserted into a separate publication, such as a newspaper. [DES]

free trade area: The area of jurisdiction encompassing a group of countries that have agreed to abolish all internal barriers to trade between the member countries. [WJK]

free-flow pattern: A store layout arrangement consisting of a series of circular, octagonal, oval, or U-shaped fixture patterns, resulting in curving aisles characterized by a deliberate absence of uniformity. [WRD]

free-on-board (FOB): Implies loading on a transportation vehicle at some designated point. After the letters F.O.B., there is generally a designation of a place where title and control pass to the buyer. For example, F.O.B. Plant means that the control and title to the goods pass to the buyer at the seller's plant origin. [DJB/BJL]

freight bill: The document used by carriers to charge for transportation services provided. [DJB/BJL]

freight classification: All products transported by common carriers are grouped together into common freight classifications based upon the characteristic of the product that influences cost of handling and transport. [DJB/BJL]

freight forwarder: Combines small shipments from different shippers into larger shipments for scale economies in the purchase of intercity transportation. The freight forwarder functions as a wholesaler of transportation services. [DJB/BJL]

freight-all-kinds rates (FAK): A mixture of different products are delivered in a combination to a single or limited number of destinations. Rather than determine the classification and rate for each product, an average rate is applied for the total shipment. This simplifies paperwork associated with the bill of lading and freight bills. [DJB/BJL]

frequency: The number of times a person, household, or target audience is exposed to an advertising medium or media schedule within a given period of time; usually presented as an "average" (number of exposures by an average prospect) or a distribution (the number of prospects exposed once, twice, and so on; called a frequency or exposure distribution). "Effective" frequency refers to an optimum level of exposure in terms of a communication criterion. [AMB]

Freudian theory: (See **psychoanalytic theory**.)

fringe sizes: These are the sizes that are either very large or very small and, if offered at all, are offered in very limited depth because of the thin market demand for them. Some stores specialize in fringe or out sizes; e.g., tall girls shops; petite size shops. (See also **out sizes**.) [WRD]

fringe stocks: Those categories of merchandise from which a small percentage of sales come. [WRD]

fulfillment: The gathering of orders or offers from a sales promotion event and the process of completing the event by distributing items integral to the event such as premiums, rebates, bounce-backs or ordered merchandise. [DES]

full-line forcing: A form of tying arrangement in which a supplier forces a dealer to carry his full line of products. This has not been treated as per se unlawful by the courts; the restriction may be upheld as reasonable where the supplier can demonstrate a legitimate business need for his dealers to carry the full line. [DC]

full-line pricing: All items in a given line are priced relative to each other, or are discounted as a total package. Changes on any one item take into consideration the prices of the other items in the line, and the seller's intention is to enhance sale of the total line.

full-line sales organization: Each company or division salesperson sells all products to all accounts in a geographic territory. This is an appropriate strategy when the product line is not large, is non-technical, and is sold through one distribution channel. It is a lower cost strategy than specializing by product, market, or type of account. [VPB]

full-service (or retailing):   The offering of an adequate number of sales people and sales supporting services to give customers the full range of expected services. Usually compared to "limited service," which implies some expected services are not offered, e.g., credit. [WRD]

full-service advertising agency: (See **advertising agency**.)

functional (or trade) discounts: Those discounts given to middlemen or others who act in the capacity of performing distributive services which would otherwise have to be performed by the manufacturer himself. These discounts sometimes prevail regardless of the quantities involved. [WRD]

functional expense classification: A type of expense classification system that identifies the purpose of an expenditure. The major functions promoted by the National Retail Merchants Association are (1) administration, (2) occupancy, (3) publicity, (4) buying, and (5) selling. [WRD]

functional middlemen: Middlemen who ordinarily assist directly in effecting a change in ownership but do not themselves take title to the goods in which they deal. They specialize in the performance of a single marketing function or a limited number of such functions, one of which is usually related to the transfer of title. [WRD]

functional organization: In a functionally organized company, the managers of each major function (such as marketing, production, R&D, and finance) report to the chief executive who provides overall direction and coordination. Similarly, in a functionally organized marketing department, the managers of the major marketing functions (such as sales, advertising, marketing research, and product planning) report to the marketing manager. Comment: The advantage of this form is that it provides specialization by function while coordination of functions is provided by the chief executive. The same can be said for the functional marketing department where direction and coordination of marketing functions is provided by the marketing manager. [VPB]

functional perceived risk: (See **perceived risk**.) [HHK]

fundraising: Techniques used to solicit contributions or other support for an organization from outside interests. [DES]

funnel approach: An approach to question sequencing that gets its name from its shape, starting with broad questions and progressively narrowing down the scope. [GAC]

Fur Products Labeling Act (1951): Gave the Federal Trade Commission jurisdiction to promulgate rules designed to disclose in labels what kind of fur is actually in a fur product. [DC]

future transaction: A commitment to take or deliver a currency at a specified future date. [WJK]

futures research: (See **futurology**.) [WL]

futurism: A philosophy or perspective that focuses on the importance of serious thinking about and planning for the future. [WL]

futurology: The prediction of future developments by an intensive study of past and present trends, using a variety of techniques, from imagination to the Delphi process to computer simulations. Perspectives of the future are useful in contingency planning and have been used for strategic long range planning. Used interchangeably with futures research. [WL]

game theoretic models: Models that use game theory to predict the actions of either cooperative or competitive individuals (or firms). In cooperative game theory, the agreements that emerge from colluding individuals are examined. Noncooperative game theory is concerned with the actions of rational, intelligent individuals competing independently. A key element of this theory is the Nash equilibrium — i.e., a set of strategies, one for each individual, such that no individual would then unilaterally like to change his strategy. Typically, the individuals are assumed to adopt strategies in accordance with this equilibrium (assuming that such an equilibrium exists). For an overview of game theory in marketing, see Moorthy (1985). [DCS/YJW]

games: A sales promotion technique which involves the collection, matching, or use of skill to complete projects or activities with the goal of a prize or reward for the player. [DES]

garment district: The leading textile center in the country located in New York City in the 34th Street area. [WRD]

gatekeeper: (See **buying roles**.)

GATT (The General Agreement on Tariffs and Trade): An institutional framework which provides a set of rules and principles committed to the liberalization of trade between countries. [WJK]

General Electric's strategic business planning grid: (See **market attractiveness-competitive position matrix**.)

general merchandise stores: Establishments primarily selling household linens and dry goods, and either apparel and accessories or furniture and home furnishings. Establishments which meet the criteria for department stores, except as to employment, are included in this classification. Included are establishments whose sales of "apparel" or of "furniture and home furnishings" exceed half of their total sales, if sales of the smaller of the two lines in combination with "dry goods and household linens" accounts for 20 percent of total sales. [WRD]

general merchandise wholesalers: Those that carry a variety of goods in several distinct and unrelated lines of business. [WRD]

general sales manager: Has overall responsibility for corporate, group, or division sales. Sales management at this level is concerned with developing sales policies, strategies, and plans that support the overall marketing plan. In a small company the general sales manager may supervise all salespeople directly. As the number of salespersons increase, however, supervision of salespeople must be delegated to field sales managers. In a functionally organized company, the general sales manager reports to the marketing manager or the chief executive. In a divisionalized corporation, the general sales manager reports to the division marketing manager or to the division manager. In a divisionalized company with a central sales force, the general sales manager reports to the chief executive or to a group executive. [VPB]

general stores: Establishments primarily selling a general line of merchandise, the most important being food. The more important subsidiary lines are notions, apparel, farm supplies, and gasoline. These establishments are usually located in rural communities. In these establishments, sales of food account for at least one-third and not more than two-thirds of total sales. [WRD]

general-line (or full-line) wholesaler: Wholesalers who carry a complete stock of one type of merchandise, corresponding roughly to a substantial majority of the total merchandise requirements of customers in a major line of trade or industry classification. [WRD]

generic brands: Products which are named only by their generic class (e.g. drip-grind coffee, barber shop). Other products have both an individual brand and a generic classification (Maxwell House drip-grind coffee, Maurice's barber shop). Generic brand products are often thought to be unbranded, but their producer or reseller name is usually associated with the product too. This approach is usually associated with food and other packaged goods, but many other consumer and industrial goods and services are marketed as generics. [CMC]

generic strategies: Generalized game plans that work across a range of industries and markets. They provide management with a set of strategic options, one (or a combination) of which can be chosen for application in a specific situation. Generic strategies do not provide specifics and the detail needed to be developed for any specific situation. [GSD]

generic terms, as brand names: (See **brand generic**.) [CMC]

geocentric: A management orientation based upon the assumption that there are similarities and differences in the world that can be understood and recognized in an integrated world strategy. The geocentric or world orientation is a synthesis of the ethnocentric (home country) and polycentric (host country) orientation. [WJK]

geographic organization: A company organized into geographical units which report to a central corporate headquarters. Normally each unit produces the same or similar products as the others, and the unit manager controls both the manufacturing and sales operations. Marketing functions other than sales are usually centralized at the corporate level. Comment: Reasons for geographic organization include high shipping costs or the need for quick delivery for reasons of freshness (e.g. baked goods), both of which require that plants be located near customers. [VPB]

GEOLINE: A model providing a decision support system for creating sales and service territory boundaries. The approach aggregates small "standard geographic units" (SGU's) into sales territories while maximizing the compactness of the territories (i.e., the ease of covering the territory from the standpoint of travel), subject to the constraint that each created territory have the same overall sales activity level (or some other single criterion) (Hess and Samuels 1971). For other salesforce planning decision support systems, see CALL-PLAN and DETAILER. [DCS/YJW]

georeference classification: For analysis purposes, data covering such things as sales, customers, product, and demographics are often classified on a geographical basis. Distribution of such data by individual markets provides the geographical structure of demand that must be serviced. The most useful geographical classification structures for logistical modeling are customer point locations, county, standard metropolitan statistical area (SMSA), economic trading area, zip code, and grid structure. [DJB/BJL]

gifts: Items of value, which are offered by the seller as an inducement to influence the consideration or purchase of a product or service. (See also **premium**.) [DES]

global marketing: Marketing which consciously addresses global customers, markets, and competition in formulating a business strategy. [WJK]

global marketing information systems: A system designed to acquire, store, catalog, analyze, and make available to decision makers information from global sources within and external to the firm for use as the basis for planning and decision making. [WJK]

GMROI (gross margin return on investment): Shows for each dollar invested in merchandise inventory, the equivalent dollars generated in gross margin. [WRD]

goals: Concrete, short term points of measurement that the business unit intends to meet in pursuit of its objectives. An overall objective converts into specific short-run goals. (See also **objectives**.) [GSD]

goods: Products that have tangible form, in contrast to services which are intangible. (See also **services**.) [CMC]

government information on industrial markets: The set of data about industrial markets that the government collects and distributes. It tends to be organized around the Standard Industrial Classification system. [GLL/DTW]

government market: Includes purchases by the governmental units—federal, state and local—that procure or rent goods and services in carrying out the main functions of the government. The federal government accounts for almost 40 percent of the total spent by all levels of government, making it the nation's largest customer. Federal, state, and local government agencies buy a wide range of products and services. They buy bombers, sculpture, chalkboards, furniture, toiletries, clothing, fire engines, vehicles, and fuel. [GLL/DTW]

grade labeling: A system of identification that describes products by their quality, using agreed-on numbers or letters. The grade classes (standards) and the requirements for each are usually assigned by a government or trade group, and the actual scoring is sometimes done by inspectors. Grade labeling leads to product standardization and ease of comparison by the buyer, often the purpose of the labeling. [CMC]

grading: The classifying of a product by examining its quality. Often done with a program of grade labeling, though individual firms can grade their own products by a private system if they wish—e.g. Good, Better, Best. (See also **grade labeling**.) [CMC]

graphic-rating scale: Scale in which individuals indicate their ratings of an attribute by placing a check at the appropriate point on a line that runs from one extreme of the attribute to the other. [GAC]

gravity models: Retailers' primary source of ideas about the structure of market areas. The model states that the volume of purchases by consumers and the frequency of trips to the outlets are a function of the size of the store and the distance between the store and the origin of the shopping trip. [WRD]

green river ordinances: Municipal ordinances regulating or forbidding house-to-house selling, canvassing, or soliciting of business. [WRD]

gridiron pattern: A store layout of fixtures and aisles in a repetitive or rectilinear pattern, best illustrated by a variety store or the grocery department in a typical supermarket. Secondary aisles run at right angles to aisles, and each aisle is usually of the same width for its length. [WRD]

gross additional markups: The original amount of additional markups taken before subtraction of any additional markup cancellations to determine net additional markups. (Retail inventory method of accounting.) [WRD]

gross cost of merchandise handled: The cost value of the opening inventory plus purchases and additions at billed cost. (Retail inventory method of accounting.) [WRD]

gross cost of merchandise sold: The gross cost of merchandise handled less the closing inventory at cost. The gross cost of merchandise sold is subtracted from net sales to calculate maintained markup. Maintained markup is then adjusted by cash discounts and workroom cost to determine gross margin of profit. (Retail inventory method of accounting.) [WRD]

gross domestic product (GDP):   Gross national product less net foreign investment. [DLS]

gross margin of profit: Difference between net sales and total cost of goods sold. [WRD]

gross markdowns: The original amount of markdowns taken before subtraction of any markdown cancellations to determine net markdown. [WRD]

gross national product (GNP):   1. An estimate of the total national output of goods and services for a year valued at market prices. 2. The sum of personal consumption expenditure on goods and services, government expenditures on goods and services, plus investments. 3. The sum of all currently produced wages, interest, rents, and profits. [DLS]

gross profit: 1. Net sales minus cost of goods sold. 2. The difference between purchase price of an item and the sale price. [DLS]

gross rating points (GRP):   The total weight of advertising that derives from a particular media vehicle or group of vehicles (media schedule) over a given period of time; the sum of the ratings for a particular vehicle or vehicles, thus including audience duplication; equals reach (in percent) times average frequency. [AMB]

group buying: The consolidating of buying requirements of several to many individual stores. [WRD]

group indepth interview: (See **focus group interview.**)

growth-share matrix: Each business or product in this portfolio matrix is classified jointly by the rate of present or forecast market growth and a measure of market share dominance. The Boston Consulting Group (BCG), which developed this model, chose market growth as an indicator of the need for cash while relative market share is an indicator of profitability and cash generating ability. Businesses are classified into one of four quadrants, and labelled according to their cash flow characteristics.

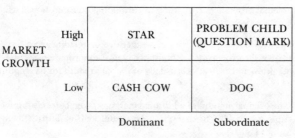

	Dominant	Subordinate

High — STAR — PROBLEM CHILD (QUESTION MARK)

MARKET GROWTH

Low — CASH COW — DOG

Dominant — Subordinate

RELATIVE MARKET SHARE

These quadrants include: **cash cow:** likely to be profitable and net cash generators, as low growth demands less cash and the business is relatively profitable; **star:** strong market share position, but in a rapidly growing market; profitable, but likely to be net cash user; **problem child (question mark):** have a large appetite for cash; **dog:** small relative share in low growth market, generates moderate amount of cash, but uses most if not all the cash generated in maintaining operations and share position. [GSD]

growth stage of product life cycle: The second stage of the product life cycle, during which sales are increasing at an increasing rate, profits are increasing, and competitors enter the market. Product differentiation takes place, and price competition begins. Industry profits usually taper off as the product category enters the third (mature) stage, during which sales increases come only at a declining rate and eventually cease. [CMC]

growth strategy: Market share expansion is the prime objective under this strategy, even at the expense of short term earnings. The firm may seem to expand market share through a number of alternative routes. Firstly, the firm may seek new users who may previously have been loyal to other brands, or tended to switch, or were not users of the category at all. The second way in which the firm can expand its market share is to expand usage by current users; for instance, by identifying and promoting new uses. [GSD]

guarantee, guaranty (warranty):   Assurance, expressed or implied, of the quality of goods offered for sale. Expressed guarantee, with definite promise of money back or other specific assurance, is often used as a sales aid, especially in nonstore selling. (See also **warranty**.) [WRD]

Guttman scale: The general deterministic procedure to determine whether or not the responses of subjects to items form a scale; the analysis is based on the response patterns of the subjects to the set of items, where a response pattern denotes the of responses given by a subject to a set of items. If the items form a scale, only a limited number of the response patterns are possible, and relative nonoccurrence of deviant patterns allows the recovery of the order of the individuals and category boundaries of the items from the observed data. [GAC]

habit: A learned response to a stimulus, that has become automatic and routine requiring little or no cognitive effort. (See also **routinized response behavior**.) [HHK]

habit formation: The process of learning a specific behavior often requiring practice or rehearsal of the response. There is considerable controversy, however, onjust how much repetition or how many trials are necessary for learning to occur. It probably differs between cognitive problem solving and simple physiological or muscular reactions. [HHK]

hand-to-mouth buying: Purchase by a business in the smallest feasible quantities for immediate requirements. [WRD]

handbills: The term commonly used to identify all promotion pieces that are either handed out to shoppers at the store or distributed door-to-door by a messenger. [WRD]

hard goods: As compared with soft goods, which have a textiles base, these goods are mainly comprised of hardware, home furnishings, and furniture and appliances. More than likely these goods are also durable goods. (See also **durable goods**.) [WRD]

hard sell: (See **high-pressure selling**.) [BAW]

Hart-Scott-Rodino Antitrust Improvements Act (1976): Requires that mergers involving corporations of a certain size must be reported in advance to the enforcement agencies. It also permitted state attorneys general to bring parens patriae suits on behalf of those injured by violations of the Sherman Act. [DC]

harvesting strategy: The maximization of short run cash flow from the business in expectation of a deterioration of market share and eventual withdrawal from the market. The cash flow raised is directed toward other areas of business where the cash flow is needed. (See also **divest strategy**). [GSD]

head of stock: In departmentized stores, this individual is usually at the very first level of the training positions; an assistant to the buyer (or department manager) who is responsible for seeing that reserve and forward stocks are maintained properly for selection and reorder and replenishment. Often performs routine control functions as well. Only large, highly specialized stores have this person who usually reports to the assistant buyer. [WRD]

health care marketing: Marketing designed to influence the behavior of target audiences where the benefits would accrue to the target audience's physical and/or mental health. Comment: Health care marketing may be carried out by individuals, by hospitals or clinics or by national agencies such as the National Cancer Institute. [ARA]

heavy equipment: Products which are typically capital goods, normally purchased by end user customers. They are treated as as asset by the purchasing firm and depreciated for tax purposes. Examples are lathes, drilling machines, and grinders. [GLL/DTW]

hedging: The sale or purchase of a currency in forward markets for future delivery to satisfy a future obligation or obtain a future payment. The purpose of hedging is to reduce risk. [WJK]

Hendry model: A model representing the amount of switching among the brands in a product category. The model postulates that, for directly competing brands (i.e., brands within the same market "partition"), the level of switching among those brands should be proportional to the product of their market shares. The exact level of switching (i.e., the proportionality constant) is assumed to be the value that maximizes the entropy (i.e., randomness or lack of information) in this probabilistic system. (The Hendry Corporation 1970, 1971; Kalwani and Morrison 1977; Rubinson, Vanhonacker and Bass 1980). [DCS/YJW]

heuristics: Propositions that connect an event with an action that usually simplify decision making. For example, "buy the cheapest brand" could be a choice heuristic that would simplify purchase. [JPP/JCO]

hierarchy of effects: 1. A concept related to the manner in which advertising supposedly works; based on the premise that advertising moves individuals systematically through a series of psychological stages such as awareness, interest, desire, conviction, and action. The DAGMAR approach (Defining Advertising Goals for Measured Advertising Results) has been used for setting advertising objectives within the context of a hierarchy of effects model (unawareness, awareness, comprehension, conviction, action).   2. An early model that depicted consumer purchasing as a series of stages including awareness, knowledge, liking, preference, conviction, and purchase. [JPP/JCO] (See also **AIDA**.)

hierarchy of needs: A theory proposed by Maslow (1943) concerning the specific order of the development of needs. He proposed that needs develop in man in a sequential order from "lower" to "higher," needs ranging from Physiological needs to Safety needs (security, order), to Belongingness and Love needs. Then Esteem needs (prestige, respect) and Self-Actualization (self-fulfillment) follow. hierarchy of needs:Higher order needs emerge as lower order ones are more or less satisfied. [HHK]

high involvement: (See **involvement**.)

high-pressure selling: A selling approach in which the salesperson attempts to control the sales interaction and pressure the customer to make a purchase. [BAW]

homemade diversification theorem: A theorem which states that (in the absence of synergy) diversification by a firm is not valuable to shareholders because they can diversify their own portfolios more cheaply by purchasing shares of stocks in the market. [PFA]

hoodoo sites: Locations that apparently have all the factors necessary for the successful operation of a retail store but in which a successive number of merchants have failed. [WRD]

horizontal buy: A purchase that is made from a direct competitor. For example, a west coast chemical company may buy a chemical compound from an east coast competitor because of a geographic supply/demand imbalance. [GLL/DTW]

horizontal competition: Rivalry to gain customer preference among entities at the same level, such as competition among competing wholesalers, or competing retailers. [WL]

horizontal diversification: (See **diversification**).

horizontal expansion: (See **horizontal integration**.) [WL]

horizontal integration: 1. Expanding a business by acquiring or developing businesses engaged in the same stage of marketing essentially the same product. The most common approach is to buy out competitors. Also known as **horizontal expansion**. [WL] 2. The combination of two or more separate enterprises at the same stage in the channel through ownership, including mergers or acquisitions. [JRN]

horizontal mergers: The joining together or combination of companies in the same industry. They may be deemed illegal if they tend to reduce competition substantially. [WL]

horizontal price-fixing: A conspiracy among competitors at the same level in the channel to set prices for a product. [DLS]

horizontal structure of the sales organization: A sales organization may incorporate an internal company sales force or outside agents. When a company sales force is used, alternative approaches to sales organization include: (1) geographical organization; (2) organization by type of product; (3) organization by type of customer; and (4) organization by selling function. [OCW]

house account: An account, usually large, not assigned to a field salesperson, but handled directly by executives or home-office personnel. [BAW]

house agency: An advertising agency that is owned or controlled by an advertiser; also called "in-house agency." [AMB]

house brand: A private brand, usually associated with retailers. [CMC]

house publications: An internally developed or produced magazine or brochure designed to communicate the views of the organization to a selected audience without outside editorial restraints. [DES]

house-to-house salesperson: A salesperson who is primarily engaged in making sales direct to ultimate consumers in their homes. [WRD]

Household Goods Carrier Operations Act (1980):   Carriers of household goods may, upon request, provide the shipper with an estimate of charges for transportation of household goods; proposed service charges for such estimates are subject to antitrust laws. [DC]

human ecology: Application of the concepts of plant and animal ecology to human collective life to seek knowledge about the structure of social systems and the way in which structures develop, paying attention to spatial configurations. Man's adaptation to the natural environment. [WL]

hypermarket: An unusually large limited service combination discount store, supermarket, and warehouse under a single roof. Typically it sells both food and nonfood items at 10-15% below normal retail prices and stacks much reserve stock merchandise in the sales area. They are a phenomenon of European origin. [WRD]

id: That arm of the personality, according to Freudian Theory, that reflects the basic physiological and sexual drives (libido) of man demanding immediate gratification. (See also **superego, ego** and **ego defenses**.) [HHK]

idea generation: That stage of the product development cycle when ideas are sought for new products. These ideas may be created in-house or sought from outsiders. This stage is often called concept generation rather than idea generation, since the new product is but a concept at this time. The activity of generation often follows some stated or implied strategic focus, and it precedes the concept evaluation stage.

idea screening: (See **screening of ideas**.)

ideal self concept: The ideas, attitudes, and perceptions people have about themselves concerning what they would be like if they were perfect or ideal. [JPP/JCO]

identification: (See **ego defenses**.) [HHK]

IIA: (See **Luce's Choice Axiom**.) [DCS/YJW]

image: Consumer perception of a product, institution, brand, business, or person which may or may not correspond with "reality or actuality." For marketing purposes the "image of what is" may be more important than "what actually is." [WL]

imperfect competition: Refers to market conditions where firms have some control, but not necessarily absolute control, over price, by such techniques as differentiating products and limiting supply. [WL]

implementation: The stage in the strategic market planning process where an action program (see definition) is designed to meet the strategic objective(s) using the available resources and given the existing constraints. The action program is intended to be both a translation of a strategic plan into operational terms as well as a means by which the strategic performance may be monitored and controlled. The action plan has three major components: (1) specific tasks— what will be done including the specification of the marketing mix to be employed; (2) time horizon—when it will be done; and (3) resource allocation and budgeting—attaching dollar figure to each income- and expense-related activity and allocating capital funds. [GSD]

implicit costs: The value of utilized economic resources which are not explicitly charged on accounting records of a firm—e.g., interest on owner's capital investment. [WRD]

implicit price index (IPI): A relative measure of changes in the general price level of goods and services produced by an economy during a given time period. [DLS]

implied warranty: A warranty (promise of performance) that is extended to the customer but unstated. It usually is assumed from common practice in the trade, or suggested by statements made about the product by the seller. [CMC]

import license: An instrument of government control which regulates access to foreign exchange and the quantity and/or value of imports. [WJK]

impulse buying: A purchase behavior that is assumed to be made without prior planning or thought. Often, it is claimed, impulse buying involves an emotional reaction to the stimulus object (product, packaging, point-of-purchase display, or whatever) in addition to the simple acquisition act. (See also **planned buying**.) [HHK]

impulse products: Convenience products (goods or services) that are bought on the spur of the moment, without advance planning or serious consideration at the time, and often by the stimulus of point-of-sale promotion or observation. [CMC]

impulse purchase: A purchase typically made in-store with little or no previous decision making involved. [JPP/JCO]

in transit: A condition that exists when merchandise has been shipped from the vendor and has not yet arrived at the buyer's receiving dock. [WRD]

in-pack premium: A small, often low value, gift placed inside a product package to encourage purchase. [DES]

in-store coupons: Certificates redeemable only at one specific retail store or chain. Generally distributed through newspaper advertisements, flyers, or within the store. [DES]

incentive pay: Any compensation plan other than straight salary wherein the salesperson is given encouragement to sell more. Examples are straight commission (the strongest incentive); a salary plus a small percentage of net sales, etc. [WRD]

incentive plans: Events offering rewards or inducements to stimulate the salesforce or channel members to achieve predetermined sales, profit, distribution or other goals. [DES]

incentive travel: Form of sales promotional activity in which large companies reward their salespeople, agents, distributors, or dealers with trips to interesting places for attaining a specific objective, usually sales volume (or purchase commitments) in excess of some predetermined quota. [WRD]

incentives: Inducements (money, premiums, prizes) offered by sellers to reward or motivate salespeople, channel members, and/or consumers to sell/purchase their products or services. (See also **bonus** and **sales contests**.) [DES]

income: A flow of money, goods, and benefits to a person or an organization. [DLS]

income differentials: Differences in income levels among people of various categories, such as different jobs, geographic areas, age classes, sexes, races and the like. [WL]

income effect: 1. The change in patterns of consumption for a product given consumers have an increase in real income. [DLS] 2. The increase or decrease in a consumer's real income as a result of the change in the price of a good or service. [WL]

income maintenance: Policies designed to raise or maintain the income levels of designated groups of individuals. [WL]

income sensitivity of demand: Refers to the relationship between a real increase in disposable income and the corresponding change in consumption. [WL]

incremental productivity method: A method of determining sales force size by adding sales representatives as long as the incremental profit produced by their addition exceeds the incremental costs. The method recognizes that there will probably be diminishing returns with the addition of salespeople. [OCW]

incrementalism: The notion that strategies are the outcome of a series of piecemeal and minor tactical decisions in response to problems and opportunities rather than through systematic, formal, prepared plans. Incrementalism holds that organizations are more reactive than proactive. [GSD]

independence from irrelevant alternatives: See Luce's Choice Axiom. [DCS/YJW]

independent carrier: Owner-operator or individual trucker who provides line-haul service for others. Under current transportation regulations, can make business arrangements with common, contract, exempt, and private carriers. [DJB/BJL]

independent sector: Collectively, all private nonprofit marketers. (See also, **third sector**.) [ARA]

independent store: Retail outlet owned individually; not a chain or branch store. [WRD]

index of retail saturation: A technique normally used in larger areas to aid retailers choose among possibilities for location of new outlets. It offers better insight into location possibilities than a simple descriptive analysis of market potential since it reflects both the demand side and the supply side, i.e., the number of existing outlets in the area and the number or income of consumers. [WRD]

indirect channels: A channel whereby goods and services are sold indirectly from producer through independent middlemen to final user. [JRN]

indirect exporting: Sales to export intermediaries who in turn sell to overseas customers. The indirect exporter has no direct contact with overseas customers. [WJK]

individual brand: The brand identity given to an individual product, as separate from other products in the market and from other items in the product's own line. A trademark. [CMC]

industrial advertising: (See **business advertising**.)

industrial (business) market segmentation: The process of separating an industrial (business) market into groups of customers/prospects such that the members of each resulting group are more like the other members of that group than like members of other segments. [GLL/DTW]

industrial buying influences: (See **buying influences**.)

industrial distributor: A wholesaler who sells primarily to business or institutional customers who purchase items for business use rather than for resale. [WRD]

industrial marketing (business marketing):   The marketing of goods and services to industrial (business) markets. [GLL/DTW]

industrial markets (business markets):   The industrial market (also called the producer or business market) is the set of all individuals and organizations that acquire goods and services that enter into the production of other products or services that are sold, rented, or supplied to others. The major types of industries making up the business market are agriculture, forestry, and fisheries; mining; manufacturing; construction, transportation; communication, public utilities; banking, finance, and insurance; and services. [GLL/DTW]

industrial products: Goods which are destined to be sold primarily for use in producing other goods or rendering services as contrasted with goods destined to be sold primarily to the ultimate consumer. They include equipment (installed and accessory), component parts, maintenance, repair and operating (MRO) supplies, raw materials, and fabricating materials. The distinguishing characteristics of industrial goods is the purpose for which they are to be used, i.e. in carrying on business or industrial activities rather than for consumption by individual ultimate consumers or resale to them. The category also includes merchandise destined for use in carrying on various types of institutional enterprises. Relatively few goods are exclusively industrial goods. The same article may, under one set of circumstances, be an industrial good, and under other conditions a customers good. (See also **installations, accessory equipment, raw materials, parts, supplies, business services**, and **semi-manufactured goods**.) [GLL/DTW]

industrial salespeople: Salespeople who are primarily responsible for making sales of goods and services to industrial customers and institutions. [BAW]

industrial user: (See **buying roles**.)

industrialized countries: Those countries whose 1987 GNP per capita ranges from $2,500 and $8,499. The industrialized countries display the following characterisics: (1) degree of urbanization increases, literacy levels are very high, often exceeding 85%, and the population engaged in agriculture drops substantially; (2) wage levels rise sharply, and ownership of every type of consumer durable, transportation, leisure time, and housing products, rises sharply; and (3) the need for labor saving methods creates new industrial product markets in existing industries, and development creates entirely new industries. (See also pre-industrial countries, underdeveloped countries, developing countries, and post-industrialized countries.) [WJK]

industry attractiveness: (See **market attractiveness**.)

industry: A set of companies that vie for market share of a given product. [DLS]

inelastic demand: 1. A situation where a cut in price yields such a small increase in quantity taken by the market that total revenue decreases. 2. A situation where the percentage of quantity taken in the market "stretches" less than the percentage drop in price. [DLS]

inferior goods: Less-expensive substitutes for products that consumers prefer. [DLS]

inflation: An economic condition characterized by continuously rising prices. [DLS]

influence, interpersonal, in the buying center: The influence of one individual member of the buying center on another is the change in behavioral and/or psychological states of other buying center members brought about by the perception of each other's power in an organizational buying situation. [GLL/DTW]

influences, buying center: (See **influence in the buying center**.) [GLL/DTW]

informal group: The interpersonal and intergroup relationships that develop within a formal group or organization. This might include cliques, "coffee-colleagues", or friendship circles. An informal group tends to form when the formal organization fails to satisfy important needs of the members. [HHK]

information processing: (See **consumer information processing**.)

information search: 1. (organizational buying): The process by which a buyer seeks to identify the most appropriate supplier(s) once a need has been recognized. The information search process may vary based upon variables such as buying situation (see **buyclasses**.) and organizational size. [GLL/DTW] 2. (consumer buying) The intentional exposure to information. Before buying a camera the consumer might be attracted to and seek out advertisements for cameras, read articles in photography magazines, and turn to *Consumers' Reports*. Seeking the advice of an expert, knowledgeable acquaintance, or salesperson can be involved. [HHK]

information seeking: (See **information search**.)

informative label: (See **descriptive labeling**.)

initial markup (initial markon):   The difference between the merchandise cost and the original retail price placed on the goods; expressed as a percentage of the retail value. (Retail inventory method of accounting.) [WRD]

inner-directedness: A system of values prevalent in production oriented societies in which members of the society are taught specific value systems dependent on self sufficiency and inner values. First developed by David Riesman in his monograph "The Lonely Crowd" and later adapted by Stanford Research Institute in their VALS program. (See also **other-directed**.) [HHK]

innovation: In the marketing literature, innovation implies the introduction of a new product, idea, or service into the marketplace. According to Robertson, it involves a new product that is very different from the established products or at least perceived to be different by consumers in the relevant market segment. New products can be referred to as continuous innovations such as Crest spearmint toothpaste,or Michelob light beer. Or they can be discontinuous innovations, a completely new product such as the electric light bulb or perhaps the computer. [HHK]

innovative imitation: The strategy or practice whereby a firm's new products are emulative of others already on the market but are significantly different in at least one aspect. Differs from pure imitation where the new item is a "me-too" or total copy, and from emulative product because the difference here is significant. (See also **adaptive products**.) [CMC]

innovativeness: 1. When applied to the seller, it is the degree to which the firm has the capability of, and follows the practice of, being innovative. 2. When applied to a buyer, it is the extent to which that person or firm is willing to accept the risks of early purchase of an innovation. [CMC] 3. A personality trait designed to account for the degree to which a consumer accepts and purchases new products and services. [JPP/JCO]

innovators: Firms, or persons, that are innovative. The term is often applied (1) to those who are the first to create a new type of product, or (2) to those who are the first to adopt a new product that has been introduced into the marketplace. Innovators are often thought to be opinion leaders. (See also **adopter categories** and **product adoption process**.) [CMC]

input evaluation measures: Objective measures of the amount of effort or resources expended by the sales force, including the number of sales calls, time and time utilization, expenses and nonselling activities such as letters written, number of phone calls, number of customer complaints received. [OCW]

inquiry: A customer request for additional information about a product or service. Comment: Inquiries are often generated through advertising in which a customer can request additional information by mailing a card or coupon. [BAW]

inquiry tests: A test of advertising effectiveness that uses inquiries returned by respondents as a measure of the communication ability of advertisements or the efficacy of media vehicles. [AMB]

inside salespeople: Salespeople who perform the selling activities over the telephone at their employers' location. Comment: Inside sales people typically answer questions and take orders; however, there is a growing trend for inside salespeople to actively solicit orders. (See also **telephone selling**.) [BAW]

installations: Non-portable industrial goods such as furnaces and assembly lines that are major, and that are bought, installed, and used to produce other goods or services. Often grouped with accessory equipment to comprise capital goods. Also called heavy eqipment. [CMC]

installment account: The resulting charge account of a customer who has purchased on an installment plan; i.e., pays a down-payment and specified amounts per month including a service charge. The customer has the use of the merchandise during the life of the installment account. (See also **revolving credit**.) [WRD]

installment sale: A sale of real or personal property for which a series of equal payments is made over a period of weeks or months; also, sale of goods on credit, often conditional (seller retaining title) with payments of the obligation in periodic portions. [WRD]

institutional advertising: Advertising that promotes the name, image, personnel, or reputation of a company or organization, instead of the actual products or services it markets; generally communicates positive attributes and attempts to present the organization in a favorable way, without raising controversial issues (as would be the case for "advocacy"advertising); when used by corporations, often called "corporate" advertising. [AMB]

institutional market: The market consisting of churches, museums, private hospitals, schools and colleges, clubs, and many other organizations that have objectives that differ basically from those of traditional business organizations. [GLL/DTW]

institutional marketing: The marketing of goods and services to institutional markets. (See **institutional markets**.) [GLL/DTW]

instrumental conditioning: (See **operant conditioning**.)

instrumental values: One of two major types of values proposed by Milton Rokeach. Instrumental values represent preferred modes of conduct or preferred patterns of behavior. (See also **terminal values**.) [JPP/JCO]

integrated division: Contains both marketing and production functions, thereby providing the division manager coordination and control of the principal factors affecting profits. [VPB]

integration: The acquisition or development of businesses, that are related to the company's current businesses, as a means of increasing sales and/or profit and gaining greater control. There are three forms of integration: (1) **backward integration**—when the company acquires one or more of its suppliers or develops its own supply capability in order to gain more profit and/or control; (2) **forward integration**—when the company acquires one or more of its "buyers" (e.g., wholesalers or retailers where the buyer is not the "ultimate buyer"); and (3) **horizontal integration**— when the company acquires one or more of its competitors. [GSD]

intensive distribution: A form of market coverage in which a product is distributed through all available wholesalers or retailers who still stock and/or sell the product in a given market area. [JRN]

intentions: The decisions to acquire specific goods/services under given terms and conditions. (See also buying intentions.) [GLL/DTW]

inter-selling: The process of selling between and among departments to facilitate larger transactions and to make it more convenient for the customer to accessorize. [WRD]

interindustry competition: Rivalry among sellers in different industries to achieve such objectives as gaining a larger share of market, increasing profits or increasing sales, by urging consumers to substitute a seller's products or services for their current choices. Examples are substituting cotton clothing for synthetics, or fish for steaks. [WL]

intermediary: (See **middleman**.)

internal data: Data that originate within the organization for which the research is being done. [GAC]

internal stimulus: (See **external stimulus**.) [HHK]

internal validity: One criterion by which an experiment is evaluated; the criterion focuses on obtaining evidence demonstrating that the variation in the criterion variable was the result of exposure to the treatment or experimental variable. [GAC]

international advertising: The advertising phenomenon which involves the transfer of advertising appeals, messages, art, copy, photographs, stories and video and film segments (or spots) from one country to another. [WJK]

International Bank for Reconstruction and Development (IBRD): A bank set up under the Bretton Woods Agreement in December 1945 for two purposes: (1) to help finance the rebuilding of war devastated areas and to aid in the advancement of less developed countries; and (2) to provide technical advice to governments or other borrowers, including general economic surveys for Governments wishing to study resources and to plan long range programs of development. [WJK]

international channel of distribution: The structure of intracompany organization units and extra-company agents and dealers, wholesale and retail, through which a commodity, product or service is marketed in international markets. [WJK]

International Court of Justice: The principal judicial organ of the United Nations. It settles disputes between the sovereign nations of the world but not between private citizens. [WJK]

International Development Association (IDA): An affiliate of the IBRD formed in 1960 to help developing nations by extending financial aid on subsidized terms. It helps countries whose credit standing does not enable them to borrow from the bank, and it is prepared to finance a wide variety of projects. [WJK]

international law: The set of rules and principles that states and nations consider binding upon themselves. [WJK]

International Monetary Fund (IMF): A multinational organization whose objective is to promote international financial cooperation, and to coordinate the stabilization of exchange rates and the establishment of freely convertible currencies. [WJK]

international product cycle: A model developed by Professor Raymond Vernon which shows the relationship of production, consumption, and trade over the life cycle of a product. Based on empirical data for the pre-1967 era, the model showed how the location of production shifted from the United States to other advanced countries and then to less developed countries. [WJK]

international retailing: Retailing activity by an organization that reaches across national boundaries. [WJK]

international trade product life cycle: A trade cycle model which suggests that many products go through a cycle where high income, mass consumption countries are initially exporters, then lose their export markets, and finally become importers of the product. [WJK]

interpersonal factors: Those influences or forces on the consumer due to other individuals within his life space or sphere or activity. Wearing a tie when others are doing so would be an example, as would a person purchasing perfume to impress someone else. [HHK]

Interstate Commerce Commission (ICC) (1887): The first independent regulatory agency established, it is required to "foster the preservation and development of a national transportation system adequate to meet the needs of the commerce of the United States, of the postal service, and of the national defense." [DC]

intertype competition: Competition between different types of firms selling the same product. For example, automobile tires may be sold through discount department stores; gasoline service stations; conventional department stores; tire, battery, and accessory dealers; and independent garages. [WRD]

interurbia: Large urban area resulting from the mingling and eventual uniting of close market areas into one large market area. [WRD]

interval scale: Measurement in which the assigned numbers legitimately allow the comparison of the size of the differences among and between members. [GAC]

intraindustry competition: Rivalry among sellers of the same product or service to achieve such objectives as increasing sales, market share or profits. [WL]

intransit storage: Facility for storing, transferring, or modifying shipments enroute to final destination, often used for break-bulk or consolidation purposes. [DJB/BJL]

intrapreneurship: The practice of entrepreneurship within a large firm. Intrapreneurship is a style of management thought to be independent, risk-taking, innovative, daring, and typical of the style used in successful start-up firms. In some situations intrapreneurship requires that the entrepreneurial unit be segregated or isolated from the others, thus permitting the unique style of management. [CMC]

intratype competition: Conflict (or competition) between firms of the same type—e.g., a department store competes with another department store; a supermarket competes with another supermarket. [WRD]

intrinsic reward: Those rewards that come from within the individual rather than externally. Practicing the piano for the sheer joy of learning and creating music rather than for a cash reward is an example. [HHK]

introductory stage of product life cycle: The first stage of the product life cycle. The new product is introduced to the market, sales are slow, promotion is usually heavy, costs are accumulated, and expectation is focused on determining when and if the product will soon enter the second(growth) stage of the cycle. [CMC]

invention: A new device, process, etc., that has been created. Can be in either physical or conceptual form. Preexisting knowledge is combined in a new way to yield something that did not heretofore exist. Not to be confused with a product innovation, which is an invention that has been converted by further management and process development into a marketable product. Invention is thought to require both engineering science and art, but scientific findings and artistic creations, alone, though they may be original, may not constitute inventions. [CMC]

invention pricing policy: A pricing policy in which the company neither fixes a single price worldwide nor remains aloof from subsidiary pricing decisions, but strikes an intermediate position. [WJK]

inventory: Value of merchandise on hand at cost or retail. [WRD]

inventory control: Procedures used to insure that desired inventory levels are maintained. Most are based on either perpetual or periodic review. (See also **stock** or **inventory control**.) [DJB/BJL]

inventory cushion: The allowance in the inventory made for uncertainties in sales or deliveries, often added to the basic low stock to provide for conditions neither controllable nor accurately predictable. [WRD]

inventory overage: Value of physical inventory in excess of the book value. [WRD]

inventory policy: A firm's standard practice regarding the level of inventory to be maintained. For example, it may be customary to hold a 60 or 90 day supply. [DJB/BJL]

inventory stock shortage: Value of the book inventory in excess of the actual physical inventory, often expressed as a percentage of net sales. The amount of theft, breakage, sales in excess of amounts charged customers, and errors in record keeping. May be either clerical (caused by miscalculation), or physical (caused by misappropriation of goods). [WRD]

inventory turnover: The number of times average inventory is sold during a specified time period (usually one year). (See also **stock turnover.**) [DJB/BJL]

investment: Any outlay of cash in the near term that is expected to generate cash inflows in future periods. Typically some or all of the cash outlay is capitalized on the balance sheet of the firm. [PFA]

involvement: The degree of personal relevance a product, brand, object, or behavior has for a consumer. A high involvement product is one that a consumer believes has important personal consequences or will help achieve important personal goals. A low involvement product is one that is not linked to important consequences or goals. [JPP/JCO]

item merchandising: The special planning and control effort employed to discover and take advantage of the sales opportunities afforded by items that are in greater consumer demand. [WRD]

item nonresponse: Source of nonsampling error that arises when a respondent agrees to an interview but refuses or is unable to answer specific questions. [GAC]

itemized rating scale: Scale distinguished by the fact that individuals must indicate their ratings of an attribute or object by selecting one from among a limited number of categories that best describes their position on the attribute or object. [GAC]

job description: (See **position description.**) [VPB]

job lots: A promotional grouping of merchandise through which some vendors dispose of end-of-season surpluses and incomplete assortments. For example, a blouse manufacturer may offer, in minimum units of three dozen garments, a miscellaneous selection of different sizes and styles at one-half the original or early season wholesale price. [WRD]

jobber: Earlier, a dealer in odd or job lots; now, a middleman who buys from manufacturers (or importers) and sells to retailers; a wholesaler. [WRD]

joint rate: A form of transportation pricing when more than one carrier is involved in the movement of freight. A joint rate means that freight moves on a through bill of lading even through multiple carriers are involved in the transport. [DJB/BJL]

joint ventures: 1. A partnership between two firms from different countries who share ownership and control in proportion to their investments. [DLS] 2. (international) A form of participation in foreign markets by means of alliance with a local partner. [WJK]

joint venturing: A linkage between two companies in order to facilitate the supply and/or sale of products to a market or market segment. A joint venture arrangement might be set up between two or more companies in order to enter a new market (e.g., a foreign market), or between two or more companies in the value chain as when the child of two corporate parents develops a new distribution or builds a supplying plant. Joint ventures can be informal sharing agreements or formal equity-sharing arrangements. [GSD]

judgment sample: Nonprobability sample that is often called a purposive sample; the sample elements are handpicked because they are expected to serve the research purpose. [GAC]

jury of executive opinion: A method of sales forecasting in which the executives of the company are polled for their assessment of likely sales. Also known as the jury of expert opinion method. [GAC]

just-in-time (JIT):   Inventory management system based upon philosophy that well-run manufacturing plants do not require the stockpiling of parts and components. Instead, they rely upon receiving necessary inventory in the exact quantity and at a specified time to support manufacturing schedules. [DJB/BJL]

key items: Items that are in greatest consumer demand. Also referred to as best sellers. [WRD]

key success factors: Those factors which are a necessary condition for success in a given market. That is, a company that does poorly on one of the factors critical to success in its market is certain to fail. [GSD]

keystone markup: The cost price is doubled or a markup of 50% of retail is obtained. For example, if an item is retailed at $20 and cost the retailer $10, then the keystone markup has been applied. [WRD]

label: The information attached to or on a product for the purpose of naming it and for describing its use, its dangers, its ingredients, its manufacturer, and the like. A label is usually thought of as printed material, but labeling in the broader sense has been ruled to include spoken information and separate promotional pieces, if they serve the information purpose and are closely allied to the product. [CMC]

labeling: (See **label**).

labor intensive: A term applied to a product or an industry where labor requirements are large relative to requirements for capital goods. [DLS]

laboratory experiment: Research investigation in which investigators create a situation with exact conditions so as to control some, and manipulate other, variables. [GAC]

laggards: The fifth, and last, group of users to adopt an innovation. (See also **adopter categories** and **product adoption process.**) [CMC]

landed cost price: The quoted or invoiced price of a commodity, plus any transportation charges. [WRD]

Lanham Trademark Act (1946): Provides for the registration and protection of trademarks. [DC]

late majority: The fourth group of users to adopt an innovation. (See also **adopter categories** and **product adoption process.**) [CMC]

lateral diversification: (See **diversification.**)

launch control: The process by which a management plans for and supervises the introduction of a new product; the product's progress is monitored against preestablished norms, variances are detected, and corrections made such that the original goals set for the product are achieved. [CMC]

law of demand: 1. (popular) Other things being equal, consumers will buy more of a product at a low price than at a high price. 2. (economic) Under the same conditions of demand, the amount of product taken by a market varies inversely with its price. [DLS]

law of diminishing marginal utility: A situation where consumption of an additional unit of a good adds less to total satisfaction than the preceding unit. [DLS]

law of diminishing returns: After a certain point has been reached, each successive application of a factor of production will add less to total output than before. [DLS]

law of effect: A technical term from learning theory in psychology often credited to Thorndike. Of the several responses made to the same situation, that which is accompanied or closely followed by satisfaction, other things being equal, will more likely be repeated, and the connections learned. Those responses which are followed by punishment will be extinguished. For example, the consumer's probability of repeating purchase of a brand would increase if he/she were satisfied with the purchase and decrease if he/she were dissatisfied. However, whether rewards and punishment are essential for learning to occur is controversial in that many learning theorists claim that reinforcement is unnecessary. [HHK]

lay-away: The purchase of an article with a down payment, but the store retains the article until full payment is made, often in a series of installments. [WRD]

layout: The plan of a print advertisement that indicates where the component parts (headline, illustrations, text, signature, etc.) are to be placed on the page for most effective communication; the layout is a presentation of the final printed advertisement. [AMB]

L.C.L. (less-than-carload-lot): Rates that apply to less than full carload shipments. [WRD]

lead time: The amount of time determined by a merchandiser that is necessary to "add on" to the purchasing period in order to assure that sufficient merchandise will be on hand until the particular order is received. If delivery time is long, or if raw materials are in short supply, "lead time" may be longer than when conditions are "normal". [WRD]

leader pricing: The practice of knowingly and intentionally marking a part of the stock at prices that will not yield the maximum profit return on these particular goods. The articles so selected for special price emphasis are identified as "leaders". (See also loss leader.) [WRD]

leading economic indicators: Those economic indicators that reach peaks or troughs before aggregate economic activity. [DLS]

leading question: A question framed so as to give the respondent a clue as to how he or she should answer. [GAC]

leads, sales: An individual or organization that is a potential customer. [BAW]

leadtime: The time required to receive inventory once an order is placed. Also called replenishment time. [DJB/BJL]

learning: According to Hilgard, learning refers to more or less permanent change in behavior which occurs as a result of practice. It is a process by which an activity originates or is changed through reacting to an encountered situation, but does not include those changes induced by maturation, genetic response tendencies, or temporary situations such as fatigue or drug influence. It includes such activities as the learning of facts and skills, brands, jingles, purchase behavior, beliefs and attitudes. [HHK]

learning curve: Typically a graph of the amount of material learned, plotted against time or number of trials. Many learning situations lead to an S-shaped curve. [HHK]

leased departments: Sections of a retail business managed and operated by an outside person or organization rather than by the store of which it is a physical part, whether conducted by an individual or a chain. [WRD]

leasing: A contract through which the asset owner (lessor) extends the right to use the asset to another party (lessee) in return for periodic payment of rent over a specific period. It is divided into financial leases and operating leases. [GLL/DTW]

less-than-truckload (LTL): Small freight shipment typically less than 10,000 pounds transported by common carriers. [DJB/BJL]

lexicographic rule: Unlike the conjunctive or disjunctive rule, the lexicographic heuristic assumes that attributes of products can be ordered in terms of importance. In making a choice, alternative brands are first compared with respect to the most important attribute. If one alternative is preferred over all others for this attribute, then that alternative is chosen regardless of the values the alternatives have on the other attributes. If two brands are equal on the most important attribute the second attribute is is considered, then the third, and so on. (See also **noncompensatory rules**.) [HHK]

licensing: 1. Selling the right to use some process, trademark, patent or other right for a fee or royalty. [JRN] 2. (international) A relatively simple, low risk linkage that allows a manufacturer to "enter" new markets (typically foreign markets). An arrangement where a licensee in a new market is given the right to use a process, trademark, patent or other proprietary item for a fee or royalty. [GSD] 3. (international) An agreement between two companies in which the licensor grants the right to the licensee to sell a patented product in specified markets for an agreed upon fee. A tool for participating in foreign markets without large capital outlays. When capital is scarce, when import restrictions forbid any means of entry, when a country is sensitive to foreign ownership, or when it is necessary to protect trademarks and patents against cancellation for non-use, licensing is a legitimate means of capitalizing on a foreign market. [WJK]

life style: 1. In general the manner in which the individual copes and deals with his/her psychological and physical environment on a day to day basis. More specifically, used by some theorists as a phrase describing the values, attitudes, opinions and behavior patterns of the consumer. [HHK] 2. The manner in which people conduct their lives, including their activities, interests, and opinions. [JPP/JCO]

life style analysis: (See **psychographic analysis**.)

light equipment: The industrial (business) product classification that includes items such as portable power tools like drills, saws, grinders, measuring instruments, typewriters, calculators, etc. [GLL/DTW]

likert scale: (See **summated ratings**.)

limited decision making: A choice involving a moderate degree of cognitive and behavioral effort. [JPP/JCO]

limited-function wholesalers: Term applied to a variety of types of wholesalers that have placed emphasis upon reducing, eliminating or modifying certain well-established functions ordinarily performed by regular wholesalers. [WRD]

limited-service advertising agency: An advertising agency that concentrates its activities on a particular advertising function, such as creative (message development) or media; a "boutique" (or creative boutique) offers creative service and a "media buying service" primarily limits its activity to media buying (although in some cases also does media planning as well). [AMB]

line authority: The authority managers need to manage the people assigned to them so as to achieve the goals for which they are held responsible by higher management. It generally encompasses the authority to hire, assign, direct, reward, demote, and fire, although company policy may require that some of these actions have the approval of higher line managers or managers with functional authority. [VPB]

line extension: A new product marketed by an organization which already has at least one other product being sold in that product/market area. Line extensions are usually new flavors, sizes, models, applications, strengths, etc. Sometimes the distinction is made between near line extensions (very little difference) and distant line extensions (almost completely new entries).

line-haul rate: Transportation rates commonly charged by common carriers (motor carriers). There are three basic types: class, exception, and commodity rates. [DJB/BJL]

linear learning model: A brand choice model that views the probability of choosing a particular brand on the current choice occasion as linearly related to the consumer's probability for choosing that brand on the previous occasion. The particular linear function applied to the previous period's choice probability depends on whether the brand of interest was actually chosen last time (in which case the "acceptance operator" is applied) or not chosen last time (causing the "rejection operator" to be applied) (Kuehn 1962). In this model the consumer's probability of selecting a particular brand on the current choice occasion is affected by the entire sequence of previous choices— hence the term "learning model" is appropriate. [DCS/YJW]

list price: The selling price for an item before any discounts or reductions in price. [KM]

literature search: Search of statistics, trade journal articles, other articles, magazines, newspapers, and books for data or insight into the problem at hand. [GAC]

LITMUS: A model for predicting the sales over time of a new (typically frequently purchased) consumer product using pre-test market data. The approach views a potential customer as moving through the stages of awareness, trial and repeat purchase. It incorporates explicitly the effect of advertising and promotion on awareness and trial of the product. The model's parameters are calibrated using a laboratory-test-market coupled with a follow-up telephone interview (Blackburn and Clancy 1982). LITMUS II adds monthly or quarterly projections, sensitivity analysis and profit analysis. For other models predicting sales of new products see ASSESSOR, NEWS, SPRINTER MOD III and TRACKER. [DCS/YJW]

live rack: A storage rack designed so product automatically flows forward to the desired selection position. The typical live rack contains roller conveyors and is constructed for rear loading. The rear of the rack is elevated; gravity causes the product to flow forward. [DJB/BJL]

living standards: A measure of the possession and distribution of the material goods among members of a society. [DLS]

lobbying: Refers to a person or group of persons seeking to influence the proceedings of legislative bodies through personal intervention. [DC]

local advertising: Advertising that is sponsored by an organization that operates mostly in a limited geographical territory, such as a particular city; where such advertising is by a retail store, it is called "retail" advertising. Local advertising does not include national advertisers who advertise in local markets as part of a national or regional campaign. [AMB]

local brand: A brand of product that is marketed (distributed and promoted) in a relatively small and restricted geographical area. May be called a regional brand if the area encompasses more than one metropolitan market. [CMC]

local rate: The advertising rate offered by media to a local advertiser and which often is lower than the rate available to a national advertiser. [AMB]

location affinities: The clustering of similar or complementary kinds of retail stores. [WRD]

logistical cost: Costs associated with providing purchasing, manufacturing support, and physical distribution services. [DJB/BJL]

logistical resource planning (LRP):   Formal plan for controlling and monitoring overall materials logistics process. Emphasis is placed on integrating the overall objectives of the enterprise with logistical requirements. [DJB/BJL]

logistics: A single logic to guide the process of planning, allocating and controlling financial and human resources committed to physical distribution, manufacturing support and purchasing operations. The Council of Logistics Management (formerly NCPDM) offers the following definition. "Logistics management is the term describing the integration of two or more activities for the purpose of planning, implementing and controlling the efficient flow of raw materials, in-process inventory and finished goods from point of origin to point of consumption. These activities may include, but are not limited to, customer service, demand forecasting, distribution communications, inventory control, material handling, order processing, parts and service support, plant and warehouse site selection, procurement, packaging, return goods handling, salvage and scrap disposal, traffic and transportation and warehousing and storage." [DJB/BJL]

logistics manager: (See **physical distribution manager.**) [VPB]

logit model: A probabilistic model for representing the discrete choice behavior of individuals. On any choice occasion the individual is assumed to choose the item for which he/she has the highest preference. Over repeated choice occasions preferences are assumed to have a probabilistic component. For the logit model this random component of preference is taken to have the double exponential distribution (i.e., the type 1 Fisher-Tippett extreme value distribution). The model can be used to predict choice probabilities based on attributes of the items being chosen (Corstjens and Gautschi 1983; Yellott 1977). This model is a substitute for discriminant analysis that in addition provides approximate standard errors of estimated model parameters. It is an alternate to regression analysis when the dependent variable is categorical as opposed to continuous. Unlike the probit model or the nested logit model or the EBA model, logit assumes that Luce's Choice Axiom holds, which is sometimes seen as a drawback to the use of this model. [DCS/YJW]

logo: A clipped or shortened form of logotype. Logo is a word or phrase that serves to identify an organization. Similar to trade name. [CMC]

long range planning: (See **planning.**)

longitudinal study: Investigation involving a fixed sample of elements that is measured repeatedly through time. [GAC]

loss leader: An item that is sold at a "loss" of markup, which would normally be obtained on the particular item, for the express purpose of increasing store traffic. (See also **leader pricing**.) [WRD]

loss leader pricing: The featuring of items priced below cost or at relatively low prices to attract customers to the seller's place of business. [KM]

low involvement: (See **involvement**.)

low involvement consumer behavior: Used to describe consumer decision making in which very little cognitive activity is involved. Those situations where the consumer simply does not care and is not concerned about brands or choices and makes the decision in the most cognitively miserly manner possible. Most likely, low involvement is situation based and the degree of importance and involvement may vary with the individual and with the situation. [HHK]

low involvement hierarchy: In the Hierarchy of Effects model, the order consists of acquiring information, leading to formation of positive attitudes and then to the behavioral act of purchase or trial. Under low involvement conditions, the process is reversed such that it is after purchase, if at all, that interest and attitudes emerge. [HHK]

Luce's choice axiom: A statement that the relative odds of an individual's choosing one particular item (e.g., brand "A") over another (e.g., brand "B") are unaffected by the presence or absence of other items (e.g., brands "C", "D", etc.) as potential choices. The property is also known as independence from irrelevant alternatives or IIA, (Luce 1977; Yellott 1977). The logit model possesses this property (which is sometimes seen as a liability), while the probit model and other choice models can avoid it. [DCS/YJW]

macroenvironment: Refers to the surroundings, conditions, circumstances or influences in the aggregate facing a person or company. It focuses on such magnitudes as the general level of prices, the amount of unemployment, the rates of economic growth and the balance of payments. It is contrasted with the microenvironment. [WL]

macromarketing: The study of marketing processes, activities, institutions and results from a broad perspective such as a nation, in which cultural, political, and social, as well as economic interaction are investigated. Marketing in a larger context than any one firm. [WL]

Magnuson-Moss Warranty-Federal Trade Commission Improvement Act (1975): Requires the seller of a consumer product who provides a written warranty to indicate clearly and conspicuously whether the warranty is a "full" or "limited" warranty. The FTC was given responsibility for administering the act as well as additional powers including the authority to promulgate "trade regulation rules" that specifically define "unfair or deceptive acts or practices." [DC]

mail questionnaire: Questionnaire administered by mail to designated respondents under an accompanying cover letter and its return, by mail, by the subject to the research organization. [GAC]

mail-order houses: Establishments primarily engaged in distributing merchandise through the mail as a result of mail orders received. [WRD]

maintained items: Specific items that are continuously maintained in assortments. [WRD]

maintained markup (maintained markon): The differential between the cost of goods sold and net sales. (Retail inventory method of accounting.) [WRD]

maintenance and repair services: Business services aimed at keeping the plant and equipment in good operating condition or repairing inoperable equipment. They are usually available from the OEM (original equipment manufacturer), but in many industries, specialized organizations perform this function as well. Examples are window cleaning, air conditioning system repairs. [GLL/DTW]

majority fallacy: A marketing strategy that directs a new product to an entire market, or to the largest segment in it, solely because of its size. Today, this shotgun approach is felt to be almost always inferior to the alternative strategy of targeting to smaller segments. [CMC]

makegood: Rescheduling or compensation offered an advertiser by the medium when an advertisement or commercial is unavoidably cancelled, preempted, or not run correctly; also, in broadcast, running an additional commercial (or commercials) because a particular vehicle did not deliver the promised audience. [AMB]

mall-type shopping center: A grouping of stores near the center of a shopping center plot with parking area surrounding the store concentration on all sides. All or most of the stores face a "mall" or pedestrian shopping area. [WRD]

management information system (MIS): Set of procedures and methods for the regular, planned collection, analysis, and presentation of information for use in making management decisions. [GAC]

management of marketing: (See **marketing management**.) [VPB]

management of products: (See **product manager** and **product planning manager**.) [VPB]

management of sales force: (See **sales management**.)

manipulation check: A measurement that is taken in an experiment to make sure that subjects accurately perceived the actual changes in the treatment variable. [GAC]

manufacturers' agent: An agent who generally operates on an extended contractual basis; often sells within an exclusive territory; handles non-competing but related lines of goods; and possesses limited authority with regard to prices and terms of sale. (See also **sales agent**.) [WRD]

manufacturer's brand: A brand owned by a manufacturer, as distinguished from a brand owned by a reseller. (See **private brand**.) [CMC]

manufacturers' sales branches and offices: Captive wholesaling operations owned and operated by manufacturers. Sales branches carry inventory whereas sales offices do not. [JRN]

manufacturing resource planning (MRP-II): An extension of standard MRP to include planning and feedback in the manufacturing system. Also integrates the manufacturing plan into the financial business plan of the firm. Sometimes referred to as "closed-loop" MRP. [DJB/BJL]

margin: The difference between the selling price and total unit costs for an item. [KM]

marginal analysis: A technique of explanation that focuses on the extra or marginal unit of cost, production, or utility. [DLS]

marginal cost (MC): The net change in total cost that results from producing and marketing one additional unit. [DLS]

marginal propensity to consume: The fraction of each extra dollar that consumers will spend on consumption, given an extra dollar of real income. [DLS]

marginal propensity to save: The fraction of each extra dollar that consumers will save, given an extra dollar of real income. [DLS]

marginal revenue (MR): The net change in total revenue that results from producing and marketing one additional unit. [DLS]

marginal unit: The last unit, i.e., that unit whose acquisition or loss is under consideration. [DLS]

marginal utility: The increase in total utility due to purchasing or consuming one additional unit of a good or service. [DLS]

markdown: 1. The amount of a reduction from the selling price. [KM] 2. A reduction in the original or previous retail price of a piece of merchandise. For management purposes, markdowns are stated as percentage of net sales in contrast with off-retail percentage. [WRD]

markdown cancellations: Upward price adjustments that are offset against former markdowns. The most common example: the restoration of a price to original retail after the goods have been marked down temporarily for purposes of a special sales event. [WRD]

markdown control: Any system ensuring that every markdown taken is accounted for, so that the book retail inventory may be kept in line with the actual physical inventory. [WRD]

market attractiveness-competitive position matrix: Each business unit or product is classified jointly by market attractiveness and the strength of the competitive position. The market attractiveness-competitive position model is a multifactor portfolio model developed jointly by McKinsey and General Electric (GE) with each dimension of the matrix being based on multiple factors. It is sometimes called a nine-block matrix because each of the two dimensions is divided into three levels. [GSD]

market attractiveness: A measure of the profit potential inherent in the structure of a market or industry. There are a multitude of factors contributing to (and which can be used to measure) market attractiveness. The major categories and some examples from each of the categories are provided in the following: (1) **market factors:** market growth rate, market size and life cycle stage; (2) **economic and technological factors:** investment intensity, industry capacity, barriers to entry/exit and access to raw materials; (3) **competitive forces:** types of direct rivals, structure of competition and substitution threats, bargaining power of buyers and suppliers; and (4) **environmental factors:** regulatory climate, degree of social acceptance and human factors. [GSD]

market concentration: The degree to which a relatively few firms account for a large proportion of the market such as in an oligopolistic situation. Also known as the **concentration ratio**. [WL]

market coverage: The number of available outlets in a given line of retail or wholesale trade, relative to a saturation level, that are marketing a manufacturer's brand in a given market area. Manufacturers typically follow one of three forms of market coverage: exclusive, selective or intensive distribution. [JRN]

market coverage strategies: Represent alternative approaches that company can use to select and target markets. Five common market-coverage strategies are: (1) **single market concentration**, focusing on one part of the market; (2) **product specialization**, making one product for all markets; (3) **market specialization**, making all products for one market; (4) **selective specialization**, making products for multiple niches; and (5) **full coverage**, making a product for every customer. [GLL/DTW]

market demand: The total volume of a given product or service bought by a specific group of customers in a specified market area, during a specific time period. [WL]

market development: The expansion of the total market served by a business, achieved by: (1) entering new segments—by expanding the geographic base of the business or by using new channels to reach unserved customers; (2) conversion of non-users—by lower prices or increased (or specially designed) promotion; and (3) increasing usage by present users—by developing and promoting new uses for the product. [GSD]

market evolution: Market (or industry) life cycles describe the evolution of the market. These cycles have a similar shape to the product life cycle (see definition) and similarly, have a number of distinct stages: (1) embryonic—the product class and industry definitions are virtually synonymous, diffusion rates are gradual and there is considerable uncertainty about the product; (2) growth—the industry structure develops, the introduction of new product classes becomes easier as consumers become more knowledgeable and the channels facilitating the marketing of new product classes established; and (3) maturity—an established infrastructure facilitates rapid introduction and diffusion of new product varients or classes, competitors jockey for position and older products have to make adjustments to protect their declining position. (See also **product life cycle**). [GSD]

market factor: A feature or characteristic in a market that is related to the demand for the product, e.g. number of households in the market is related to the demand for many products. [GAC]

market index: A mathematical expression that combines two or more market factors into a numerical index, typically by forming a linear combination of the factors where the weights assigned each factor would reflect their relative importance in affecting demand for a product or products. [GAC]

market management organization: Market managers are responsible for developing marketing plans, implementing the plans (or coordinating their implementation by functional departments), and monitoring performance for their assigned markets. The market manager may be a staff position for planning and for providing authoritative market information to the functional departments that implement plans. Or it may be a line position with its own (for example) sales and advertising personnel. Market managers may report directly to the marketing manager or (if numerous) to an intervening level of management such as a group marketing manager. Or market managers may report to a product manager of a major product line which is sold to different markets. Comment: The market management form of organization may be appropriate where company products are sold to different markets through different channels of distribution. This is often the case with industrial goods companies who sell the same or similar products to different industries (i.e. markets) and where knowledge of industry product application is essential to successful market penetration. With expert knowledge of the needs and practices of a particular market, the market manager provides feedback from customers for the guidance of R&D, sales engineers, and technical service personnel. [VPB]

market manager: Within an organization, a person assigned responsibility for overseeing all functional activities (e.g. manufacturing, pricing, service) that relate to a particular market (customer group or product application). The market manager is to a market what a product manager is to a product, and delineating their respective roles in industrial firms is difficult. (See also **product manager**.) [CMC]

market niche strategies: (See **niche strategies**.)

market opportunity analysis: Analysis and evaluation of probable future situations by a variety of techniques to identify market opportunities that a company can profitably cultivate.

It is part of the strategic analysis of the company's strengths, weaknesses, opportunities and threats. [WL]

market opportunity: (See **situation analysis**.)

market opportunity index: The use of relevant criteria by a company to rank future opportunities that have been identified and facilitate the selection of the most promising opportunities. [WL]

market penetration strategy: The move by management to increase its market share held by current products in currently serviced markets. Market share may be increased some combination of: (1) attracting users of competitive brands, (2) persuading current users to increase usage, or (3) attracting non-users of the product category. [GSD]

market positioning: Positioning refers to the customer's perceptions of the place a product or brand occupies in a market segment. In some markets, a position is achieved by associating the benefits of a brand with the needs or life style of the segments. More often, positioning involves the differentiation of the company's offering from the competition by making or implying a comparison in terms of specific attributes. [GSD]

market potential: An estimate of the maximum possible sales of a commodity, a group of commodities, or a service for an entire industry in a market during a stated period. [GAC]

market research: Systematic gathering, recording, and analyzing data with respect to a particular market, where market refers to a specific customer group in a specific geographic area. [GAC]

market rollout: Introduction of a new product into a market sequentially. The rollout may be by geographical areas, by applications or uses, or by individual customers. Over time, depending on the speed of the rollout, the entire market is covered. [CMC]

market segmentation: The process of subdividing a market into distinct subsets of customers, that behave in the same way or have similar needs. Each subset may conceivably be chosen as a market target to be reached with a distinct marketing strategy. The process begins with a basis of segmentation—a product-specific factor that reflects differences in customers requirements or responsiveness to marketing variables (possibilities are purchase behavior, usage, benefits sought, intentions, preference or loyalty). Segment descriptors are then chosen, based on their ability to identify segments, to account for variance in the segmentation basis, and to suggest competitive strategy implications (examples of descriptors are demographics, geography, psychographics, customer size and industry). To be of strategic value the resulting segments must be measurable, accessible, sufficiently different to justify a meaningful variation in strategy, substantial and durable. [GSD]

market segmentation strategies: Having segmented a market, the task is then to determine which segments are profitable to serve. The business can adopt one of three market segmentation strategies: (1) **undifferentiated marketing**: where the business attempts to go after the whole market with a product and marketing strategy intended to have mass appeal; (2) **differentiated marketing**: where the business operates in several segments of the market with offerings and market strategies tailored to each segment; (3) **concentrated marketing**: where the business focuses on only one or a few segments with the intention of capturing a large share of these segments. [GSD]

market share: The proportion of the total quantity or dollar sales in a market that is held by each of the competitors. The market can be defined as broadly as the industry, or all substitutes, or as narrowly as a specific market segment. The choice of market depends on which level gives the best insight into competitive position. [GSD]

market structure: The pattern formed by the number, size, and distribution of buyers and sellers in a market. [DLS]

market test: Controlled experiment, done in a limited but carefully selected sector of the marketplace; its aim is to predict the sales or profit consequences, either in absolute or relative terms, of one or more proposed marketing actions. [GAC]

market testing: The phase of new product development when the new item and its marketing plan are tested together. Prior testing, if any, involved separate components. A market test simulates the eventual marketing of the product, and takes many different forms, only one of which bears the name test market. [CMC]

market-crystallization: A market development stage that refers to the effort needed to identify a latent market (i.e. organizations that share a similar need or want for something that does not yet exist) and to work to "crystalize" that need. The result is a new method or service that can satisfy all or part of the market. For example, the videotex market is in the market crystallization phase. It appears to have some market-benefits, but those benefits have not been fully developed. [GLL/DTW]

marketing: The process of planning and executing the conception, pricing, promotion, and distribution of ideas, goods, and services to create exchanges that satisfy individual and organizational goals. [AMA]

marketing (only) division: Contains the usual marketing functions, including sales, but its products are supplied by a centralized production operation which supplies two or more marketing divisions. When standardized products can be mass produced by a centralized facility, economies of scale are the usual result. Comment: When a growing company breaks into two or more divisions, the products of a division may be so few as to allow for functional organization. But as the division grows it may turn to product or market management. Eventually it may grow to the point where it is broken into two or more new divisions which, in turn, revert back to the functional organization. [VPB]

marketing and consumer satisfaction: (See **consumer satisfaction** and **post purchase evaluation**.) [HHK]

marketing conduct: A legal view of marketers' decisions on marketing mix variables and the process by which they make these decisions. [DLS]

marketing ethics: 1. Standards of marketing decision-making based on "what is right" and "what is wrong," and emanating from our religious heritage and our traditions of social, political and economic freedom. [DC] 2. The use of moral codes, values and standards to determine whether marketing actions are good or evil, right or wrong. Often standards are based on professional or association codes of ethics. [WL]

marketing goals: (See **goals**.)

marketing information system (MkIS):   Set of procedures and methods for the regular, planned collection, analysis, and presentation of information for use in making marketing decisions. [GAC]

marketing information systems (MkIS) manager: Responsible for the administration of a system that collects, classifies, selectively stores, and retrieves the kinds of information needed for marketing decisions. The marketing information systems manager normally reports on a line basis to the executive in charge of company management information systems and on a dotted line basis to the chief corporate or division marketing executive. [VPB]

marketing intelligence system: Refers to the development of a system to gather, process, assess and make available marketing data and information in a format that permits marketing managers and executives to function more effectively. Marketing data, when analyzed, may yield information which can then be processed and put into a format that gives intelligence for planning, policy making, and decision purposes. [WL]

marketing management: The process of setting marketing goals for an organization (considering internal resources and market opportunities), the planning and execution of activities to meet these goals, and measuring progress towards their achievement. Comment: The process is ongoing and repetitive (as within a planning cycle) so that the organization may continuously adapt to internal and external changes that create new problems and opportunities. [VPB]

marketing manager: The generic title for the line executive responsible for designated marketing functions (such as marketing research, product and market planning, pricing, distribution, promotion, and customer services) and for coordinating with other departments that perform marketing related activities (such as packaging, warehousing, order filling, shipping, design of new and improved products, credit, billing, collections, accounting, legal, transportation, purchasing, product repair, warranty fulfillment, technical assistance to customers). The marketing manager may have an officer title (such as vice president of marketing) and usually reports to the chief executive officer in a functionally organized company or to the division manager (president) in a divisionalized company. Comment: The above definition describes the marketing manager with full responsibility for marketing. However, the title is sometimes used for jobs of lesser scope; for example, in a multiproduct division a manager may be in charge of a line of products or a business segment and report to the division marketing manager. Also, it is not uncommon for the sales and marketing functions to report separately to a common supervisor such as the division manager. In such a case the marketing manager may be in charge of marketing functions other than personal selling. This dichotomy most often occurs in industrial or consumer shopping goods businesses where personal selling is the key aspect of promotion. [VPB]

marketing manager, corporate level executive: Some large divisionalized companies have a corporate marketing vice president who performs a staff role designated by the corporate chief executive officer. In general the principal role is to view marketing problems and opportunities from a broader perspective than that of division management. It may also include specific functions such as: providing marketing counsel to corporate management, monitoring divisional marketing performance, critiquing divisional marketing plans, evaluating potential acquisitions, assisting with or directing the corporate strategic planning function, searching for new product and business opportunities outside of present division charters, assisting with setting R&D priorities, and administering the corporate advertising and/or corporate image programs. This position usually reports to the corporate chief executive. **marketing manager, corporate level executive:** [VPB]

marketing mix: The mix of controllable marketing variables that the firm uses to pursue the desired level of sales in the target market. The most common classification of these factors is the four factor classification called the Four P's—price, product, promotion, and place (or distribution). Optimization of the marketing mix is achieved by assigning the amount of the marketing budget to be spent on each element of the marketing mix so as to maximize the total contribution to the firm. "Contribution" may be measured in terms of sales, profits or in terms of any other organizational goals. [GSD]

marketing mix models: The determination of an optimal marketing mix is often aided by models that take into account the market response to the various marketing mix elements and their interactions. These models include econometric market response models to the marketing mix variables of the firm (and its competitors) as well as specialized models such as ADVISOR and BRANDAID, microsimulation models, various optimization models, and customized applications of the AHP and other resource allocation models. [DCS/YJW]

marketing objectives: (See **objectives**.)

marketing organization, forms of: No two companies are likely to have identical structures. Most utilize one or more of the classic structural forms with the choice at any one time having to do with the stage of company development. (For the more frequently used forms, see **functional organization, product/brand management organization, market management organization, divisional organization, geographic organization,** and **matrix organization**.) It should be noted that larger companies may be using different forms in different parts of the company at the same time. [VPB]

marketing plan: A document composed of an analysis of the current marketing situation, opportunities and threats analysis, marketing objectives, marketing strategy, action programs and projected or pro-forma income (and other financial) statements. This plan may be the only statement of the strategic direction of a business, but it is more likely to apply only to a specific brand or product. In the latter situation, the marketing plan is an implementation device that is integrated within an overall strategic business plan. [GSD]

marketing planning: The process that leads to the development of the marketing plan. (See also **marketing plan**.) [GSD]

marketing research: The function which links the consumer, customer, and public to the marketer through information—information used to identify and define marketing opportunities and problems; generate, refine and evaluate marketing actions; monitor marketing performance; and improve understanding of marketing as a process. Marketing research specifies the information required to address these issues; designs the method for collecting information; manages and implements the data collection process; analyzes the results; and communicates the findings and their implications. [AMA]

marketing research manager: Responsible for providing professional research services to executives who require objective and timely market information to assist with planning, problem resolution, and decision making. Normally the marketing research manager reports to the marketing manager. In larger companies, however, there may be multiple marketing research managers reporting, for example, to the corporate marketing or strategic planning executive, to division managers, and to the R&D director. Comment: The types of research carried out will vary by type of company, industry, and the organizational unit to which the manager is assigned. With the growth of computerized marketing information systems and the availability of outside research organizations that report repetitive market data, the marketing research manager assembles the information needed for a particular problem and, when necessary, directs the development of information that must be obtained via special studies. The typical marketing research manager works with a small staff and uses outside research firms to carry out all or parts of field studies. [VPB]

marketing services: Sometimes called "customer services," it is an all-inclusive term that covers different sets of functions for different companies. Historically it has included some or all of the functions needed to service channel intermediaries and/or end customers, such as inventory planning and control; order processing, shipping, and delivery information; product installation, maintenance, repair, replacement, and warranty administration; and answering customer inquiries. Organizationally most of these services are provided by functional departments other than marketing. They may or may not be coordinated by a "marketing services" or "customer services" manager reporting to the marketing manager. Comment: While the above named services are basic to providing marketing services to channels and customers, another use of the term applies to a centralized department that provides "in-house" services to company divisions. (See **marketing services department** for a definition of this use of the term.) [VPB]

marketing services department: A unit in a multidivision company that performs marketing functions for divisions which can be performed better or at less cost when carried out centrally. While the functions of this unit may vary by company, they may include some or all of the following: media planning, coordination of media buying, sales promotion planning and counselling, providing sales promotion materials, package design, control of advertising production costs, advertising research, creative services, and advertising claims substantiation. For small divisions with limited personnel, the marketing services department may serve as their advertising, sales promotion, product publicity, or marketing research department. [VPB]

marketing services director: Manages the marketing services department and may report to a corporate executive, group executive, or to the manager of a major division. Irrespective of the reporting level, this manager provides the services for all divisions that require them. [VPB]

marketing strategy: A statement (implicit or explicit) of how a brand or product line will achieve its objectives. The strategy provides decisions and direction regarding variables such the segmentation of the market, identification of the target market, positioning, marketing mix elements and expenditures. A marketing strategy is usually an integral part of a business strategy that provides broad direction to all functions. (See also **strategy**.) [GSD]

marketing tactics: (See **tactics**.)

markon: (See **markup** and **cumulative markon**.)

Markov model: Brand switching matrices (from time t-1 to t) are sometimes envisioned as arising from a stationary first order Markov model. This model assumes that only the brand chosen in t-1 affects brand choice at t. The transition probability matrix describes the brand choice. Higher order models (i.e., in which choice at t is dependent on several previous choices) with varying transition probabilities have also been proposed. For example, see Kahn, Kalwani and Morrison (1986) and Lattin and McAlister (1985). [DCS/YJW]

markup: 1. (general) The amount of an increase in price over total unit costs. [KM] 2. (retail) The difference between merchandise cost and the retail price. Also referred to as Markon. (See also **initial markup** and **maintained markup**.) [WRD]

markup percentage: The difference between cost and retail, expressed either as a percentage of cost or, commonly, as a percentage of retail. [WRD]

markup table: A tabulation giving markup percentages on cost price with the corresponding markup percentages on retail price. (See also **markup wheel** and **profit flashers**.) [WRD]

markup wheel: A tabulation giving markup percentages on cost price with the corresponding markup percentages on retail price. (See also **markup table**.) [WRD]

Maslow's need hierarchy: A popular theory of human needs developed by Abraham Maslow. The theory suggests that humans satisfy their needs in a sequential order starting with physiological needs (food, water, sex), and ranging through safety needs (protection from harm), belongingness and love needs (companionship), esteem needs (prestige, respect of others), and finally, self-actualization needs (self-fulfillment). [JPP/JCO]

master carton: A container that is used primarily for protective purposes in transportation and warehousing. It contains multiple, usually identical, products which may be individually packaged for resale. [DJB/BJL]

master production schedule: A detailed listing of how many end items are to be produced and when they will be produced. An materials requirements planning (MRP) system requires a valid and detailed master production schedule as critical first input in the system. [DJB/BJL]

materials handling: A term applied to the study of physical flow in a logistics system. It is usually used to describe a mechanical or electro-mechanical set of devices which facilitate the physical handling of products in a logistics environment. [DJB/BJL]

materials management: Describes either an organizational component or approach to managing the material flow process of the firm. A distinctive characteristic of the term is that it includes the purchasing function as an integral part of the material flow process. The term materials manager is also used to describe a related job function. [DJB/BJL]

materials requirements planning (MRP):   A production and inventory planning system that integrates product components, manufacturing and procurement schedules, lead times and capacities against output requirements. [DJB/BJL]

mathematical programming: A set of optimization models whose aim is to find the maximum (or minimum) of an objective function subject to certain constraints. The most commonly used mathematical programming technique is Linear Programming (LP)—a linear objective function subject to linear constraints. LP provides both the values of the decision variables for the optimal solution and the shadow prices for the constraints (i.e., the change in value of the objective function per unit change in the value of the constraint). Other mathematical programming techniques include integer programming (for integers as opposed to continuous values), nonlinear programming, quadratic programming, and dynamic programming. Dynamic programming is a general type of approach to solve multistage problems in continuous or discrete space under certainty or uncertainty. Uncertainty can be incorporated in linear programming as well as either stochastic programming (some of the parameters are random variables) or chance constrained programming (feasible solutions are allowed to have a small probability of violating the constraints). Mathematical programming has been used in marketing, especially in media selection and salesforce allocation problems. [DCS/YJW]

matrix organization: Attempts to combine functional and product forms of organization to obtain the advantages of each. Teams of functional personnel (e.g. manufacturing, R&D, finance, and sales) report to a product manager with profit responsibility. These functional personnel also report to their functional bosses who are responsible for maintaining the quality of functional performance. Comment: This arrangement means that functional personnel report to two bosses which require a high order of understanding and cooperation if it is to be effective. Matrix organization has met with mixed results and has both its critics and champions. [VPB]

maturity stage of product life cycle: The third stage of the product life cycle, when initial rapid growth is over and when sales level off (though there may be intermittent surges and declines over the years before final decline sets in.) During the maturity stage price competition becomes very strong, similar products are made available by competition, the adoption process is mostly over, and profits fall. [CMC]

maximum operating stock: The largest quantity that should ever be on hand during normal operating conditions, usually at the stockkeeping unit level; consists of merchandise to sell during the buying period, the cushion, and the basic low stock. [WRD]

maximum system of stock control: The system of setting, for each item of staple merchandise carried, an amount large enough to take care of probable demands of customers, and of reordering, periodically, the difference between the actual stock and the maximum set. [WRD]

McGuire-Keogh Fair Trade Enabling Act (1952):   Declared that exemption of resale price maintenance agreements from antitrust laws as provided under the Miller-Tydings Act would be extended to non-signer agreements (whereby all dealers are bound to the contract if only one signs) in states that have non-signer clauses in their fair trade statutes. [DC]

MCI (Multiplicative Competitive Interaction) model: An attraction model for explaining and predicting market share. In an MCI model each brand's attractiveness is modelled as a multiplicative function of some explanatory variables (e.g., brand attributes) (Nakanishi and Cooper 1974). These authors show how such a nonlinear model can be estimated by least squares regression techniques. [DCS/YJW]

means-ends chains: An approach that organizes consumer product knowledge by linking product attributes to more abstract consequences and finally to high level consumer values. [JPP/JCO]

measurement: Rules for assigning numbers to objects to represent quantities of attributes. [GAC]

Meat Inspection Acts (1906): Required inspection and approval of live stock, carcasses and canned or packaged meat products as well as sanitary conditions in slaughterhouses. [DC]

media buying service: (See **limited-service advertising agency.**)

media mix: The strategy used to determine the various media types—for example, network television, consumer magazines, and newspapers—for a particular advertising campaign and the decisions made regarding the amount of funds to allocate to each type. [AMB]

media models: A description and/or explanation of the process, typically in quantitative terms, as to how one or more advertising media activities function in reality. Media models attempt to estimate, from a limited amount of data, the actuality of a media situation; models have been developed to estimate the media delivery of various schedules—in terms of such things as reach, average frequency, exposure distribution—as well as those that seek to arrive at optimal solutions of vehicle selection and scheduling. [AMB]

media plan: The process involved in determining the objectives, strategies, and tactics related to the advertising media effort; the blueprint for establishing and carrying out media strategy and buying. Media plans generally include a statement of goals, the target market definition, the media types to be used and their allocation (media mix), the media vehicles to be used and their allocation, and the scheduling of the media. [AMB]

media representative: An individual or firm that serves as a space or time sales representative, typically on a commission basis, for a particular advertising media vehicle; media representatives ("reps") handle noncompeting vehicles in a particular market (e.g., would sell time for only one television station in a city) and primarily sell national advertisers (often by making sales presentations to the advertiser's agency). [AMB]

MEDIAC: A model providing a decision support system for the advertising media selection and scheduling decision (Little and Lodish 1969). Little and Lodish (1966) describe the perspective adopted by the model: "The population is divided into 'market segments'. Each segment has its own sales potential and media habits. . . A media schedule consists of insertions in 'media vehicles'. . . An insertion brings about exposures in the various market segments. The exposures serve to increase what we shall call 'exposure value' in the market segments. However, people are subject to 'forgetting,' and so the retained exposure level decays with time in the absence of new exposures. The 'anticipated sales' to a market segment increases with exposure level but with diminishing returns." For other advertising decision support systems see ADBUDG and ADMOD. [DCS/YJW]

medium: (See **advertising media.**)

membership group: A small group of individuals in which the individual is psychologically and formally a member. A fraternity, the Rotary Club, prison clique, or bowling team are examples of membership groups. It is those groups in which the individual has direct, face-to-face psychological relations and interdependence with other members. [HHK]

memorandum purchase and dating: Indicates that merchandise shipped to a buyer is returnable within a specified period of time; and payment for goods kept longer or sold need not be made until this time, though legal title usually transfers at the time of shipment. [WRD]

memorandum terms: A special form of indefinite future dating under which the title of the merchandise passes to the buyer, and he assumes all risk of ownership. [WRD]

mercantile trade credit: The credit one businessperson extends to another when selling goods on time for resale or commercial use. [WRD]

mercantilism: A set of economic policies designed to give a country an advantage by developing a favorable balance of trade, encouraging agriculture and manufacturing, creating a merchant marine, and establishing foreign trading monopolies. [DLS]

merchandise budget: A statement prepared by management containing planned commitments for all the components of the merchandise plan (sales, reductions, stocks, margins, and purchases) for a period (usually a six month season). [WRD]

merchandise classification: A subdivision of a selling department; a dissection of a department's inventory, purchase, and/or sales figures for the purpose of closer control. [WRD]

merchandise control: The determination and direction of merchandising activities, both in terms of dollars (dollar control) and in terms of units (unit merchandise control). [WRD]

merchandise cost: The billed cost of merchandise less any applicable trade or quantity discounts, plus inbound transportation costs if paid by the purchaser. [WRD]

merchandise dissection: (See **merchandise classification.**)

merchandise in-transit: Merchandise with its legal title passed to the retailer, but which has not been charged to a merchandise selling department. [WRD]

merchandise mix: Refers to the breadth of merchandise carried by retailing establishments. [WRD]

merchandise plan: A plan, generally for department stores, for a six-month period, by months, in which the chief elements enter into gross profit. The essentials are sales, markdowns, retail stocks at the first of each month, purchases, and markup percentages. Inventory shortages, cash discounts, and alteration costs may also be budgeted. [WRD]

merchandising: A term of many varied and not generally adopted meanings. It can (1) relate to the promotional activities of manufacturers that bring about in-store displays, or (2) identify the product and product line decisions of retailers. [CMC]

merchant middlemen: Middlemen who buy the goods outright and necessarily take title to them. [WRD]

merchant wholesalers: Wholesalers who take title to the products they sell. [JRN]

merchant: A business unit that buys, takes title to, and resells merchandise. [WRD]

merger: The joining together of two or more independent business organizations into a single entity. (See also **acquisition**.) [WL]

method variance: The variation in scores attributable to the method of data collection. [GAC]

metropolitan statistical area (MSA): A freestanding metropolitan area surrounded by nonmetropolitan counties, including a large central city or urbanized area of 50,000 or more people. [DLS]

MFN Principle: The most favored nation principle whereby each country agrees to extend all countries the most favorable terms that it negotiates with any country. [WJK]

micromarketing: The study of marketing activities of an organization. [DLS]

middleman: 1. A business concern that specializes in performing operations or rendering services directly involved in the purchase and/or sale of goods in the process of their flow from producer to consumer. [WRD] 2. An independent business concern that operates as a link between producers and ultimate consumers or industrial users. There are two levels of middlemen: wholesalers and retailers. [JRN]

military buying: The purchase of goods and services by the Defense Department largely through the Defense Logistics Agency, the General Services Administration, and the three military departments; Army, Navy, and Air Force. [GLL/DTW]

Miller-Tydings Resale Price Maintenance Act (1937): Resale price maintenance contracts prescribing minimum prices for name brand commodities were made exempt from the Sherman and FTC Acts in those states having fair trade laws permitting such contracts. [DC]

minimum and maximum system of stock control: A system whereby for each item of staple merchandise carried, a minimum quantity of inventory is established which, when reached, indicates a need to reorder. Maximum stock consists of the minimum and the predetermined reorder quantity. [WRD]

minimum charge: In most transportation tariffs, the minimum charge which is the lowest price at which a carrier will accept a shipment for delivery. A minimum charge reflects the fixed cost component of the transportation carrier's cost of doing business and is often used as an incentive to encourage the shipper to consolidate multiple shipments. [DJB/BJL]

minimum order: The smallest unit of sales permitted by a manufacturer or wholesaler. Sometimes expressed in units, in dollar amount and, sometimes a weight. [WRD]

misredemption: Improper claiming of price savings, premiums, prizes or other sales promotion rewards after the specified time period or by persons not eligible for the incentive. [DES]

mission statement: An expression of a company's history, managerial preferences, environmental concerns, available resources, and distinctive competencies to serve selected publics. Used to guide the company's decision making and strategic planning. [DES]

mission: (See **corporate purpose**.)

missionary salespeople: Salespeople who are employed by manufacturers to call on end-users with the objective of stimulating demand for the manufacturer's offerings even though the purchases will be made from other firms in the channel of distribution. [BAW]

model stock approach to space allocation: A method of determining space allocation for departments in a retail store. Is based upon an analysis of an ideal stock necessary to achieve projected sales volume, of how much stock should be displayed versus how much should be kept in reserve space, of how much physical space will be required to display the merchandise, and of how much physical space will be needed for any service requirements. [WRD]

model stock plan: An outline of the composition of an ideal stock in terms of general characteristics or assortment factors, usually with optimum quantities indicated in an amount that reflects balance in relation to expected sales. [WRD]

model system: The part of a decision support system that includes all the routines that allow the user to manipulate the data so as to conduct the kind of analysis the individual desires. [GAC]

modeling: (See **vicarious learning**.)

modified rebuy: (See **buyclasses**.)

monetary policies: Pursuit of a course of action by a government acting through its central bank to control money and credit. [DLS]

money income: Used by the Bureau of the Census publications to cover money income received exclusive of certain items such as capital gains, social security and the like. It does not include non cash benefits. [WL]

monopolistic competition: Competition among many sellers, each of whom accounts for relatively small market share. [DLS]

monopoly: 1. A market situation where one firm markets all the goods or services and can influence price. [WL] 2. Complete control of an economic good for which there is no substitute. [DLS]

monopsony: A single buyer with monopoly-buying-power.[DLS]

mores: Cultural norms which specify behavior of vital importance to society and which embody its basic moral values. The prohibition against bigamy or child abandonment in some cultures are examples. Mores often are codified into law such that legal as well as social sanctions can be applied to assure conformity. In comparison, folkways are cultural norms that specify behavior not vital to the welfare of the groups and the means of enforcement are not clearly defined (according to Krench, Crutchfield and Ballachey). For example, folkways specify that a student shall wear specifically defined clothes on campus. If he does not he may be considered a boor or a nerd, but his nonconformity is not regarded as having important consequences for the group. The punishment for nonconformity is informal, mild and variable. [HHK]

motivating of salespersons: (See **sales force motivation.**)

motivation: The positive or negative needs, goals, desires, and forces that impel an individual toward or away from certain actions, activities, objects or condition. It is the needs and wants of the individual, the driving force, guided by cognitions, behind the behavior to purchase, approach, or avoid products and ideas and things. [HHK]

Motor Carrier Act (1980): Designed to "reduce unnecessary regulation by the federal government" in the trucking industry; however, it introduced new and complex regulations. [DC]

MRO (maintenance, repair, and operating) items and supplies: **Maintenance** items are the supplies used to preserve the plant and equipment in good working condition such as paint, mops, and brooms. **Repair** items are the materials or replacement items used to keep equipment in good operating condition or to repair inoperable equipment such as light bulbs, new switches, new valves. **Operating** items are the supplies used to operate the equipment such as fuel oil, typing paper. [GLL/DTW]

multi-unit establishment: One of two or more establishments in the same general kind of business operated by the same firm. [WRD]

multiattribute attitude models: Models designed to predict attitudes toward objects (such as brands) based on various evaluations of product attributes or expected consequences. [JPP/JCO]

multibrand strategy: Having more than one brand of product, competing with each other, in a given market. Contrasts with the strategy of family branding where the separate items are given a common line identity and are usually each directed to one segment within the market. Under multibrand strategy there may not even be manufacturer identification, unless required by law.

multibusiness organization: A corporation engaged in more than one class of business. Each business may be organized as a division of the corporation or as a subsidiary company. Comment: Organizationally there may be no difference in the way a division and a subsidiary is viewed by corporate management even though the subsidiary is a separate legal entity controlled by the parent corporation through majority or full ownership. [VPB]

multichotomous question: Fixed-alternative question containing three or more alternatives in which respondents are asked to choose the alternative that most closely corresponds to their position on the subject. [GAC]

multidimensional scaling: Approach to measurement in which people's perceptions of the similarity of objects and their preferences among the objects are measured, and these relationships are plotted in a multidimensional space. [GAC]

multiple basing-point pricing system: In a multiple basing-point pricing system several locations are designated as basing points. The choice of a basing point is the point that yields the lowest delivered cost to the buyer. (See also **basing-point pricing**.) [KM]

multiple channels: Use of a combination of channels to reach different and isolated target markets with different demands for service outputs. [JRN]

multiple packaging: Usually refers to multiple-unit packaging, but also refers to situations where a product has a primary package such as foil, bottle, or polyurethane, a secondary package such as a paper carton, and tertiary package such as a corrugated shipping carton. [CMC]

multiple purchasing: The strategy of dividing annual purchasing requirements of a good or service among more than one supplier. This is done to create a more competitive environment among suppliers and to reduce the buying firm's dependence on a single source of supply. (Also called **multiple sourcing**). [GLL/DTW]

multiple-unit packaging: The practice of putting two or more finished packages of a product into a larger packaged unit (such as a six-pack of soda). The new wrap may vary from a band to a larger completely closed container. Multiple packaging may be temporary, related to a promotional program. [CMC]

multiple-unit pricing: 1. (general) The practice of pricing several items as a single unit. (See also **price bundling**.) [KM] 2. (retail) The combination of several like products as a unit of one, involving at least a slightly different markup that is obtained when the items are sold separately. [WRD]

multiple-zone pricing system: In a multiple-zone pricing system, delivered prices are uniform within two or more zones. (See also **single-zone pricing**.) [KM]

national accounts: Important customers, usually industrial firms and institutions, of the manufacturing company who have business operations that span several sales territories with selling efforts coordinated in a central office. [BAW]

National Advertising Division (NAD):   (See **National Advertising Review Board (NARB)**.)

National Advertising Review Board (NARB):   An organization that aims to provide for the self-regulation of national advertising in contrast to federal governmental regulation; works in conjunction with another self-regulatory body—the National Advertising Division (NAD) of the Council of Better Business Bureaus. Complaints regarding advertising, for example in terms of truthfulness or accuracy of information, first are reviewed by NAD; advertising that is not resolved within the NAD is sent to the NARB for final adjudication. [AMB]

national advertising: Advertising that is sponsored by an organization that operates on a national or regional basis; could include advertisements placed in a particular locale, such as a city, but the advertiser likely would be doing this as part of a national or regional campaign; sometimes called "general" advertising. [AMB]

national brand: A brand that is marketed throughout a national market. Contrasts with regional brand and local brand. Usually is advertised and usually is owned by a manufacturer, though neither is necessary for the definition since K mart's brands, for example, are obviously national, even international. [CMC]

National Environmental Policy Act (1969):   The act in which Congress applied at the national level an across-the-board policy of environmental protection for the federal government and all its agencies. Environmental quality under the NEPA has become a major factor in agency decision making. [DC]

national income (NI):   1. Net national product less indirect business taxes and business transfer payments plus government subsidies. [DLS]2. The aggregate of labor and property earning from the current production of goods and services. It comprises employee compensation, proprietors' income, rental income, profits and net interest. [WL]

national rate: The advertising rate offered by media to a national advertiser; often higher, per unit of space or time, than that available to a local advertiser. [AMB]

National Traffic and Motor Vehicle Safety Act (1966):   An act designed to improve the safety of automobiles, roads and tires, delegating the responsibility for implementing standards to the Department of Transportation. [DC]

natural selection theory: A theory of retail institutional change, which states that retailing institutions that can most effectively adapt to environmental changes are the ones most likely to prosper or survive. [WRD]

NBD model (Negative Binomial Distribution Model):   A probability mixture model representing the frequency and timing of product purchases, primarily applied to frequently purchased consumer goods. It assumes that sequential purchases made by an individual occur randomly in time, and also assumes that purchase rates have a gamma distribution across individuals (Ehrenberg 1972; Greene 1982). With these two assumptions the distribution for the number of purchases made by a randomly chosen set of customers in a fixed time period has the negative binomial distribution. The model can be used to predict future purchase patterns for customers with a given purchase history (Morrison and Schmittlein 1981). [DCS/YJW]

near-pack premium: A gift or other item generally too large to be included with or in the product package which is offered as an inducement to purchase. Commonly, the premium is placed near the product's in-store location. [DES]

need satisfaction selling: A selling approach in which the salesperson first identifies the prospective customer's needs, and then tries to offer a solution that satisfies those needs. [BAW]

needs and wants: (See **motivation.**) [HHK]

negative reference group: (See **reference group.**) [HHK]

negative authorization: In credit verification systems, if only poor credit risks are noted in the credit check, it is called negative authorization. Any credit not negatively reported is assumed to be verified. [WRD]

negative disconfirmation: (See **disconfirmation.**)

negotiation: The process of trying to find mutually agreeable terms in an exchange situation. Negotiation leads either to mutually acceptable terms (agreement) or a decision not to transact (disagreement). [GLL/DTW]

neighborhood shopping center: The smallest type of shopping center—30,000 to 100,000 square feet. It provides for the sale of convenience goods (food, drugs, and sundries) and personal services which meet the daily needs of an immediate neighborhood trade area. A supermarket is the principal tenant. [DLH]

nested logit model: A probabilistic model for representing the discrete choice behavior of individuals. On any choice occasion the individual is assumed to behave as though choice alternatives were considered in a hierarchical manner. At each stage of the hierarchy the choice to eliminate a set of items from consideration is made according to the logit model (McFadden 1986). The nested logit model arises as a random utility model where the random component of utility has the generalized extreme value distribution. Guadagni (1983) used this model to represent jointly brand choice and purchase incidence decisions, and Dubin (1986) employed the model to represent consumers' choice of home water heating fuel (gas, oil or electricity) given the type of space heating system in the home. [DCS/YJW]

net national product (NNP):   Gross national product less depreciation, i.e., capital consumption allowance. [DLS]

net operating income (profit):   Net sales less net cost of goods sold less operating expenses. [WRD]

net present value technique: The method of choice in financial economics for analyzing an investment project. Comment: Net present value (NPV) is calculated as follows:

$$NPV = \sum_{i=0}^{n} \frac{A_i}{(1+k)^i}$$

where A_i equals the net after-tax cash flows in year i, n is the expected life of the project in years, and k is the risk-adjusted, after-tax required rate of return on the investment. [PFA]

net terms: Terms calling for the billed amount of the invoice. No cash discount is allowed. [WRD]

net unduplicated audience: (See **reach.**)

never-out lists: "Key items" or "best sellers" listed separately from a model stock plan or basic stock list, or that are especially identified on the basic stock list by colored stars or other suitable means, sometimes referred to as a list of key items, checking-list items, or best seller list. [WRD]

new product development: The overall process of strategy, organization, concept generation, concept and marketing plan evaluation, and commercialization of a new product. Occasionally is restricted in meaning to that part of the process done by technical (R&D) departments. New product development concerns activity within an organization, in contrast to the acquisition of finished new products from outside. [CMC]

new product failure: A new product that does not meet the objectives of its developers. Depending on what those objectives are, a profitable new product can be a failure, and an unprofitable new product can be a success. [CMC]

new product forecasting models: Models for forecasting the performance (e.g., trial, repeat, sales, share) of new products and services include three major types of models: a) those based on management subjective estimates; b) those based on analogy to a similar product which had been previously introduced to the market; and c) those based on consumer studies. There are four types of consumer based models: i) concept test based forecasting models, including models such as POSSE; ii) pre-test market based models, especially those categorized as simulated test market models such as LITMUS; iii) test market based forecasting models such as NEWS and TRACKER; and iv) early sales based forecasting models, which include the various diffusion models. For a review of these models, see Wind, Mahajan,and Cardozo (1981). [DCS/YJW]

new product manager: Responsible for identifying new product needs, developing new product concepts, and testing the concepts with panels of consumers before turning to R&D for technical development. If a satisfactory product evolves from R&D, the new product manager arranges for consumer product and package testing; and, if these are successful, prepares market introduction plans. When ready for commercialization the new product usually is assigned to a product manager. The new product manager reports to the marketing manager or (if there are several) to a group new products manager. This position is most likely to be found in consumer packaged goods companies producing low technology products. [VPB]

new product organization, forms of: New product organization provides for the planning scheduling, coordination, and control of the new product process from idea to commerciali zation (or abandonment along the way), as well as getting participation from the interna functional departments and external agencies that must do the work. Comment: Interna participation is required of top management (corporate and/or divisional), major functiona departments such as marketing, R&D, production, engineering, finance, and physical distri bution (logistics). External participation may involve, for example, advertising agencies industrial design firms, independent laboratories, market research agencies, new product consultants, and new product development companies. [VPB]

new products committee: Made up of high level executives, it sets new product policies establishes priorities, reviews progress, eliminates logjams, decides whether to abandon o commercialize a new product, and provides impetus to the overall new product program Members typically include the chief executive, director of the new products department, and the managers of major functional departments. Comment: Usually the new products commit tee will be in addition to one or more other forms of new product organization described in this section. While the committee does not actually manage the new product program, i serves to spotlight the performance of the committee members whose departments are responsible for carrying out parts of new product development projects. [VPB]

new products department: Responsible for planning and coordinating the new product program for the company. The director has the functional authority to obtain the participa tion of other company departments and the line authority to hire outside agencies as needed. The director may have a staff of market research and technical people for conducting preliminary investigations before deciding to involve functional departments in full scale development. The director reports to the corporate chief executive. This provides an avenue for the chief executive to be directly involved in the new product program and provides the director with top management backing when needed to get action from functional managers. [VPB]

new-task purchase: (See **buyclasses.**)

NEWPROD: A model for predicting market share of a new product using test market data. The approach views potential customers as progressing through the stages of awareness, trial and repeat purchase. It considers the effect of advertising and promotion on awareness and trial, and the effect of the level of distribution on trial and repeat purchase (Assmus 1975). For other models predicting sales of new products see ASSESSOR, LITMUS, NEWS, SPRINTER MOD III and TRACKER. [DCS/YJW]

NEWS: A model used to predict the level of awareness, trial, repeat purchase, and market share over time for a new frequently purchased consumer product. It considers explicitly the effect of advertising and promotion on brand awareness and product trial, and also incorpo rates the effect of the level of distribution on trial and repeat purchase. For any particular new product, the model's parameters can be calibrated either using pretest market data (i.e., a telephone survey, advertising copy test, concept test, and in-home product-use test) in the NEWS/Planner version, or using test market data in the NEWS/Market version (Pringle, Wilson and Brody 1982). (For other models predicting sales of new products see **ASSESSOR, LITMUS, SPRINTER MOD III** and **TRACKER.**) [DCS/YJW]

news clips: A film presentation where editorial content is controlled by the sponsor. Provided to broadcast media for their use as deemed appropriate. [DES]

news release: Information of timely value distributed by an organization to promote its views or product/services. Used to influence the media to communicate favorably about the material discussed. [DES]

newsletters: Brief digests of important or noteworthy information. Maybe developed by individuals for sale or distributed free by associations, professional societies and companies as a method of reaching various publics quickly. [DES]

niche strategies: A game plan employed by a firm that specializes in serving particular market segments in order to avoid clashing with the major competitors in the market. "Nichers" pursue market segments that are of sufficient size to be profitable while at the same time are of less interest to the major competitors. [GSD]

nominal credit terms: Terms applied to the date on which full payment of the account is due; for vendors that bill customers on a monthly basis, full payment is usually due by the tenth day after billing. [WRD]

nominal scale: Measurement in which numbers are assigned to objects or classes of objects solely for the purpose of identification. [GAC]

non-compensatory rules: In evaluating alternatives, non- compensatory rules suggest that positive and negative consequences of alternatives do not compensate for each other. Among the types of non-compensatory rules include conjunctive, disjunctive, and lexicographic. The **conjunctive rule** suggests that consumers establish a minimum acceptable level for each choice criterion and accept an alternative only if it equals or exceeds the minimum cutoff level for every criterion. The **disjunctive rule** suggests that consumers establish acceptable standards for each criterion and accept an alternative if it exceeds the standard on at least one criterion. The **lexicographic rule** suggests that consumers rank choice criteria from most to least important and choose the best alternative on the most important criterion. [JPP/JCO]

non-price competition: Competition on the basis of variables other than price, such as quality, brand, selection or services. It implies that a company can influence demand by its marketing activities. [WL]

non-signer clause: A clause in state fair trade laws permitting the enforcement of resale price maintenance contracts against all dealers in a state when such a contract had been signed by any one of them. [DC]

non-tariff trade barriers: (See NTBs.)

nonbusiness marketing: (See **nonprofit marketing**.) [ARA]

noncoverage error: Nonsampling error that arises because of a failure to include some units, or entire sections, of the defined survey population in the actual sampling frame. [GAC]

noncumulative quantity discount: A discount granted for volume purchased (measured either in units or dollars) at a single point in time. [KM]

nondurable goods: Goods that are (1) made from materials other than metals, hard plastic and wood, (2) are rather quickly consumed or worn out, or (3) become dated, unfashionable or in some other way no longer popular. An awkward term that includes a highly varied set of goods, and is useful primarily as a contrast with durable goods. (See also durable goods.) [CMC]

nonmonetary transaction: A marketing exchange where the costs paid by the target audience do not include a transfer of economic assets. [ARA]

nonobservation error: Nonsampling error that arises because of nonresponse from some elements designated for inclusion in the sample. [GAC]

nonprice competition: Vying for sales through better products, promotion, service, and convenience. [DLS]

nonprobability sample: Sample that relies on personal judgment somewhere in the element selection process and therefore prohibits estimating the probability that any population element will be included in the sample. [GAC]

nonprofit marketer: An individual or organization conducting nonprofit marketing. [ARA

nonprofit marketing: Marketing of a product or service where the offer itself is not intended to make a monetary profit for the marketer. Comment: Nonprofit marketing may be carried out by any organization or individual and may or may not be designed to have a positive social impact. A decision by a for-profit organization to only break even on a new product venture would come under this definition. A nonprofit marketer may undertake specific ventures that are for-profit as when a museum markets reproductions or offers food and beverages at a profit. A nonprofit marketer that is an organization may be incorporated privately or may be a governmental (public) agency. [ARA]

nonresponse error: Nonsampling error that represents a failure to obtain information from some elements of the population that were selected and designated for the sample. [GAC]

nonsampling errors: Errors that arise in research that are not due to sampling; nonsampling errors can occur because of errors in conception, logic, misinterpretation of replies, statistics arithmetic and errors in tabulating or coding, or in reporting the results. [GAC]

nonselling area: Floor space, other than selling area, used in the conduct of business in a store building or in remote service or warehouse buildings, including entrances, show windows, vertical transportation facilities, offices, boiler and engine rooms, alteration and work rooms, repair shops, receiving and marking rooms, and stockrooms. [WRD]

nonselling department: Any department of a store engaged in work other than the direct selling of merchandise—e.g., receiving department. [WRD]

nonstore retailing: A form of retailing in which consumer contact occurs outside the confines of the retail store, such as vending machines and electronic shopping, at home personal selling, and catalog buying. [WRD]

norms: The rules of behavior that are part of the ideology of the group. Norms tend to reflect the values of the group and specify those actions that are proper and those that are inappropriate, as well as the rewards for adherence and the punishment for nonconformity. (See also **mores.**) [HHK]

not-at-home: Source of nonsampling error that arises when replies are not secured from some designated sampling units because the respondents are not at home when the interviewer calls. [GAC]

NTBs (Non Tariff Barriers): (l) Ongoing administrative, discriminatory and ad hoc "safeguard" actions and practices to protect home industries. Typical NTBs include exclusion orders, standards (requiring, for example, that products admitted to the country meet exact specifications that either cannot be met in the case of some natural products or that are very expensive to meet in case of manufactured products), exclusionary distribution, and administrative delays (when the French decided that the Japanese imports of VCRs were excessive, they simply "applied the rules" and gave each VCR a complete inspection. The number of VCRs entering the country dropped from thousands to six per day. (2) Any measure, public or private, that causes internationally traded goods and services to be allocated in such a way as to reduce potential real world income. [WJK]

objective-and-task budgeting: Advertising appropriation method in which advertising expenditures are determined directly from the established objectives; also called "objective" method. [AMB]

objectives: Desired or needed results to be achieved by a specific time. Objectives are broader than goals, and one objective can be broken down into a number of specific goals. Like goals, objectives serve to provide guidance, motivation, evaluation and control. (See also goals.) [GSD]

observation: Method of data collection in which the situation of interest is watched and the relevant facts, actions, or behaviors recorded. [GAC]

observation error: Nonsampling error that arises because inaccurate information is secured from the sample elements or because errors are introduced in the processing of the data or in reporting the findings. [GAC]

obsolescence: The act or process of a product's becoming out-of-date, discarded, no longer in use. The rejection is for some reason other than being worn out or inoperable. May apply to an individual item or to all of the items in a given class or group. The active verb form, less widely acceptable, is to obsolete or to make obsolete. [CMC]

odd lot: Dealing with broken lots or unbalanced assortments reduced in price for quick turnover. [WRD]

odd-even pricing: Refers to a form of psychological pricing that suggests buyers are more sensitive to certain ending digits. Odd price refers to a price ending in an odd number (e.g., 1,3,5,7,9), or to a price just under a round number (e.g., $0.89, $3.99, $44.98). Even price refers to a price ending in a whole number or in tenths (e.g., $.50 $5.00, $8.10, $75.00). [KM]

off-retail percentage: The markdown as a percentage of the original price. For example, an item originally retails for $10 and is marked down to $5; off-retail percentage is 50%. [WRD]

office error: Nonsampling error that arises in the processing of the data because of errors in editing, coding, tabulation, or in some other part of the analysis. [GAC]

oligopolistic situation: A market condition where only a few large sellers vie and collectively account for a relatively large market share. [DLS]

oligopoly: A market situation where there are so few marketers that each is conscious of price decisions by the others. [DLS]

oligopsony: A market situation where there are so few buyers that each is conscious of the actions of the others. [DLS]

on order: When the retailer has ordered merchandise and it has not been received, it is considered to be "on order" and thus a commitment against a planned purchase figure. Thus, the Open-to-Buy figure is affected by the amount of the on-order dollars. [WRD]

on-pack premium: A gift attached to the product or product package in some way such as banding, taping, or other adhesive. Used to influence product purchase. [DES]

on-percentage: The result of multiplying together the complements of a given series of discount percentages. To find the net merchandise price, the list price is multiplied by the on-percentage. [WRD]

one hundred percent location: The retail site in a major business district that has the greatest exposure to a retail store's target market customers. [WRD]

one price policy: At a given time, all customers pay the same price for any given item of merchandise. [WRD]

open account: The sale of goods on credit; the seller giving the buyer no written evidence of indebtedness, instead he debits his account; Open Credit. [WRD]

open dating: The practice of putting onto a product information that reveals the date beyond which it should no longer be sold or used. Applies primarily to perishable products, those which lose some important attribute over time while awaiting sale in the channel between maker and user. Open dating is common to certain industries (for example dairy products and pharmaceuticals), and is sometimes mandated by law. [CMC]

open order: An order sent by a store to a market representative to be placed with whatever vendor the latter finds can best fill it. In department store buying, authority granted to a resident buyer to purchase merchandise required by the store. [WRD]

open rate: The highest advertising media rate before discounts are earned; refers to a rate structure, with the open rate being the highest, whereby advertisers receive discounts for advertising volume and/or frequency; contrasts with flat rates, under which no discounts are available. [AMB]

open stock: Items kept on hand in retail stores and sold either in complete sets or in separate pieces—e.g., china, glassware. [WRD]

open-code dating: A date marked on food products to indicate the last day that the food can be sold in the store. It some times indicates use date. (See also **open-date labeling**.) [WRD]

open-date labeling: A date marked on food products to indicate the last day that the food can be sold in the store. (See also **open code dating**.) [WRD]

open-ended question: Question characterized by the condition that respondents are free to reply in their own words rather than being limited to choosing from among a set of alternatives. [GAC]

open-to-buy: The residual balance of current purchase allotments; total planned purchases for a period, less receipts and merchandise on order. [WRD]

open-to-buy report: Statement of existing or expected relations between dollar inventory and sales, used to calculate open-to-buy amounts. [WRD]

operant conditioning: The process of altering the probability of a behavior being emitted by changing the consequences of the behavior. [JPP/JCO]

operating supplies: (See **MRO (maintenance, repair and operating) items and supplies**.)

operational definition: Definition of a construct that describes the operations to be carried out in order for the construct to be measured empirically. [GAC]

opinion: An opinion is a belief or emotionally neutral cognition the individual holds about some aspect or object in the environment. Those things he/she "knows" to be true have been defined as knowledge and those things he/she "thinks" are true or he/she is "pretty sure are true" are defined as opinions. [HHK]

opinion leaders: Not all individuals in a group or all consumers in a society wield equal personal influence on the attitudes, opinions and behavior of others. Those who are most influential are termed the opinion leaders; it is those to whom others turn for advice and information. [HHK]

opportunity analysis: (See **situation analysis.**)

opportunity cost: The cost attributable to doing a thing caused by foregone opportunities that are sacrificed in order to do this one thing. [DLS]

option: A contract which allows the holder to buy or sell a specific stock at a fixed price at or before a stated maturity date. [PFA]

options pricing models: A class of models designed to calculate the value of an option. Comment: The empirical adequacy of these models is an unresolved issue in financial economics. [PFA]

order entry: The order entry phase is the beginning phase of the order cycle process. Order entry refers to the process of actually entering an order into the seller's order processing system. This may be done by a salesperson writing an order, a customer ordering by phone, a telemarketing solicitation, or by the buyer's computer communicating directly with the seller's computer (EDI). [DJB/BJL]

order register: A form on which orders placed with vendors are recorded; includes the date of each order, the name of the vendor, the total amount of each order, the month in which shipment is to be made, the amount to be delivered each month, and a serial number. [WRD]

order-processing: The system of the firm which generally refers to the way orders are recorded by the firm and how this information is used to provide customer service and manage various functional elements of the business. It includes the management of the order entry process as well as the information flows which surround and support the order fulfillment objectives of the firm. [DJB/BJL]

order-shipping-billing cycle: Describes the paperwork or information cycle of the order processing system. [DJB/BJL]

ordinal scale: Measurement in which numbers are assigned to data on the basis of some order (for example, more than, greater than) of the objects. [GAC]

ordinary dating: Illustrated by such terms as "1/10, net 30" or 2/10, net 60". The two specified time elements are the cash discount and the net credit period. The cash discount may be deducted if the bill is paid within the discount period (10 days in both examples); otherwise, the full amount is due at the end of the credit period (30 and 60 days in the examples given). Both the cash discount and the net credit periods are usually counted from the date of the invoice, which, in most cases, is also the date of shipment. [WRD]

organization: When used as a noun, implies the framework or structure within which people are assigned to positions and their work coordinated in order to carry out plans and achieve goals. [VPB]

organization chart: A visual representation of an organizational structure. It identifies the organizational unit and portrays each position in relation to others. Positions are usually represented by squares or rectangles (although circles or ovals are sometimes used) which contain the position title; they may show the name of the incumbent as well. Each position is connected by a solid line running to the immediate supervisor and topossitions supervised, if any. Broken or dotted lines may be used to show other than line relationships (e.g. advisory or functional). [VPB]

Organization of Economic Cooperation and Development (OECD): An organization which came into being on September 30, 1961, succeeding the OEEC with the objectives to promote policies designed to achieve the highest sustainable economic growth and employment and a rising standard of living in member countries while maintaining financial stability. [WJK]

Organization of Petroleum Exporting Countries (OPEC): An association of countries formed in 1960 for the purpose of promoting the interests of the oil exporting countries. Member countries include Algeria, Bahrain, Brunei, Ecuador, Gabon, Indonesia, Iran, Iraq, Kuwait, Libya, Nigeria, Oman, Quatar, Saudi Arabia, Trinidad and Tobago, United Arab Emirates, and Venezuela. [WJK]

organization structure: The formal and informal framework within which people work to achieve organization objectives. It includes the establishment of positions along with descriptions of their duties, responsibilities, authority, reporting relationships, and assignment to groups. (See also **position description**.) Organizational charts are used to show where positions fit within the structure. (See also **organizational chart**.) [VPB]

organizational (industrial) buying behavior: The buying decision-making process of an organization rather than by an individual consumer. Organizational buying behavior differs from consumer buying behavior in that (a) normally, multiple individuals are involved, (b) buying decision rules or standards may be applicable, and (c) purchases occur as a result of derived demand. [GLL/DTW]

organizational behavior: Management theory and practice relating to how and why people behave as they do within organizational structures and how managers can bring about improvements in individual and group performance. [VPB]

organizational climate: The general internal organizational environment that is determined by the organization's structure, leadership, philosophy, technology, people and the like. [WL]

organizational markets: Consist of **industrial markets**, **reseller markets**, and **government markets**. Industrial buyers buy goods and services to aid them in producing other goods and services (derived demand). Resellers buy goods and services to resell them at a profit. Government agencies buy goods and services to carry out mandated governmental functions. [GLL/DTW]

organized market: A group of traders operating under recognized rules in buying and selling a single commodity or related commodities; a commodity exchange. [WRD]

original equipment manufacturer (OEM):   An organization that purchases industrial goods in order to incorporate them into other products that are sold in the industrial (business) or ultimate consumer markets. For example, IBM acting as an OEM buys microprocessors for its personal computers from Intel. [GLL/DTW]

original retail: The first price at which merchandise is offered for sale and accounted for as the retail value of receipts. [WRD]

O.T.B.:   (See **open-to-buy.**)

other-directedness: A mode of conformity to the culture in which one draws values and beliefs from the peer group rather than from the family group. Tradition, inner, and other direction are part of the conceptualization of David Riesman in his monograph, "The Lonely Crowd." (See also **inner-directed**.) [HHK]

out sizes: The sizes that are either very large or very small and, if offered at all, are offered in very limited depth because of the thin market demand for them. Some stores specialize in fringe or out sizes; e.g., tall girls shops, petite size shops. (See also **fringe sizes**.) [WRD]

out-of-stock costs: Costs which can be directly or indirectly attributed to not having a product available when the buyer wants to purchase the product. May include cost of lost future sales. [DJB/BJL]

outlet store: (1) A store specializing in job lots and clearance merchandise. (2) A store controlled by a vendor to dispose of surplus stocks or for other reasons to be in the retail business. [WRD]

output evaluation measures: Objective measures of sales force performance including number of orders, average size of orders, number of cancelled orders, and number of active, new, lost, overdue and prospective accounts. [OCW]

outside salespeople: (See **field salespeople.**) [BAW]

over, short, & damage (OSD):   A traditional term used in transportation and warehousing to describe an inventory situation. After a physical inventory, it is possible to be "over" (have too much in inventory), be "short" (have a shortage of inventory), or have damaged inventory which is not usable. The same term may be applied to a shipment received by the buyer or an intermediary. May be an accounting adjustment in some systems. [DJB/BJL]

overage: The amount by which a physical inventory exceeds the book inventory figure, as opposed to shortage; also may refer to cash excess. [WRD]

overbought: (1) A condition where a buyer has become committed to purchases in excess of planned purchase allotment for a merchandising period. (2) The purchase of merchandise in excess of demand. [WRD]

overcoming objections: The process of successfully handling reasons given by customers for not buying the salesperson's offering. [BAW]

overcoverage error: Nonsampling error that arises because of the duplication of elements in the list of sampling units. [GAC]

package: The container used to protect, promote, transport, and/or identify a product. May vary from a plastic band wrap to a steel or wooden box or drum. May be primary (contains the product), secondary (contains one or more primary packages) or tertiary (contains one or more secondary packages). [CMC]

packaged goods: Goods that are usually sold in smaller packages, carry low unit prices, are distributed through food and drug stores, are heavily promoted (usually in mass media), and are bought and consumed frequently. [CMC]

packaging: The process by which packages are created. Occasionally is used as synonymous with package. [CMC]

pallet: A platform usually made out of wood, but also made out of other materials, upon which product is stacked to provide a unit load in the transportation and distribution system. [DJB/BJL]

panel (omnibus):   Fixed sample of respondents who are measured repeatedly over time but on variables that change from measurement to measurement. [GAC]

panel (true):   Fixed sample of respondents who are measured repeatedly over time with respect to the same variables. [GAC]

PAR ROI: A regression model based on the PIMS (Profit Impact of Marketing Strategy) data, which relates ROI (return on investment) to a set of independent variables. PAR ROI specifies the ROI and associated cash flow that could be expected for a business with a given market position, competitive conditions, and other specified conditions. In addition to allowing a comparison of PAR (based on the businesses in the PIMS sample used for analysis) and actual ROI, the model allows the identification of the impact on ROI that various factors (such as attractiveness of the business environment, strength of competitive position, effectiveness of use of investment, etc.) will have (Day 1986, pp. 115-166). [DCS/YJW]

parasite store: Those that live on existing traffic flow which originates from circumstances other than their own promotional effort, store personality, merchandising effort, or customer service. [WRD]

Parfitt-Collins model: A model for predicting the market share of a new product, based on early panel data sales results. The model views market share as the product of three quantities: the brand's penetration level (i.e., proportion of buyers of this product class who try this brand), the brand's repeat purchase rate (i.e., the proportion of repurchases going to this brand by consumers who once purchased this brand), and the buying-rate index of repeat purchasers of this brand (where the average rate across consumers $= 1.0$. This index shows the extent to which the consumer is a relatively heavy buyer (rate > 1.0) or light buyer (rate < 1.0) of the product category) (Parfitt and Collins 1968). Panel data are used to make a projection over time for each of these quantities, from which the ultimate market share is calculated. [DCS/YJW]

partially integrated division: Contains production and marketing functions except for sales. Personal selling is provided by a centralized sales force selling the products of two or more divisions. A centralized sales force can be more cost effective when the divisions produce products which are sold to similar markets through the same channels of distribution. [VPB]

parts: Manufactured products such as bicycle sprockets and lenses that are bought as components of other goods being produced. Parts are often sold simultaneously in industrial (original equipment) channels and in consumer channels for replacement purposes. [CMC]

parts, component: Products (or sub-assemblies) bought by industrial users to be installed in the finished product completely with no further change in form. For example, tires, batteries, carburetors, and the like are component parts for automobiles. [GLL/DTW]

party selling: A direct selling approach that involves demonstrating and selling products to a group of consumers attending a party at a neighbor's or friend's house. [BAW]

party-plan selling: A practice in which salespersons arrange to have a party in a home, at which merchandise is demonstrated to a group of the host's or hostess' friends. [WRD]

pass-along deal: A seller's offer where an item of value such as a price reduction, gift, premium, coupon, etc. is offered to the middle-man channel member with the intent that the incentive be passed along to others in the channel. [DES]

pass-along readers: Readers of a print advertising media vehicle who acquire a copy other than by purchase or subscription; also called "secondary" readers; contrasted to primary readers. [AMB]

patent: The legal right of exclusive use and license granted by a government to the person who invents something. An invention is patentable if it is a useful, novel, and nonobvious process, machine, manufacture or composition of matter. [CMC] 2. patents (and patent laws) provide the owner the exclusive right to produce and sell his invention for a period of seventeen years. Patents are considered as incentives to inventors, and the law recognizes the inherent inconsistency between antitrust laws which are designed to foster competition and patent laws which restrict competition. [DC]

patronage discount: The offering of a price reduction based on previous customer relationship or preferred customer standing. Such a discount is usually offered because of an established relationship between the seller and buyer. [KM]

patronage dividends: Any surpluses accrued from the spread between prevailing market prices and cost of merchandise and store operation that are paid to members (of a cooperative) in proportion to their volume of purchases. [WRD]

patronage motives: Those motives that drive an individual toward selection of a particular outlet, retailer, or supplier of services. [HHK]

pay, of salespeople: (See **sales force compensation.**)

payback: The time, usually in years, from the point of full scale market introduction of a new product until it has recovered its costs of development and marketing. The market-testing stage is usually considered to be a part of the evaluation process (and not in the payback period), but if a rollout is used, practice varies on when the payback period should begin. [CMC]

payout budgeting: A method of advertising appropriation in which advertising dollars are treated as an investment in advance of sales and profits; typically used in new brand introductions. [AMB]

penetration pricing: The strategy of setting a product's price relatively low in order to generate a high sales volume. This strategy is commonly associated with pricing new products that do not have identifiable price-market segments. [KM]

per capita income: A nation's total income divided by the number of persons in its population. Gross national product is a popular, but technically incorrect, surrogate for total income. [DLS]

per se illegality: An act that is illegal by, of, for, or in itself. [DLS]

per se rules: 1. Rules that define clear cut business violations. For example, restraint upon price competition when sought to be affected by combination or conspiracy is per se unlawful. [DC] 2. A rule under which the prosecution needs to show only that the alleged act was performed. (See also **rule of reason**.) [DLS]

perceived risk: 1. The expected negative consequences of performing an action such as purchasing a product. [JPP/JCO] 2. Most if not all decisions contain some risk, be it monetary, physical, psychological, social or whatever. The degree of risk that is perceived to exist by the individual making a purchase or behavioral decision has been termed perceived risk in the consumer behavior literature. [HHK]

perceived role accuracy: The degree to which the salesperson's perception of role set member demands- particularly company superiors—is accurate. [OCW]

perceived role ambiguity: The degree to which a salesman feels he does not have the information necessary to perform the job adequately. The salesman may be uncertain about what some role set members expect of him in certain situations, how he should go about satisfying those expectations, or how his performance will be evaluated and rewarded. [OCW]

perceived role conflict: The degree to which a salesperson believes that the role demands of two or more members of his or her role set are incompatible. [OCW]

perceived-value pricing: A method of pricing where the seller attempts to set price at the level that the intended buyers value the product. Also called value-oriented or value-in-use pricing. (See also **demand oriented pricing**.) [KM]

percent-of-sales budgeting: Method of advertising appropriation whereby expenditures are a fixed percentage of past, current, or estimated future sales; can be based in terms of dollars or units sold. [AMB]

perception: Based on prior attitudes, beliefs, needs, stimulus factors, and situational determinants, individuals perceive objects, events or people in the world about them. Perception is the cognitive impression that is formed of "reality" which in turn influences the individual's actions and behavior toward that object. [HHK]

perfect competition: A market model that assumes pure competition plus perfect knowledge, perfect freedom of movement, and perfect substitutability of the factors of production. (See also **pure competition.**) [DLS]

periodic inventory system: An inventory system where orders are placed at scheduled intervals (e.g., first day of month) but the amount of product ordered will be variable.[DJB/BJL]

peripheral route to persuasion: One of two types of cognitive processes by which persuasion occurs. In the peripheral route, the consumer does not focus on the product message in an ad but on other stimuli such as attractive or well-known celebrities or popular music. The presence of these other stimuli may change the consumer's beliefs and attitude about the product. (See also **central route to persuasion.**) [JPP/JCO]

permanent income hypothesis: A hypothesis that postulates that consumption patterns are relatively stable over time, or that consumer expenditures are based on average income expectations over time. [WL]

perpetual inventory system: A stock control system that is designed to keep continuous track of all additions and deletions to inventory. [DJB/BJL]

person marketing: Marketing designed to influence target audiences to behave in some positive manner with respect to the positions, products or services associated with a specific person. Comment: Attempts by an individual or organization to educate target audiences or change their attitudes about a person are not marketing. (See also **public relations.**) [ARA]

personal consumption expenditures: The aggregate amount spent each year by consumers to buy goods and services in the marketplace. [DLS]

personal disposable income: Current money income less all taxes and money spent for the purchase of necessities. [DLS]

personal income: 1. National income adjusted for corporate profits and government transfer payments. 2. Current income received by persons from all sources less contributions for Social Security taxes. [DLS]

personal influence: The influence of one individual upon another in face-to-face interactions. It is the informal social influence transmitted among peers. (See also **opinion leader** and **two step flow of communication.**) [HHK]

personal interview: Direct, face-to-face conversation between a representative of the research organization (the interviewer) and a respondent or interviewee. [GAC]

personal relationships (in organizational buying): Personal Relationships in business marketing have a strong influence on organizational buying behavior. Positive or negative relationships between members of the buying and selling organizations often represent the deciding factor in supplier's choice. [GLL/DTW]

personal savings: That part of disposable income that is not used for current consumption purposes. [WL]

personal selling: Selling that involves a face-to-face interaction with the customer. [BAW]

personality: Personality can be defined as man's consistency in coping with his environment. Personality is the consistent pattern of responses to the stimuli from both internal and external sources. It is this consistency of response that allows us to type people as aggressive or submissive, as obnoxious or charismatic. The particular theory or philosophy of motivation and personality held by scholars in this field colors their views, research and even definitions of the term. Nevertheless, "a consistent pattern of responses in coping with perceived reality" is a good working definition. [HHK]

persuasion: Changes in consumers' beliefs and attitudes caused by promotion communications. [JPP/JCO]

phantom freight: Occurs in basing-point pricing when the seller quotes a delivered price that includes a freight charge greater than the actual transportation costs. [KM]

physical distribution: Describes a concept or approach to managing the finished goods inventory of the firm. Typically it includes transportation, warehousing, inventory, and order processing functions of the firm. [DJB/BJL]

physical distribution agencies: Third party agencies which support the physical distribution objectives of the firm. These may include transportation companies, public warehousing companies, and companies that manage information flows between buyer and seller as third-party intermediaries. [DJB/BJL]

physical distribution (or logistics) manager: Plans the flow of materials in a manufacturing organization (beginning with raw materials and ending with delivery of finished products to channel intermediaries or end customers) and coordinates the work of departments involved in the process, such as procurement, transportation, manufacturing, finance, legal, and marketing. In the more limited marketing sense, physical distribution management is concerned with the efficient movement of finished product from the end of the production line to customers. This is usually a staff position, reporting to corporate or division management, with the functional authority needed to coordinate the execution of distribution plans by functional departments so as to provide good customer service at acceptable cost. [VPB]

physical inventory: An inventory determined by actual count and evidenced by a listing of quantity, weight, or measure; usually compiled in dollars as well as units. [WRD]

physiological motives: Those needs that must be satisfied if the organism is to survive. These are the basic biological drives such as the need for food, air, relief of pain, bowel and bladder, and other basic physiological processes. The sex drive, although driven by hormones and other biological processes, is heavily overladen with social needs and drives and hence can be classified either a physiological or a social drive. [HHK]

physiological needs: (See **physiological motives.**) [HHK]

physiological reaction technique: Method of assessing attitudes in which the researcher monitors the subject's response, by electrical or mechanical means, to the controlled introduction of some stimuli. [GAC]

piggyback: The transportation of highway trailers or detachable trailer bodies on special rail cars designed for this service. This type of service usually involves a combination rail-highway movement of goods. [DJB/BJL]

pilferage: The stealing of a store's merchandise. (See also **shoplifting**.) [WRD]

PIMS (Profit Impact on Market Strategies) Program: Operated by The Strategic Planning Institute (SPI), the PIMS program provides individual companies with a data base describing the financial and market performance of over 2,800 businesses. Each business can extract information about the experience of their "strategic peers" (i.e., businesses facing similar strategic positions but possibly in different industries). Three basic sets of variables have been found to account for 75 to 80 percent of the variance in profitability and cash flow in the sample of businesses: (1) the competitive position of the business, as measured by market share and relative product quality; (2) the production structure, including investment intensity and productivity of operations; and (3) the relative attractiveness of the served market, comprising the growth and customers' characteristics. [GSD]

pioneering innovativeness: A strategy of trying to be the first to market new types of products. The highest order of innovativeness (others are adapting, emulating, and imitating), it is often based on technical breakthroughs. [CMC]

pioneering stage: A non-specific period early in the life cycle of a new type of product, during which the pioneers are trying to build primary demand for the product type more than secondary demand for their particular brands. [CMC]

pipeline: A line of pipe connecting shipper and intermediate point or end user. Used primarily for shipment of liquids such as oil and gas. [DJB/BJL]

place marketing: Marketing designed to influence target audiences to behave in some positive manner with respect to the products or services associated with a specific place. Comment: Attempts by an individual or organization to educate target audiences or change their attitudes about a place are not marketing. (See also **public relations**.) [ARA]

planned buying vs. unplanned buying: Planned buying is purchasing activity undertaken with a problem previously recognized and a buying intention previously formed. Most organizational buying is planned buying. Unplanned buying is buying activity that occurs as a result of exposure to an advertisement, a salesperson's visit. Trial of new supplies or consumables may begin as unplanned buying. [GLL/DTW]

planned economy: An economy in which a central authority makes economic decisions, as contrasted with a market economy. [WL]

planned obsolescence: A product strategy that seeks new products to make prior products obsolete. Usually applied to a product category where annual product changes make prior years' models less desirable. [CMC]

planned stock: The dollar amount of merchandise a buyer desires to have on hand at a given time in a certain department, merchandise classification, price line, or other control unit. [WRD]

planning: A systematic process for relating the competences of the business with the threats and opportunities of the market environment. Most planning processes use the following sequence: (1) business definition-implementation— including the specific action plans or programs, budgets and timetables; (2) situation assessment—the analysis of internal and environmental factors that influence business performance; (3) preliminary performance objectives-based on past performance and corporate expectations; (4) strategy development—the identification and evaluation of strategic options, and the choice of an option for implementation; (5) which establishes the initial scope of the planning activities; and (6) monitoring of performance—compared with strategies and objectives. [GSD]

planning horizon: (See **planning**.)

plus-one dialing: Technique used in studies employing telephone interviews in which a single randomly determined digit is added to numbers selected from the telephone directory. [GAC]

point of diminishing returns: That point at which total product begins to increase at a decreasing rate with successive application of inputs. (See also **law of diminishing returns**.) [DLS]

point of negative returns: That point at which total product decreases absolutely with successive applications of inputs. See also law of diminishing returns.) [DLS]

point of sale transfer: The payment for retail purchases by using an electronic funds transfer card. [WL]

point-of-purchase advertising: Advertising usually in the form of window and/or interior displays in establishments where a product is sold to the ultimate consumer. [WRD]

point-of-purchase display: On- and off-shelf display materials or product stockings generally at the retail level which are used to call special attention to the featured product. Sometimes referred to as **point-of-sale display**. [DES]

point-of-sale display: (See **point-of-purchase display**.)

polarity of retail trade: A trend in retailing that indicates that the predominate retailing institutions are on one hand (pole) high yield mass distribution outlets and, on the other hand (pole), high yield specialty, single-line, boutique type retail institutions. [WRD]

policy adjustment: An exception to the usual complaint adjustment practice or policy which is made nevertheless for the purpose of retaining the customer's goodwill. [WRD]

political environment: Refers to the government/business surroundings that affect and shape market opportunities, including government's role as both a controller and as a customer of business. [WL]

political marketing: Marketing designed to influence target audiences to vote for a particular person, party or proposition. Attempts by an individual or organization only to educate or change attitudes are not political marketing. (See also **lobbying**.) [ARA]

pollution: Refers to befouling the pure state of the environment. A workable definition of pollution is dependent on the public's decision as to what use it wants to make of its environment. [DC]

polycentric: The unconscious bias or belief that it is necessary to adopt totally to local culture and practice. A "host" country orientation in management. [WJK]

polycentric pricing policy: (See **adaptation pricing policy.**)

pooled buying: The practice of independent merchants informally pooling their orders. [WRD]

pooling: Refers to a process of combining shipments which are consigned to the same destination. This service, often provided by a third party, improves physical distribution productivity in the handling of multi-unit shipments. [DJB/BJL]

population: Totality of cases that conforms to some designated specifications. [GAC]

portfolio: A set of things that are developed and/or marketed in relationship to each other. Most often applied to that group of projects currently active in a research laboratory, but may apply to all new projects underway. [CMC]

portfolio analysis: More diversified companies are more usefully considered as being composed of a portfolio of strategic business units (SBUs). Portfolio analysis is used to assess needs and to allocate resources in recognition of differences in the contributions of different SBUs to the achievement of corporate objectives for growth and profitability. Portfolio analyses are often performed using models which classify SBUs and product-markets within a two dimensional matrix in which one dimension represents the attractiveness of the market and the other dimension, the strength of competitive position. The position of the SBU within the matrix has direct implications for the generic investment strategy of the business—that is, whether it is appropriate to "invest/build," "hold," "harvest" or "divest." Some of the best known models for portfolio analysis include the Boston Consulting Group's (BCG) growth-share matrix and General Electric's (GE) market attractiveness-competitive position matrix (see definitions). [GSD]

portfolio management: The arrangement of investments so as to achieve a balance of risks and rewards acceptable to the investor. The term can be applied to a global product portfolio. [WJK]

position analysis: The analysis of existing products including the manufacturing program of the present company and of the subsidiaries, analysis of competitor's market shares, a technical and economic evaluation of all products in comparison with competitor's products, assessment of manufacturing capacity, sales capacity, in the field and in the home organization, appraisal of product knowledge within the group, analysis of custom duties and tariffs and some study of innovations to be expected in the future. [WJK]

position description: A written description which helps the incumbent of a position know what is expected of him/her. It includes the organizational unit, position title, purpose of the position, reporting relationships, duties and responsibilities, and authority (if any). [VPB]

positioning: (See **product positioning**.)

positioning analysis: (See **market positioning**.)

positive disconfirmation: (See **disconfirmation**.)

POSSE: A decision support systems for making product design decisions. The approach uses conjoint analysis to identify the relation between the attributes possessed by a product and the desirability of that product, for each of a set of potential customers. In a second step, the level of market demand for any potential product is estimated by aggregating the individual preference models across customers. An optimization routine then reveals the most desirable product (or products) in terms of some specific management objective (e.g., maximizing incremental market share). This objective may take into account the presence of specific other products in the market and/or any cannibalization effect of the new product on specific existing products. Finally, the market segment most attracted to this optimal new product is identified (Green, Carroll and Goldberg 1981). [DCS/YJW]

post purchase evaluation: The evaluation of a product or service after the behavior is consummated. This may involve remorse as well as the feeling of satisfaction or disssatisfaction. (See also **cognitive dissonance** and **satisfaction**.) [HHK]

postindustrial society: A concept referring to the next stage in our societal evolution where the production of knowledge will be our major activity and most of the employment opportunities will be in the service sector. [WL]

post-industrialized countries: Those countries where the 1987 per capita GNP is greater than $8,500. Characteristics of this type of an economy are: (1) the importance of the service sector is to the extent of more than 50% of the GNP; (2) the crucial importance of information processing and exchange; and (3) the ascendancy of knowledge over capital as the key strategic resource; of intellectual technology over machine technology; of scientists and professionals over engineers and semiskilled workers; and of theory and models over empiricism. (See also **pre-industrial countries, underdeveloped countries, developing countries** and **industrialized countries**.) [WJK]

postponement: 1. An economic term used to describe a strategy whereby the seller "postpones" any customization of the product until a firm demand is received from the buyer. A common example would be where the consumer buys paint which is custom mixed at the hardware store after the order is placed by the customer. [DJB/BJL] 2. This concept holds that changes in the form and identity of a product and inventory location are shifted to the latest possible point in the marketing process in order to reduce the costs of the marketing system. [JRN]

posttesting advertising: The testing of advertising effectiveness after the final audience is exposed to the advertising; posttests include measures of communication as well as sales effects, and seek to measure such things as message impact, media delivery, or both simultaneously. [AMB]

poverty level: The poverty level is based solely on money income, and updated every year, to reflect changes in the Consumer Price Index; reflects the consumption requirements of families based on their size and composition. It is used to classify families as being above or below the poverty level. [WL]

pragmatic validity: Approach to validation of a measure based on the usefulness of the measuring instrument as a predictor of some other characteristic or behavior of the individual; it is sometimes called predictive validity or criterion related validity. [GAC]

preapproach: Activities preceding the sales call that include prospecting, collecting information, and planning the sales presentation. [BAW]

predatory pricing: The practice of selectively pricing a product below that of competition so as to eliminate competition, while pricing the product higher in markets where competition does not exist or is relatively weaker. [KM]

preemptive pricing: The practice of setting prices low so as to discourage competition from entering the market. [KM]

preferential tariff: A reduced tariff rate applied to imports from certain countries. [WJK]

preindustrial countries: Those countries with 1987 incomes under $500 per capita. The characteristics exhibited by this group of countries are: (1) low literacy rates and high percentage of employment in agriculture; (2) low population density and low degree of urbanisation; (3) linguistic heterogeneity and a small percentage of working age population; (4) industrial sectors virtually nonexistent and undeveloped; and (5) heavy reliance upon foreign sources for all manufactures and principal engagement in agricultural endeavors. (See also **underdeveloped countries, developing countries, industrialized countries,** and **post-industrialized countries.**). [WJK]

premarking: Price marking by the manufacturer or other supplier before goods are shipped to a retail store. Also called "prepricing." [WRD]

premium: An item of value, other than the product itself, given as an additional incentive to influence the purchase of a product. [DES]

prepaid rate: A transportation charge which is paid before a shipment is delivered, usually by the shipper or seller. [DJB/BJL]

preprint advertising: Advertising material printed ahead of a publication's regular press run, often on a press other than the publication's, and then inserted into the publication for distribution to its circulation; preprint advertising involves a variety of types, including multipage inserts, free standing inserts (FSI), reply cards and envelopes, and those advertisements printed on paper stock that is different from that which generally appears in the publication (e.g., heavy, high-gloss ads printed with special inks). [AMB]

preretailing: The practice of determining prices and placing them on a copy of the purchase order at the time that goods are bought (orders placed). [WRD]

presentation, sales: The core of the personal selling process in which the salesperson verbally transmits the information about the product and attempts to persuade the prospect to become a customer. [BAW]

press conference: The convening of media representatives by a person or organization to explain, announce, or expand on a particular subject. [DES]

press parties: The convening of media representatives at a social event to distribute information or material for possible future use or to influence their opinion of the sponsoring organization. [DES]

pretest: Use of a questionnaire (observation form) on a trial basis in a small pilot study to determine how well the questionnaire (observation form) works. [GAC]

pretesting advertising: The testing of advertising effectiveness before exposure to the final audience; often used to test an advertisement or commercial, or even specific parts, before producing the final version. [AMB]

price: The formal ratio that indicates the quantities of money goods or services needed to acquire a given quantity of goods or services. [KM]

price code: A symbol or code placed on a price ticket or bin ticket to indicate the cost price of an item. [WRD]

price competition: Rivalry among firms seeking to attract customers on the basis of price, rather than by the use of other marketing factors. [WL]

price controls: Legal limits on prices in the market. [DLS]

price cutting: The practice of reducing the prices of established products or services. [KM]

price discrimination: The practice of charging different buyers different prices for the same quantity and quality of products or services. [KM]

price elasticity of demand: Provides a measure of the sensitivity of demand to changes in price. It is formally defined as the percentage change in quantity demanded relative to a given percentage change in price. (See also **elastic demand**.) [KM]

price fixing: The practice of two or more sellers agreeing on the price to charge for similar products or services. [KM]

price guarantee: The practice of vendors offering their customers guarantees against price declines. [WRD]

price guidelines: Suggested targets for price levels directed at marketers by government officials. [DLS]

price leader: 1. In competitive situations, the seller who normally initiates price changes in the market. [KM] (2) (retail) An item of merchandise priced abnormally low for the purpose of attracting customers. [WRD]

price leadership: The practice in an industry of recognizing and adopting the price established by one or more members of the industry. [WRD]

price lining: 1. A limited number of predetermined price points at which merchandise will be offered for sale—e.g., $7.95, $10.95, $14.95. [WRD] 2. The offering of merchandise at a number of specific but predetermined prices. Once set, the prices may be held constant over a period of time, and changes in market conditions are adapted to by changing the quality of the merchandise. [KM]

price maintenance: The determination by the manufacturer of the price at which an identified item shall be resold by wholesalers and/or retailers. [WRD]

price offs: A stated reduction in the price of a product generally offered by the manufacturer and printed directly on the product package. [DES]

price structure: A price structure includes the time and conditions of payment, the nature of discounts to be allowed the buyer, and where and when title is to be taken by the buyer. [KM]

price thresholds: The lowest and highest prices that buyers are willing to pay for a particular good or service. [KM]

price-quality relationship: The degree that product or service quality covaries with price. [KM]

primary advertising: Advertising whose purpose is to promote generic demand for products or services; often used by industry trade associations to build demand for products made by their members or to enhance the image of the industry. [AMB]

primary buying motives: Those motives which induce an individual to buy a certain kind or general class of article or service, as opposed to the selection of brands within a class. (See also **physiological drives.**) [WRD]

primary data: Information collected specifically for the purpose of the investigation at hand. [GAC]

primary metropolitan statistical area (PMSA): An area of at least one million people that includes a large urbanized county or a group of counties that have strong economic and social ties to neighboring communities. (See also **consolidated metropolitan statistical area (CSMA)**). [DLS]

primary readers: Readers of a print advertising media vehicle who are in a household which acquired the publication through purchase (e.g.,newsstand sale or subscription); contrasted to pass-along or secondary readers. [AMB]

private brand: A brand that is owned by the product's reseller rather than by its manufacturer. In rare instances, the reseller may be the manufacturer as well. The term is often associated with (1) advertised versus unadvertised brands (a private brand is most often unadvertised), and (2) national versus regional or local brands (a private brand is usually less than national). These distinctions have become clouded by large retail and wholesale organizations (e.g. Sears, Kroger, K mart, Ace) who advertise their private brands and market them nationally and internationally. [CMC]

private (or distributor) brands: Brands that are the property right of middlemen in the channel of distribution; they may be sponsored by retailers, wholesalers, or cooperative buying groups. [WRD]

private carrier: A corporate-owned and corporate-managed transportation capability. Private carriage usually refers to trucking, but corporate ownership of other modes is also found in rail and water transportation. [DJB/BJL]

private nonprofit marketer: A nonprofit marketer incorporated privately. Comment: Nonprofit marketers collectively have been defined as the "third sector" or the "independent sector." (See also **independent sector** and **private nonprofit marketer: third sector**.) [ARA]

private sector: All the economic activities that are outside the so-called public sector, or those activities that are independent of government control. They are usually, but not exclusively, carried on for profit. [WL]

prizes: The reward structure of cash and/or merchandise offered in a contest, game, or sweepstakes sales promotion. [DES]

probability mixture model: A stochastic model for representing the behavior (e.g., brand choice or media viewing) of a set of individuals. This type of model is characterized by two components. First, a particular family of probabilistic models (such as a Poisson process) is selected to represent the behavior of any single individual (for example, the number of product purchases made by the individual.) Second, there is an explicit realization that individuals differ from each other (heterogeneity). That is, a distribution is selected to represent the variation across individuals in the particular probabilistic model followed, within the family of models noted above. (For example, the Poisson purchase rate varies from individual to individual.) Probability mixture models have been used to predict brand choice, product purchase, and media viewing patterns over time (Greene 1982; Massy, Montgomery and Morrison 1970). (For examples, see **Beta Binominal model** and **NBD model**.) [DCS/YJW]

probability sample: Sample in which each population element has a known, non-zero chance of being included in the sample. [GAC]

probe: A question or verbal expression intended to elicit information from a customer. [BAW]

probit model: A probabilistic model for representing the choice behavior of individuals. On any choice occasion the individual is assumed to choose the item for which he/she has the highest preference. Over repeated choice occasions preferences are assumed to have a probabilistic component. For the probit model this random component of preference, for the set of items being considered, is taken to have the multivariate normal distribution (Thurstone 1927). The model can be used to predict choice probabilities (or market share, as an average of these probabilities) based on the distribution of preference levels, and also to link average preference to attributes of the items being chosen (Currim 1982; Daganzo 1979). Unlike the logit model, probit does not require that Luce's Choice Axiom hold, which is sometimes seen as an appealing feature of probit. On the other hand, this feature comes at the cost of significant additional computational complexity and more parameters to estimate, relative to the logit model. [DCS/YJW]

problem child: (See **growth-share matrix**.)

problem recognition, in organizational buying: The recognition that the current product or service can be replaced by a better product or service or that a cheaper way to operate exists. It is followed by a search for information and evaluation of whether new purchases are justified. Problem recognition may be stimulated internally (by a value analysis, or audit, for example) or externally, (by exposure to an ad or by a salesperson's visit). (See also **buy grid**.) [GLL/DTW]

problem solution approach: A selling approach in which the salesperson identifies the customer's problems and several alternative solutions, then analyzes the advantages and disadvantages of the solution and helps the customer select the best option. (See also **consultative selling**.) [BAW]

processed materials: Manufactured materials that have been partially processed before reaching an ultimate producer. In contrast to component parts, they must be processed further before becoming part of a finished product. Examples are steel, cement, wire, and textiles. [GLL/DTW]

procurement: The functions in the material acquisition cycle from the time an item is requisitioned until it is delivered. It includes responsibility for selection of vendor, negotiation of price, and assurance of quality and delivery; it may also include responsibility for transportation, receiving, inspection, and inventory control. It is a function usually performed by the purchasing department. (See also **purchasing department**.) [GLL/DTW]

producer market: (See **industrial markets**.)

producer price index: A monthly price index of about 2,800 commodities prepared by the U. S. Bureau of Labor Statistics, formerly known as the wholesale price index. [WL]

producers goods: (See **installations** and **accessory equipment**.)

producers' cooperative marketing: Type of cooperative marketing which primarily involves the sale of products of the membership; may perform only an assembly or brokerage function, but in some cases, notably milk marketing and citrus fruits, extends into processing and distribution of the members' output. [WRD]

product: (1) A bundle of attributes (features, functions, benefits and uses) capable of exchange or use; usually a mix of tangible and intangible forms. Thus a product may be an idea, a physical entity (a good), or a service, or any combination of the three. It exists for the purpose of exchange in the satisfaction of individual and organizational objectives. (2) Occasional usage today implies a definition of product as that bundle of attributes where the exchange or use primarily concerns the physical or tangible form, in contrast to a service where the seller, buyer, or user is primarily interested in the intangible. Though to speak of "products and services" is convenient, it leaves us without a term to apply to the set of the two combined. The term for tangible products is "goods", and it should be used with services to make the tangible/intangible pair, as subsets of the term product. (See also **services**.) [CMC]

product adaptation: The strategy of developing new products by modifying or improving on the product innovations of others. Contrasts with the strategies of pioneering and imitation. (See also **adaptive products**.) [CMC]

product adoption process: The sequence of stages that individuals and firms go through in the process of accepting new products. The stages vary greatly in usage, but tend to include

(1) becoming aware of the new product, (2) seeking information about it, (3) developing favorable attitudes toward it, (4) trying it out in some direct or indirect way, (5) finding satisfaction in the trial, and (6) adopting the product into a standing usage or repurchase pattern. [CMC]

product and business portfolio models: Portfolio models of products, market segments, or businesses, not unlike the financial portfolio models, are designed to help allocate resources among the portfolio units (e.g., stocks, products, businesses) and select an optimal portfolio. In marketing, product and business portfolios have included standardized portfolio models (e.g., BCG Growth-Share Matrix, the McKinsey/GE Business Assessment Array, A. D. Little Business Profile Matrix, and Shell International Directional Policy Matrix), marketing driven modified financial portfolio models (e.g., modified risk return and stochastic dominance models), and customized portfolio models (e.g., conjoint analysis based simulation models or an AHP based approach). Whereas the standardized models offer no more than product or business classification systems, the customized models and more recent hybrid models (combining models from the three classes—the GE/McKinsey with stochastic dominance and AHP) can provide operational guidelines for resource allocations. [DCS/YJW]

product assortment: The collection of products (items, families, lines) that comprise the offering of a given seller. Though sometimes thought to be only a collection of categories of products, more common usage makes the term similar to product mix. Product assortment is used more by resellers, product mix more by manufacturers. [CMC]

product attributes: The characteristics by which products are identified and differentiated. Usually comprised of features, functions, benefits, and uses. [CMC]

product brand: (See **brand**.)

product champion: A person who takes an inordinate interest in seeing that a particular process or product is fully developed and marketed. The role varies from situations calling for little more than stimulating awareness of the item to extreme cases where the champion tries to force the item past the strongly entrenched internal resistance of company policy or that of objecting parties. [CMC]

product class: That group of products which are homogeneous or generally considered as substitutes for each other. The class is considered as narrow or broad depending on how substitutable the various products are. For example, a narrow product class of breakfast meats might be bacon, ham and sausage. A broad class would include all other meat and meat substitutes even occasionally sold for breakfast use. [CMC]

product concept: A verbal or pictorial version of a proposed new product. Consists of (1) one or more benefits it will yield, (2) its general form, and (3) the technology used to achieve the form. A new product idea becomes a concept when it achieves at least one benefit and either the form or the technology. Further work in the development process gradually clarifies and confirms those two and adds the third. A concept becomes a product when it is sold successfully in the market place; prior to that, it is still undergoing development, even if marketed. [CMC]

product deletion: (See **abandonment**.)

product design models: Optimal product design models are often based on consumers' perceptions and preferences data and have typically been formulated in the context of multidimensional scaling methods or conjoint analysis. In the latter case, simulation and various optimization programs have been used. As an example of a conjoint analysis based approach, see the **POSSE model**. [DCS/YJW]

product development: (See **new product development**.)

product differentiation: One or more product attributes that make one product different from another. The differentiation may or may not be favorable, and thus constitute a **differential advantage**. The difference may or may not be promoted to the consumer. [CMC]

product elimination: (See **abandonment**.)

product evolution: The gradual change in a product, as it is modified by its seller, to keep it competitive or to permit it to enter new markets. Similar to the patterns of evolution in nature. [CMC]

product form: The physical shape or nature of a good or the sequential steps in a service. Form is provided by one or more technologies and yields benefits to the user; for example, many technologies go to make a front-wheel drive form of an automobile. Products of the same form make up a group within a product class (e.g., all front-wheel drive automobiles). Differences in form of service separate discount and full-service stock brokers. [CMC]

product hierarchy: An organizational-chart type of array of the products offered in a given market, breaking first into class, then form, then variations on form, then brand. For the transportation market, the top layer is broken into cars, trucks, busses, etc. The second layer breaks cars by form (sedans, station wagons, convertibles), trucks by form (semis, heavy duty, pick-up), etc. The third layer breaks each of these class/form groupings one more time, for example showing automobile sedans as two-door, four-door, etc. The fourth layer breaks each of these smaller groups into brands (Ford, Chevrolet, etc.). There are various options within these product hierarchy dimensions, so that the array can be designed to fit the needs of the analyst. The hierarchy concept fits services as well as it does goods. [CMC]

product idea: (See **product concept**.)

product innovation: (1) The act of creating a new product or process; includes invention as well as the work required to bring an idea or concept into final form. (2) A particular new product or process. An innovation may have various degrees of newness, from very little to highly discontinuous, but that must include at least some degree of newness to the market, not just to the firm. [CMC]

product introduction: The first stage of the product life cycle, during which the new item is announced to the market and offered for sale. Most methods of market testing are considered pre-introduction, but many marketers call the roll-out an introduction because of the commitment implied in the method. If successful during the introduction, the new product enters the second (growth) stage. (See also **product life cycle**.) [CMC]

product liability: 1. Concerned with injuries caused by products that are defectively manufactured, processed or distributed. Liability for such injuries attaches to all members of the distributive chain from manufacturers to retailers. [DC] 2. The obligation a seller incurs regarding the safety of a product. The liability may be implied by custom or common practice in the field, stated in the warranty, or decreed by law. If injury occurs, various defenses are prescribed by law and judicial precedent. Sellers are expected to offer adequate instructions and warnings about a product's use, and these too have precise legal bases. [CMC]

product life cycle: 1. (From biology) the four stages that a new product is thought to go through from birth to death: introduction, growth, maturity and decline. Controversy surrounds whether products do indeed go through such cycles in any systematic, predictable way. The product life cycle concept is primarily applicable to product forms, less to product classes, and very poorly to individual brands. [CMC] 2. Describes the stages in the sales history of a product. The product life cycle (PLC) has four premises: (1) that products have a limited life; (2) that product sales pass through distinct stages, each stage having different implications for the seller; (3) that profits from the product vary at different stages in the life cycle; and (4) that products require different strategies at different stages of the life cycle. The PLC has four stages: (1) **introduction:** the slow sales growth that follows the introduction of a new product; (2) **growth:** the rapid sales growth that accompanies product acceptance; (3) **maturity:** the plateauing of sales growth when the product has been accepted by most potential buyers; and (4) **decline:** the decline of sales that results as the product is product life cycles: replaced (by a substitute) or as it goes into disfavor.(See also **market evolution**.) [GSD]

product line: A group of products marketed by an organization to one general market. The products have some characteristics, customers, and/or uses in common, and may also share technologies, distribution channels, prices, services, etc. There are often product lines within product lines. [CMC]

product line optimization: Models to establish the optimal product line (in terms of number of products and their specific characteristics and positioning) have been typically developed in the context of conjoint analysis and have taken two forms: a) buyer's welfare models (how to maximize the buyer's utility, utilizing, for example, integer programming or search heuristics); and b) seller's welfare models which involve the selection of the best set of products to maximize the profits of the firm, utilizing, for example, dynamic programming or search heuristics. For a review of these approaches and a particular example that has been applied, see Green and Krieger (1985). [DCS/YJW]

product manager: Responsible for the planning, coordination, and monitoring of performance of a product in a multiproduct company or division. Reports to the marketing manager or (if there are numerous product managers) to an intervening level of supervision such as group product manager. Some multibrand companies use the term "brand manager" rather than "product manager" to denote this position. (See also **product/brand management organization**.) **Note:** Because the product manager does not have line authority over the functional units that execute plans, this manager's success in achieving product goals (e.g. sales, profits, and market share) is largely dependent on his/her expert knowledge and persuasive ability. Types of functional units with which the product manager has working relationships include R&D, engineering, production, physical distribution, packaging, finance, marketing research, sales, advertising, and sales promotion. The product manager may be the principal point of contact between marketing management and the advertising agency. [VPB]

product mix: The full set of products offered for sale by an organization. Includes all lines and categories. May be defined more narrowly in specific cases to mean only that set of products in a particular line or a particular market.(See also **product line**.) [CMC]

product modification: The altering of a current product so as to make it more appealing to the market place. Contrasts with creating a line extension and with repositioning a current product, both of which can be used to achieve the same purpose. [CMC]

product planning: A term of many meanings, but generally used to designate a staff position charged with part or all of the task of managing product innovation within an organization. In some firms, it also includes acquisition of products or processes. [CMC]

product planning manager: In a functionally organized department (with no product managers), represents the marketing manager in contacts with functional units within and outside the marketing department with respect to product line planning, development of new products, improvement of existing products, and pruning the product line. Reports to the marketing manager and assists this executive with the development of overall product strategy. Comment: This position usually is not present in a product management setup where the functions listed above are the responsibility of product managers, except for new product development which is usually assigned to a new products manager. [VPB]

product portfolio analysis: (See **portfolio analysis**.)

product portfolio: (See **product mix**.)

product positioning: (1) How consumers, users, buyers, and others, view competitive brands or types of products. As determined by market research techniques, the various products are plotted onto maps, using product attributes as dimensions. This use of product positioning is perceptual, not necessarily valid as based on measured product attributes. Historically, the competitive product positionings were based on sales rank in the market (rungs on a ladder), but this limited perception has long since given way to the full range of product assessments, including psychological ones. (2) For new products, product positioning means how the innovator firm decides to compare the new item to its predecessors. For the new item, the mental slates of persons in the market place are blank; this is the only chance the innovator will have to make a first impression. Later, after the introduction is over, the earlier definition of positioning will take over, as persons make their own positioning decisions. (3) For both new and established products, a product's positioning may be combined with a target segment to integrate the marketing tool decisions. Its earlier use exclusively in advertising is no longer appropriate. [CMC]

product proliferation: A charge sometimes leveled against organizations for marketing so many new products that economic resources are wasted; the consumer becomes confused and mistakes are made in the purchase of products. [CMC]

product publicity manager: Responsible for obtaining favorable publicity for new, improved, or existing products through such means as news stories, pictures and captions in newspapers and magazines, product exposure in TV programs and movies, direct mail, videocassettes, promotional events in shopping malls, and satellite programs beamed to local

TV stations. This manager may report to the marketing manager, advertising manager, or public relations manager. [VPB]

product quality: (1) The measure of any particular attribute a product has (what flavor, how much, how lasting). (2) The measure of the intended customer's reactions to that attribute, how it is liked, its affect. On manufactured goods, the quality assessment is most often made on the quality of the product's physical features as created by the manufacturing process; the judgments are made by managers using proprietary standards. (3) Product quality may also be related to price, in which any particular lower-price item might be said to have good quality, for the money; this use equates product quality with product value. [CMC]

product safety: (See **product liability**.)

product symbolism: The sum total of what a product means to consumer and what the consumer experiences in purchasing and using it. [JPP/JCO]

product use test: One of several key evaluation steps in the product development process. Involves giving a prototype or pilot plant product to persons or firms in the intended target market and asking them to use it for a time and report their reactions to it. The purposes of a product use test are (1) to see if the item developed by the organization has the attributes prescribed for it, (2) to learn whether it satisfies the market needs that were identified during the ideation process, and (3) to disclose information about how and by whom the item is used. [CMC]

product-market concentration strategies: (See **PIMS program**.)

product-market definition: The boundaries of a market are defined by choices of distinct categories along four dimensions: (1) customer function, or the pattern of benefits being provided to satisfy the needs of customers; (2) technology, which represents the various ways a particular function can be performed; (3) customer segment, which describes whose needs are being served and where they are geographically located; and (4) the sequence of stages of the value-added system. A product-market boundary is crossed when distinctly different competitive strategies are required. Within this market there may be sub-markets composed of customers with similar patterns of uses or applications for the product. [GSD]

product-market expansion grid: A two by two matrix that allows the identification of expansion opportunities as follows: [GSD]

	Current Products	**New Products**
Current Markets	Market Penetration	Product Development
New Markets	Market Development	Diversification

product-market grid: One method of segmenting the market to identify strategically important target markets. Market segments are identified by crossing the two variables - products (which relates to customer needs) and markets (which relates to customer groups):

MARKETS (Customer Groups)

		I	II	III
	1			
PRODUCTS (Customer Needs)	2			
	3			
	4			

The product-market grid implies five different patterns of market coverage that a firm can adopt: (1) single product market concentration—one product-market combination is targeted (i.e., one cell in the grid); (2) product-specialization—one product for all customer groups is produced and marketed (i.e., a row in the grid); (3) market specialization—a range of products are produced and marketed to one customer group (i.e., a column in the grid); (4) selective specialization—a number of product/market combinations are targeted (i.e., two or more cells); (5) full coverage—every product for every customer group (i.e., all cells). [GSD]

product/brand management organization: Product or brand managers are responsible for developing marketing plans, coordinating implementation of the plans by the functional departments, and monitoring performance of their assigned products. Product managers report to the marketing manager unless there are large numbers of them in which case they report to an intervening level of supervision such as the group product manager. (The terms "product management" and "product manager" are interchangeable with "brand management" and "brand manager.") Comment: The advantage of this form of organization is that each product receives the full attention of one person responsible for its success. The disadvantage is that the product manager has no authority over the functional departments that design, produce, finance, distribute, sell, and service the product. Yet the system works well enough that it is widely used by multi-product companies. Product management is most appropriate where products are sold to the same or similar market(s) through the same or similar channel(s) of distribution. Hence the more frequent use of product management occurs in consumer packaged goods companies. [VPB]

product/market matrix: A two-by-two matrix in which the column designations are current products and new products, and the row designations are current markets and new markets. The matrix thus defines four types of new product opportunities ranging from the upper-left quadrant of improved versions of "current products to current users" to the lower right quadrant of "diversification". [CMC]

production: 1. (economic definition) The addition of utilities to goods or the rendering of services possessing utility. 2. (marketing definition) The creation of form utility, i.e., all activities used to change the appearance or composition of a good or service with the intent of making it more attractive to potential and actual users. [DLS]

production function: The technical relationship, given a state of technical knowledge, telling the amount of output capable of being produced by every set of specified inputs. [DLS]

production scheduling: A process that specifies a specific target output for the production capability of the firm. It is an important operational tool in planning the short-term resource and location focus in a manufacturing environment. [DJB/BJL]

productivity: A ratio of output per unit of input employed. Measured by the U. S. Bureau of Labor Statistics as output per hour and output per combined unit of labor and capital per hour (multifactor productivity) for the business sector as a whole and for its major subsectors. [WL]

professional advertising: (See **business advertising**.)

professional discounts: A discount granted to people in a specified professional field, especially those who are users of products in that field; for example, discounts given to physicians by drugstores, especially to those who favor the store with prescription references. [WRD]

professional services marketing: Marketing of advisory services offered by licensed or accredited individuals or organizations. [ARA]

profit maximization objective: Where a firm sets as its major objective the maximization of long-run profits. If not stated, this is often the assumed objective of a firm. There are, however, many other variables which may provide the basis of objectives for a firm. Other objectives relate to such variables as sales growth, market share, risk diversification, innovation, etc. (See also **objectives**.) [GSD]

profiteering: Taking advantage of a situation such as famine or natural disaster to charge exorbitant prices and realize excessive profits. [WL]

program delivery: (See **rating**.)

programmed merchandising: The careful planning and concentration of purchases with a limited number of preferred, or key, vendors; usually for an entire line of merchandise and for extended periods of time, such as a year. [WRD]

project: A unit of activity in the product development process, and usually deals with creating and marketing one new product. A project involves a multidisciplinary group of people, tightly or loosely organized, dedicated to the new product assignment that created the project. A project is often part of a larger unit of work, a program, which delivers a stream of new products, one from each project. [CMC]

projection: The ego defense of projecting onto others the needs, hostilities and anxieties that are sub-conscious to the individual. A mode of coping with these perceived undesirable feelings. (See also **ego defenses.**) [HHK]

projective method: Term used to describe questionnaires containing ambiguous stimuli that force subjects to rely on their own emotions, needs, motivations, attitudes, and values in framing a response. [GAC]

projective techniques: Psychological methods of uncovering sub-conscious material within subjects. Ambiguous stimuli such as the Thematic Apperception Test, sentence completion test, word association tests or Rorschach ink blots are presented to subjects who are asked to verbalize their perceptions and reactions. The assumption is that if psychological needs, values and anxieties affect perception of reality, those can be uncovered by analysis of responses to vague stimuli. [HHK]

promotion mix: Various communication techniques such as advertising, personal selling, sales promotion, and public relations/product publicity available to a marketer which are combined to achieve specific goals. [DES]

promotion models: Models to estimate the effect of a promotion (e.g. temporary price change, etc.) include models based on market response functions, or a combination of empirical data with management subjective judgment as in BRANDAID. Promotion models often are stochastic and based on behavioral assumptions regarding retailers and consumers. Many of these models decompose the value of the promotion into components such as increased loyalty among current customers, attraction of deal prone switchers, etc. Inventory control based promotion models have also been proposed, incorporating the inventory carrying costs of consumers and retailers. The increased availability and popularity of scanner data has focused attention on promotion models. [DCS/YJW]

promotion, word-of-mouth: Product/service information, experience, and opinions discussed by consumers in social contexts. [DES]

promotional advertising: Intended to inform prospective customers of special sales; announce the arrival of new and seasonal goods; and feature, create, and promote a market for the merchandise items in regular stock. [WRD]

promotional allowance (or discount):   Given by vendors to retailers to compensate the latter for money spent in advertising a particular item in local newspapers, or for preferred window and interior display space used for the vendor's product. [WRD]

promotional allowances: Payments, price reductions or other inducements used to reward channel members for participation in advertising and/or sales promotion programs. [DES]

promotional campaign: The combination of various advertising, public relations, sales promotion and personal selling activities used by the marketer over a period of time to achieve predetermined goals. [DES]

promotional elasticity of demand: A measure of the change in quantity demanded relative to the change in promotional activity. [DLS]

promotional package: The collection of sales promotion materials and offers developed by the seller to influence retailers, wholesalers, or sales people to support a particular promotional theme. [DES]

promotional stock: Retailer's stock of goods offered at an unusually attractive price in order to obtain volume trade; generally represents special purchases from vendors. [WRD]

proof of purchase: Some element of the product or package used as evidence that the buyer has purchased the product. Common proofs-of-purchase are labels, boxtops, ingredient listings, etc. [DES]

propaganda: Ideas, information or other material dissiminated to win people over to a given doctrine or point of view. [DES]

propensity to consume: The relationship between consumption and saving at all levels of income. [DLS]

proprietary: Refers to private or exclusive ownership of such things as a process, design or patent that competitors cannot duplicate. In the pharmaceutical industry proprietary products are those over-the-counter products that are differentiated from prescription products. [WL]

proprietary drugs: Drug products not requiring a physician's prescription, patent medicines, or "over the counter" remedies. [WRD]

proprietary store: Establishment selling the same merchandise as drug stores, except that prescriptions are not filled and sold. [WRD]

prospecting: The process of identifying and qualifying potential customers. [BAW]

prospects: Potential qualified customers who have the willingness, financial capacity, authority and eligibility to buy the salesperson's offering. [BAW]

prosperity: A phase of the business cycle characterized by high-level production, increased demand for capital goods, and a tendency toward full employment. [DLS]

protection department: The operating unit of a retail store that is responsible for protecting the merchandise from pilferage (internal or external). Those working in the department may be store employees or outside people. (See also **security**.) [WRD]

prototype: The first physical form or service description of a new product, still in rough or tentative mode. Occasionally a prototype may precede R&D, if making it is easy (e.g. cake mixes). With complex products, there may be component prototypes as well as one finished prototype. On services, the prototype is simply the first full description of how the service will work, and comes from the systems design or development function. [CMC]

proximo dating: Specifies the date in the following month on which payment must be made in order to take the cash discount—e.g., terms of "2%, 10th Proximo, net 60 days," meaning that the bill must be paid prior to the tenth day of the month following purchase in order to take the discount, but that a credit period of 60 days from the first of the month is allowed. [WRD]

pruning decision: The act of deciding which products to delete from the line. (See also **abandonment**.) [CMC]

psychic income: The intangible gratification or value that is derived from products, services or activities, such as the improvement in a consumer's self image as a result of purchasing certain highly desirable products. [WL]

psychoanalytic theory: A psychological theory developed by Sigmund Freud that emphasizes unconscious motivation. [JPP/JCO]

psychogenic drives: (See **psychological drives**.) [HHK]

psychographic analysis: Technique that investigates how people live, what interests them and what they like; it is also called lifestyle or AIO analysis since it relies on a number of statements about a person's Activities, Interests, and Opinions.

psychographic segmentation: Dividing markets into segments on the basis of consumer lifestyles. [JPP/JCO]

psychological drives: Those drives that are not based on the basic biological needs of the individual but rather are social in origin. The need for self actualization, status, and belongingness are examples. [HHK]

psychological perceived risk: (See **perceived risk**.) [HHK]

P.U.A. (production unit accounting): A specific philosophy of making use of expense figures beyond their accumulation into expense centers. Involves utilizing the expense data through units of measure to determine productivity for the purpose of controlling expense; common in department store expense management. [WRD]

public affairs: A management function concerned with the relationship between the organization and its external environment, and involving the key tasks of intelligence gathering and analysis, internal communication, and external action programs directed at government, communities, and the general public. [DES]

public convenience and necessity: A phrase used in the regulated environment which describes the certificate required to qualify as a common carrier. A carrier desiring to enter into business in the pre-1980 regulated transportation environment was required to prove "public convenience and necessity." [DJB/BJL]

public domain: The status of works on which copyrights have expired, do not exist, or do not have copyright protection. Also land owned by the government. [DC]

public market: A wholesale or retail market primarily for foodstuffs, supervised or administered by a municipality which rents space or stalls to dealers; also, municipal market, community market. [WRD]

public nonprofit marketer: A nonprofit marketer that is a unit of a national, state or local government. [ARA]

public opinion: The consensus view of a population on a topic. [DES]

public policy: A course of action pursued by the government pertaining to people as a whole on which laws rest. [DC]

public relations manager: Oversees plans and programs designed to promote a favorable image for a company or institution among its various publics such as customers, dealers, investors, government, employees, and the general public. The marketing aspects of the public relations job are concerned with obtaining publicity for marketing programs (such as for a new product launch). The responsibility for product publicity may reside with the public relations manager or with the product publicity manager. The public relations manager would normally report to corporate management whereas the product publicity manager would normally report to the marketing manager. (See also **product publicity manager**.) [VPB]

public relations: That form of promotion that seeks to make use of publicity and other non-paid forms of communication to influence the feelings, opinions, or beliefs about the company, its products or services, or about the value of the product or service to the buyer or prospect. [DES]

public sector: Connotes those marketing activities that are carried out by government agencies for public service rather than for profit. [WL]

public service advertisements (PSAs):   Advertisements and commercials that are run without charge by a medium; for example, public service advertising created by volunteer agencies for The Advertising Council is carried by many media at no charge. [AMB]

public warehouse: A storage facility generally privately owned that does not take title to the goods it handles; may issue receipts which can be used as security for loans. [WRD]

publicity: Non-paid-for communication of information about the company or product, generally in some media form. [DES]

publics: 1. Refers to groups of people with common interest in a specific area. [DC] 2. Those groups that have an actual or possible interest in or impact on the company's efforts to achieve its goals. [DES]

pull strategy: Communications and promotional activities by the marketer to persuade consumers to request specific products or brands from retail channel members. [DES]

pulsing: An advertising timing or continuity pattern in which there is noted variation of media spending over the campaign schedule, but where there is at least some media delivery during all periods of the campaign; contrasted to a "continuous" media pattern, where approximately equal amounts of media effort are scheduled each period over the life of the plan. [AMB]

purchase analysis: (See **value analysis**.)

purchase contract: A (written) agreement between the buying and supplying organizations that specifies the terms of the transactions: product specifications, price, payment schedule, delivery terms, penalties and the like. It differs from the purchase order in that it is generally written by and signed by both parties. (See **purchase order**.) [GLL/DTW]

purchase decision, in organizational buying: That phase of the organization's buying process in which alternative offers of suppliers are evaluated and a selection of one (or more) supplier is made. [GLL/DTW]

purchase intentions: A cognitive plan created through a choice/decision process that focuses on buying a particular product or brand. [JPP/JCO]

purchase order: A (generally standard) document that is issued by a purchasing organization to a supplier requesting items in the quantities, prices, time and other terms agreed upon. [GLL/DTW]

purchase requisition: An internal document issued by the user (or requiring) department to the purchasing department, specifying goods or services required. It authorizes the expenditure, and often includes suggested suppliers and prices. [GLL/DTW]

purchase stage, in organizational buying: (See **buygrid framework**.)

purchasing: A generic term used to describe a title, a function, or a process by which a firm acquires the factors necessary to produce and distribute goods and services. (See also **procurement**.) [DJB/BJL]

purchasing agent: 1. A member of the purchasing department responsible for one or more categories of products purchased. [GLL/DTW] 2. An independent middleman, buying broker for a principal or principals (usually wholesalers), paid a commission or fee for services. [WRD]

purchasing department: The organizational unit responsible for learning the needs of operating units, locating and selecting supplier(s), negotiating price and other pertinent terms, and following up to ensure delivery. (See also **procurement**.) [GLL/DTW]

purchasing manual: An internal document specifying rules for the relationships between the purchasing department, using departments and suppliers. It details the principles and approved procedures associated with procurement. [GLL/DTW]

purchasing power: Refers to a consumer's ability to buy goods and services as distinguished from the amount of money a consumer has. (See also **buying power**.) [WL]

pure competition: A market model where (1) a lower price is the only element that leads buyers to prefer one seller to another, and (2) the amount that each individual seller can offer constitutes such a small proportion that acting alone he is powerless to affect the price. (See also **perfect competition**.) [DLS]

Pure Food and Drug Act (1906):   Banned adulteration and misbranding of foods and drugs sold in interstate commerce.[DC]

push money: Cash paid directly to retail salespeople by the manufacturer to encourage sales of the manufacturer's brand over competitive brands. Also used to influence the retail sale of specific products in a line. (See also **spiff**.). [DES]

push strategy: Communications and promotional activities by the marketer to persuade wholesale and retail channel members to stock and promote specific products. [DES]

PX (post exchange):   A retail store operated by the Armed Forces primarily for the convenience of military base personnel and their families. [WRD]

Q-sort technique: General methodology for gathering data and processing the collected information; the subjects are assigned the task of sorting a number of statements by placing a specific number of statements in each sorting category; the emphases are on determining the relative ranking of stimuli by individuals and in deriving clusters of individuals who display similar preference orderings of stimuli. [GAC]

qualifying: The process of determining whether a suspect has the characteristics that enable them to be classified as prospects. [BAW]

quality: (See **product quality**.)

quality control: A function located somewhere in or close to the operations unit. Its primary purpose is to verify that the goods or services produced meet the specifications established for them. For goods, the process involves statistical sampling and measurement of parts of the output from manufacturing. For services, quality control involves actual field sampling of ongoing operations. A secondary purpose of quality control is to analyze the operations function, seek causes for product deficiencies, answer customer complaints, etc. [CMC]

quality of life: A sense of well being about a person's or society's way of life and life style, often estimated by social indicators. The governing factors include income, wealth, safety, parks, education, health, aesthetics, leisure and the like. [WL]

quantity discount: The reduction in price for volume purchases. (See also **cumulative quantity discounts** and **noncumulative quantity discounts**.) [KM]

question mark: (See **growth-share matrix**.)

questionnaire: A document that is used to guide the questioning of respondents in a survey; the document contains the questions to be asked and in what order, and sometimes lists the alternative responses that are acceptable. [GAC]

quota: 1. (sales) A target level of performance and/or activity that the salesperson is expected to achieve. Comment: Quotas can be established for various performance measures such as sales, gross margin, and new accounts. The quotas can be used in a variety of sales management functions including forecasting sales, motivating salespeople, and evaluating their performance. [BAW] 2. (international) A trade term which denotes a specific numerical or value limit applied to a particular type of good either in the case of exports or imports of goods. [WJK]

quota sample: Nonprobability sample chosen in such a way that the proportion of sample elements possessing a certain characteristic is approximately the same as the proportion of the elements with the characteristic in the population; each field worker is assigned a quota that specifies the characteristics of the people he or she is to contact. [GAC]

quota-bonus compensation: A plan which involves a basic salary and commissions paid on sales in excess of predetermined quota. [WRD]

quotation: A promise from a potential supplier stating his willingness to supply and deliver the item(s) required (by a potential buyer) within a certain period of time at a certain price. It is a response to a buyer's request for quotation (RFQ). (See **request for quotation**.) [GLL/DTW]

rack jobber: A wholesale middleman operating principally in the food trade, supplying certain classes of merchandise that do not fit into the regular routine of food store merchandise resource contacts; commonly place display racks in retail stores providing an opening inventory on a consignment or on a guaranteed-sale basis, periodically checks the stock, and replenishes inventories. Somewhat archaic with trade acceptance of term "service merchandiser." [WRD]

random digit dialing: Technique used in studies employing telephone interviews in which the numbers to be called are randomly generated. [GAC]

randomized response model: Interviewing technique in which potentially embarrassing and relatively innocuous questions are paired, and the question the respondent answers is randomly determined. [GAC]

rate: A charge usually expressed in dollar terms for the performance of some transportation or distribution service. [DJB/BJL]

rate card: A printed listing of the space or time charges, as well as other sales conditions, for an advertising media vehicle. [AMB]

rate differential: The difference between local and national advertising rates; most typically refers to the newspaper medium. [AMB]

rate of return pricing: A method of determining prices by adding a markup which will produce a predetermined return on investment. [WRD]

rate regulation: Refers to the process by which rates are administered. In a highly regulated economy, this could include extensive rules and policies on pricing and related services. Regulation occurs at the federal, state, and local levels. [DJB/BJL]

rating: The percentage of the total potential audience who are exposed to a particular advertising vehicle; in network television, for example (with television households used as the measurement base), a rating (or "program delivery") is the number of households with their sets tuned to a particular program for a specified length of time, divided by the total number of households that have television. Ratings may be applied to print as well as broadcast media provided that audience figures, in contrast to circulation, are used in the computation. [AMB]

ratio scale: Measurement that has a natural or absolute zero and therefore allows the comparison of absolute magnitudes of the numbers. [GAC]

rational appeals: 1. (industrial) Claims (in contrast with emotional appeals) that attempt to show that a specific product will yield certain functional benefits. Rational appeals form the basis of most organizational sales messages. [GLL/DTW] 2. (consumer) The concept of rational or irrational appeals does not exist in modern consumer behavior thinking but rather this is a term carried over from economics. From the point of view of the consumer, all behavior is rational although it may not appear so to the observer. [HHK]

rationalization: An ego defense in which unattainable goals are perceived to be undesirable (sour grapes) and those that are attainable are perceived to be remarkably adequate (sweet lemons). (See also **ego defenses**.) [HHK]

rationing: Systems of allocating goods and services that are in short supply, other than by price, to prevent prices from rising to unreasonable levels and prevent inequitable distribution. Often used in periods of emergency. [WL]

ratios of output and/or input measures: Objective measures of sales force performance which incorporate common ratios used to evaluate salespeople. These ratios include expense ratios, account development and servicing ratios and call activity and/or productivity. [OCW]

raw materials: 1. Products such as lumber and minerals that are bought for use in the production of other products, either as part of the finished item or in the industrial process. [CMC] 2. The natural products (coal, iron, crude oil, fish) and farm products (wheat, cotton, fruits) that are sold in their natural state. They are processed only to the level required for economical handling and transport. [GLL/DTW]

reach: The number of different persons or households exposed to a particular advertising media vehicle or media schedule at least once during a specified period of time; also called cumulative audience, cumulative reach, net audience, net unduplicated audience, unduplicated audience. Reach is presented as a percentage or total number of persons/households. [AMB]

readership tests: A test of advertising effectiveness, typically used as a posttesting measure, in which the noticing and reading of the advertisement is ascertained among respondents; also called "recognition" test. [AMB]

readiness-to-buy stage: (See **buyer readiness stage**.)

real cost: The cost of a product or service adjusted for changes in purchasing power and taking into consideration alternative uses of funds. [WL]

real income: The power of one's income to command other goods in the market. [DLS]

real self concept: The ideas, attitudes, and perceptions people have about themselves concerning what they are really like. (See also **ideal self concept**.) [JPP/JCO]

rebate: A return of a portion of the purchase price in the form of cash by the seller to the buyer. [KM]

rebuy purchase: (See **buyclasses**.)

recall tests: A test of advertising effectiveness, generally given in a posttesting situation, whereby the respondent is asked to recall exposure to the advertisement or to various elements within it. Where the respondent is not prompted by being shown the advertisement in question, the method is called "unaided" recall. [AMB]

recession: A turning point in a business cycle characterized by dropping production and increasing unemployment. [DLS]

reciprocity: A buying arrangement when two organizations agree to purchase one-another's products. [GLL/DTW]

recovery: A phase of the business cycle characterized by increasing gross national product, lessening unemployment and a leveling out of previously falling prices; popularly called upturn or revival. [DLS]

redemption stores: Establishments operated by a trading stamp company redeeming stamps for merchandise. [WRD]

redlining: The arbitrary exclusion of certain classes of customers, often those from poor neighborhoods, from such economic activities as borrowing money or getting real estate mortgages. [WL]

reference group: A reference group is one that the individual tends to use as the anchor point for evaluating his/her own beliefs and attitudes. One may or may not be a member and may or may not aspire to membership in a reference group, nevertheless it can have great influence on one's values, opinions, attitudes and behavior patterns. A reference group may be positive, that is the individual patterns his or her own beliefs and behavior to be congruent with those of the group; or it may be negative. A negative reference group is just as influential, but in a negative direction. The church, labor union, political party or sorority are examples of both positive and negative reference groups for specific individuals. [HHK]

reference price: The price that buyers use to compare the offered price of a product or service. The reference price may be a price in a buyer's memory, or it may be the price of an alternative product. [KM]

referral: A lead for a prospect given to the salesperson by an existing customer. [BAW]

refund: 1. A return of the amount paid for an item. [KM] 2. (**refund/rebate**): An offer made by the seller to return a certain amount of money to the purchaser when the product is purchased alone or in combination with some other product. [DES]

regiocentrism: An attitude or orientation toward internationalization with the focus on regional orientation. [WJK]

regional editions: The splitting of a magazine's national circulation into geographical portions, such that an advertiser can purchase one or more territories in which the advertising will appear without having to purchase the rest of the magazine's circulation; a "region" can be a group of contiguous states, a single state, or in some instances the circulation within a specific city or metropolitan area. "Demographic" editions operate on the same principle, except that the splitting is in terms of a demographic variable (e.g., that portion of a magazine's circulation that is identified as "students"). [AMB]

regional shopping center: 1. This type of shopping center ranges from 300,000 to more than 1,000,000 square feet. It provides shopping goods, general merchandise, apparel, furniture, and home furnishings in full depth and variety. It is built around at least one full-line department store with a minimum of 100,000 square feet. [DLH] 2. A class of planned shopping centers, usually with major department store units and with usually 50 to 100 stores, serving a very large trading area. Larger than community centers. [WRD]

regression analysis: Statistical technique used to derive an equation that relates a single, continuous criterion variable to one or more continuous predictor variables. [GAC]

reinforcement: 1. A consequence that occurs after a behavior that increases the probability of future behavior of the same type. [JPP/JCO] 2. Term from learning theory denoting the reward available to an organism for the response that the experimenter was trying to create or encourage. (See also **law of effect**.) [HHK]

reliability: Similarity of results provided by independent but comparable measures of the same object, trait, or construct. [GAC]

remarking: The practice of re-marking merchandise due to price changes, lost or mutilated tickets, or customer returns. [WRD]

reorder unit: The unit in which an item is reordered, the exact amount depending on trade practices—e.g., dozen, gross, nearest hundred-weight, or foot. [WRD]

repeat sale: The subsequent sale of a product after the initial purchase. The level of repeat sales for a product is often used as a measure of customer satisfaction—the higher the level of repeat sales, the more satisfied customers are. [GLL/DTW]

replacement level fertility (zero population growth, or ZPG): A total fertility rate of 2,110 or 2.11 births per 1,000 women. The rate at which our population reaches zero population growth. [WL]

replacement sales: Sales which take place when a product becomes physically or economically obsolete. The timing of replacement is influenced by a customer's business prospects, its cash flow, product alternatives in the market, as well as the seller's financing terms, and sales efforts. [GLL/DTW]

replenishment cycle: Term used in inventory management which describes the process by which stocks are resupplied from some central location. This process often involves the development of quantitatively based inventory models designed to optimize this resupply process. [DJB/BJL]

repossession: The recovery of merchandise by the store after delivery, owing to a customer's failure to complete payment. [WRD]

request for quote (RFQ): A document transmitted to a potential supplier requesting price and delivery terms on a specific item or set of items. A supplier responds to an RFQ with a quotation. (See also **quotation**.) [GLL/DTW]

requisition: (See **purchase requisition**.)

resale price maintenance: The determination or suggestion by the manufacturer of the price at which an item will be resold by wholesalers and/or retailers. [WRD]

resale price maintenance laws: Federal and state statutes permitting agreements between a supplier and a retailer that the latter should not resell commodities below a specified minimum price. (See also **fair trade laws, Miller-Tydings Act and McGuire Act**.) [DC]

research and development (R&D): The function of working through various sciences and technologies to design new products. This usually involves some basic research for creating new technologies, and some applied research for converting those basic discoveries (and others) into specific new products. The applied (or developmental) phase begins after new product concepts have been screened and desirable attributes set up for them. It ends when scientific personnel deliver to manufacturing the necessary process specifications and finished product specifications. R&D departments also have many other duties, not so directly related to new products. [CMC]

research design: Framework or plan for a study that guides the collection and analysis of the data. [GAC]

reseller market: Composed of the individuals and organizations that acquire goods for the purpose of reselling or renting them to others at a profit. [GLL/DTW]

reservation price: The highest price a buyer is willing to pay for a product or service. (See also **price thresholds**.) [KM]

reserve system of stock control: Method of controlling amount of stock in the reserve stockroom by keeping records of all goods sent to the selling floor and all goods received from vendors; stock in reserve is determined without counting the goods, but by adding the number of pieces received to the past physical inventory and subtracting the number sent to the selling floor. [WRD]

resident buying office: One that represents many retailers in the same line of business in the central market providing information about market developments and guidance in purchasing and actual placing of some orders for their clients. [WRD]

resource allocation models: Models for guiding the allocation of marketing resources. Mathematical programming, decision calculus models, and the Analytic hierarchy process are often used. [DCS/YJW]

resource rating: The evaluation of resources through the statistical measurement and rating of vendors according to their respective contributions to store volume and profits and quality or dependability of service. [WRD]

respondent: A person in a survey who is asked for information using either written or verbal questioning, typically employing a questionnaire to guide the questioning. [GAC]

respondent conditioning: (See **classical conditioning**.)

restraint of trade: A concept with origin in common law and which embraces acts, contracts, conspiracies, combinations or practices which operate to prejudice the public interest by unduly restricting competition or unduly obstructing the due course of trade. [DC]

retail accordion theory: A theory of retail institutional change which suggests that retail institutions go from broad based outlets with wide assortments to specialized narrow line store merchants and then back again to the more general wide assortment institution. Is also referred to as the general-specific-general theory. [WRD]

retail advertising: (See **local advertising**.)

retail establishment: A single or separate place of business principally engaged in the performance of marketing functions, where in or out sales are made primarily to ultimate consumers. [WRD]

retail method (of inventory): A type of accounting system whereby the closing inventory at cost is determined by the average relationship between cost and retail value of all goods available for sale during the period. [WRD]

retail reductions: The total of markdowns, discounts to employees and other classes of customers, and stock shortages. [WRD]

retail salespeople: Salespeople employed by a retailer who are involved in selling goods and services to the ultimate consumer in retail stores. [BAW]

retail store: A place of business (establishment) open to and frequented by the general public, and in which sales are made primarily to ultimate consumers, usually in small quantities, from merchandise inventories stored and displayed on the premises. [WRD]

retailer: Merchant middleman who is engaged primarily in selling to ultimate consumers. One retailer may operate a number of establishments. [WRD]

retailer sponsored cooperatives: A form of contractual vertical marketing system that is an example of backward integration. Independent retailers organize contractually to form a cooperative which gives them greater market power in dealing with suppliers. [WRD]

retailers' handling charges: A sum of money above the face value of a coupon paid by the manufacturer to the retailer as a fee for accepting and initially processing manufacturer-originated coupons. [DES]

retailing: The final part of the marketing process in which the various functions of the seller, usually a store or service establishment, and the buyer, an individual consumer, are primarily oriented to accomplishing the exchange of goods and services for purposes of personal, family, or household use. [WRD]

retailing mix: Those variables that a retailer can combine in alternative ways to arrive at a strategy for attracting its consumers. The variables usually include product, price, promotion, place (location), operating policy, buying, and human resource considerations. [WRD]

retailing the invoice: (1) The practice of writing the unit selling prices on vendors' invoices which serves as the market's authorization. (2) Also refers to extensions of price-quality relationships to ascertain total retail value for purposes of retail inventory method of accounting. [WRD]

return to stock: When a customer returns merchandise to the store for an exchange, credit, or money-back, the process of placing the merchandise into stock again is accompanied by a transaction to "return to stock" so that the item and the dollar amount is added back to inventory levels. [WRD]

returns and allowances from suppliers: The sum of purchased goods returned to the supplier and unplanned reductions in purchase price; represents a reduction in the cost of purchased items or total purchases. Also referred to as purchase returns and allowances. [WRD]

returns and allowances to customers: The dollar sum of goods returned to the store and of reductions in price allowed customers by the store; deducted from gross sales to get net sales. Also referred to as sales returns and allowances. [WRD]

reusable containers: A form of premium in which the product is packed in a container that has additional uses or value after the product has been consumed. [DES]

reverse logistics: The process of returning products in a physical channel. In many logistics systems, there are two- way flows of product and service. In some systems, products must be returned to a central location for repair and refurbishing. In other systems, products may be recalled and returned to a central processing area. [DJB/BJL]

revolving credit: A consumer credit plan which combines the convenience of a continuous charge account and the privileges of installment payment; commonly used for purchase of merchandise on a nonsecured basis. (See also **installment account**.) [WRD]

risk analysis: As a stage in the preparation of a strategic plan, internal vulnerabilities of the business and external threats need to be identified. The risks with the highest probability of occurring and/or those that would cause the most damage need to be identified in order that appropriate action may be taken. The importance of any specific risk factor is equal to the negative (or positive) consequences of a particular risk factor multiplied by the likelihood of its occurrence. [GSD]

risk reduction: (See **perceived risk**.) [HHK]

Robinson-Patman Act (1936):   An amendment to the Clayton Act which prohibits price discrimination where the effect "may be substantially to lessen competition or create a monopoly;" prohibits payments of broker's commission where an independent broker is not employed; forbids sellers to provide allowances or services to buyers unless these are available to all buyers on"equally proportional terms;" and prohibits a buyer from inducing or receiving a prohibited discrimination in price. [DC]

R.O.G. dating: Receipt-of-goods dating; denotes the discount period does not begin until the day the customer receives the shipment. [WRD]

role set: The salesperson's role set consists of people who have a vested interest in how the representative performs the job. These people include the individual's immediate superior, other executives in the firm, purchasing agents and other members of customers' organizations, and the salesperson's family. They all try to influence the person's behavior, either formally through organizational policies, operating procedures, training programs, and the like, or informally through social pressures, rewards, and sanctions. [OCW]

roles: The behavior that is expected of people in standard situations. It is the patterns of needs, goals, beliefs, attitudes, values, and behavior that is expected of an individual occupying a particular position in society. [HHK]

robotics: The use of sophisticated custom-designed machines to do specific tasks in the production, materials handling, and distribution areas of the business. [DJB/BJL]

ROP (run of press) coupon: A couponed advertisement placed in a publication where the location is at the discretion of the publisher. [DES]

routing: 1. (sales) A plan describing how salespeople will travel through their territory. [BAW] 2. (logistics) A process of directing either an employee or a vehicle along some predesignated path. The path is usually designed to minimize cost or effort given some overall objective of the system. [DJB/BJL]

routinized choice behavior: A choice involving little cognitive and behavioral effort. [JPP/JCO]

routinized response behavior: After a sufficient number of trials or purchases of a particular brand, the decision process requires very little cognitive effort and little or no decision making is involved. The behavior becomes habitual or routine. [HHK]

rule of reason: 1. A principle for determining the legality of business practices. Illegality is determined by evidence concerning the country, competitors, and consumers. (See also **per se rule**.) [DLS] 2. A standard applied to the Sherman Act which interprets it to prohibit only "unreasonable restraints of trade" rather than every restraint of trade. The courts have not consistently defined the term unreasonable. [DC]

run-of-press (ROP): The positioning of advertising anywhere within the pages of a newspaper and determined by the newspaper, as opposed to an advertiser securing a special position; when used to refer to color advertising ("ROP color"), the term generally means advertisements run on the newspaper presses, during the regular press run, in contrast to preprint advertising. [AMB]

run-of-schedule (ROS): The placement of broadcast commercials for which a particular time, or program, is not specified; the commercial will be scheduled at the discretion of the station's management. [AMB]

runners: Styles, especially in fashion apparel, for which there are many repeat wholesale purchases of the same item. [WRD]

rural population: Comprises that part of the total population not classified as urban. [WL]

safety stock: A measurement used in inventory management. It is the average amount of inventory on hand when a new shipment arrives. Higher levels of safety stock to protect against out of stock condition require additional dollar investment in inventory. [DJB/BJL]

saleable sample: A regular or specially sized quantity of the product offered at a low price to induce trial. [DES]

sales agent: An independent channel member, either an individual or company, that is responsible for the sale of a firm's products or services but does not take title to the goods sold. [BAW]

sales analysis: Involves gathering, classifying, comparing and studying company sales data. It may simply involve the comparison of total company sales in two different time periods. Or it may entail subjecting thousands of component sales (or sales related) figures to a variety of comparisons among themselves, with external data, and with like figures for earlier periods of time. (See also **sales force evaluation.**) [OCW]

sales aptitude: The overall limit of an individual's ability to perform a given sales job. Sales aptitude is a function of such enduring personal and psychological characteristics as physical factors, mental abilities and personality characteristics. [OCW]

sales budget: The portion of a firm's total marketing budget allocated for sales force training, compensation, travel, entertainment expenses and the costs of administering sales force activities. [OCW]

sales call, interaction, or interview: A meeting between a customer and a salesperson who engages in selling. [BAW]

sales compensation: A financial reward or incentive program based on salesperson performance and tenure. Comment: A major purpose of any sales compensation program is to motivate or influence the sales force to do what management wants, how they want it done, and within the desired time. The three major methods of compensating salespeople are: (1) straight salary, (2) straight commission, and (3) a combination of salary and incentive pay in the form of commissions, bonuses, or both. [OCW]

sales contests: Short-term incentive programs designed to motivate sales personnel to accomplish very specific sales objectives. Although contests should not be considered part of the firm's ongoing compensation plan, they do offer sales people the opportunity to gain financial as well as nonfinancial rewards. Contest winners often receive prizes in cash or merchandise or travel, which have monetary value. Winners also receive nonfinancial rewards in the form of recognition and a sense of accomplishment. [OCW]

sales engineers: Salespeople who have extensive product knowledge and use this knowledge as a focal aspect of their sales presentations. [BAW]

sales force administration: (See **sales management.**) [OCW]

sales force composite: A method of sales forecasting that uses the opinions of each member of the field sales staff regarding how much the individual expects to sell in the period as input. [GAC]

sales force efficiency: (See **sales analysis** and **cost analysis**.) [OCW]

sales force evaluation: An assessment of the overall personal selling effort. The evaluation process helps to measure whether the selling effort is on target with respect to the goals established and also provide strong clues of where and how it can be improved. Sales and cost analyses are major techniques sales managers use to evaluate sales force efforts. To supplement these analyses, objective measures such as output measures, input measures, and ratios of output and/or input measures. [OCW]

sales force management: (See **sales management**.) [OCW]

sales force models: Models for allocation of sales efforts include: a) models such as CALL-PLAN for allocation of time among various customer and prospect segments; b) models such as DETAILER, or those more geared for resource allocation such as the Analytic hierarchy process, for allocation of sales efforts across products; and c) models for design of and allocation of resources among sales territories. These models include various applications of linear and integer programming as well as specialized models such as GEOLINE. In addition to these types of models, a number of compensation/incentive models have been prepared typically as an optimization model. [DCS/YJW]

sales force organization: An arrangement of activities and job positions involving the sales force. The starting point in organizing a sales force is determining the goals or objectives to be accomplished; these are specified in the firm's overall marketing plan. The selling activities necessary to accomplish the firm's marketing objective can then be divided in such a way that the objectives can be achieved with as little duplication of effort as possible. The organizational structure provides for specialization of labor, stability and continuity in selling efforts and coordination of the various activities assigned to different salespeople and departments within the firm. (See also **horizontal structure of the sales force** and **vertical structure of the sales organization**.) [OCW]

sales force recruitment and selection: The activities necessary to attract and hire potential members of the sales force. The starting point in the recruitment process is a thorough analysis of the job to be filled and a description of the qualifications that a new hiree should have. The next step is to find and attract a pool of qualified job applicants. The final stage in the hiring process is to evaluate each applicant through personal history information, interviews, reference checks, and/or formal tests. [OCW]

sales force size: (See **equalized workload method** and **incremental productivity method**.) [OCW]

sales force supervision: (See **sales management**.) [OCW]

sales forecast: An estimate of the dollar or unit sales for a specified future period under a proposed marketing plan or program. [GAC]

sales job satisfaction: All of the characteristics of the job itself that representatives find rewarding, fulfilling, satisfying, or frustrating and unsatisfying. [OCW]

sales management: The planning, direction, and control of the personal selling activities of a business unit, including recruiting, selecting, training, equipping, assigning, routing, supervising, paying, and motivating as these tasks apply to the personal sales force. Comment. Sales Management involves three interrelated processes: (1) Formulation of a Strategic Sales Program; (2) Implementation of the Sales Program; and (3) Evaluation and Control of Sales Force Performance. In formulating the strategic sales program, sales management involves a number of activities including development of account management policies, demand forecasts, quotas and budgets; sales organization; sales planning; territory design; deployment; and routing. In implementing the sales program, sales management activities include supervising, selecting, recruiting, training and motivating the sales force. In addition, implementation requires the development of compensation systems and sales force incentive programs. The evaluation and control of sales force performance involves the development and enforcement of methods for monitoring and evaluating sales force performance. Sales management activities typically required for evaluation and control include Sales Analysis, Cost Analysis, and Behavioral Analysis. (See also **strategic sales program**, **sales analysis**, **cost analysis**, and **behavioral analysis**.) [OCW]

Sales Management Survey of Buying Power: Published annually by *Sales Management Magazine,* this survey contains market data for states, a number of counties, cities, and standard metropolitan statistical areas. Included are statistics on population, retail sales and household income and a combined index of buying power for each reported geographic area. The index of buying power is a weighted index calculated with the formula: 5(percentage of disposable personal income in an area) + 2(percentage of U.S. population) + 3(percentage of total retail sales)/10. [OCW]

sales manager: Responsible for planning, organizing, directing, and controlling the personal selling function. There are usually several levels of sales management ranging from the general sales manager to the first line field supervisor of salespeople. (See also **general sales manager** and **field sales manager**.) [VPB]

sales organization, forms of: Sales forces may be centralized at the corporate level or decentralized at the division level. In either case they may be organized to sell the full product line through one salesperson in each territory, or they may be organized to specialize by product, market, or type of account. [VPB]

sales organization specialized by account: Each salesperson is assigned to one or more accounts of the same type, often without regard to geographic location. An account specialist, for example, may call only on chain store headquarters, or only on automobile company headquarters. This may be an appropriate strategy when the account potential is large and when experienced salespeople are needed to deal with high level customer executives. While this is the highest cost sales organization strategy it is usually justified by the large sales potential of the accounts assigned in this manner. [VPB]

sales organization specialized by market: Different salespeople specialize in the sale of the product line to different markets, such as consumer, institutional, and industrial markets. They may report to the same supervisor or there may be separate sale organizations for each market. Specialization may be an appropriate strategy when market knowledge is more important than product knowledge. Sales costs are higher than for a full-line strategy because two or more salespeople travel over the same geographic area; and more supervisors are needed if there is more than one sales force. [VPB]

sales organization specialized by product: Different salespeople specialize in the sales of different products. They may report to the same supervisor or there may be a separate sales organization for each product line. This may be an appropriate strategy when technical expertise is required for each line, or when there are too many products for one person to sell effectively. Sales costs are higher, however, than they are for a full-line strategy because two or more salespeople travel over the same geographic area; also more supervisors are needed if there is more than one sales force. [VPB]

sales planning: (See **strategic sales program**, **sales potential**, **sales quotas**, and **sales forecast**.)

sales potential: The portion of the market potential that a particular firm can reasonably expect to achieve. [GAC]

sales promotion: Media and non-media marketing pressure applied for a pre-determined, limited period of time at the level of consumer, retailer or wholesaler in order to stimulate trial, increase consumer demand or improve product availability. [DES]

sales promotion, in organizational buying: Refers to those activities other than advertising and personal selling aimed at stimulating product sales. Some of the components of sales promotion are: trade shows, premiums, incentives, give-aways, and specialty advertising (where a firm's name may be printed on a calendar, for example). [GLL/DTW]

sales promotion manager: A staff specialist responsible for providing market communication ideas, programs, and materials not otherwise defined as personal selling, advertising, or publicity. The sales promotion manager may report to the marketing manager, advertising manager, or there may be an advertising and sales promotion manager reporting to the marketing manager. [VPB]

sales quota: A sales goal or objective that is assigned to a marketing unit. The marketing unit in question might be an individual sales representative, a sales territory, a branch office, a region, a dealer or distributor, or a district. Sales quotas apply to specific periods and may be expressed in dollars or physical units. Thus, management can specify quarterly, annual and longer term quotas for each of the company's field representatives in both dollars and physical units. It might even specify these goals for individual products and customers. (See also **sales volume quota**, **activity quota**, and **financial quota**.) [OCW]

sales reports: Reports submitted by salespeople which tell management what is happening in the field. Most managers expect salespeople to report competitive activities, reactions of customers to company policies and products and other information management should know. In addition, sales reports can provide records for evaluating sales force performance. Sales reports often include information such as the number of calls made, number of orders taken, miles traveled, days worked, new prospects called on, and new accounts sold. [OCW]

sales representative: (See **salesperson**.) Comment: The term sales representative is a generic term that includes both direct salespeople and sales agents. [BAW]

sales response function: Describes the relationship between the sales volume of a business and the determinants of the sales volume of that business. The determinants of most interest to a business are those over which they have some control, i.e., the decision variables that comprise the marketing mix. [GSD]

sales returns and allowances: (See **returns and allowances to customers**.)

sales skill level: An individual's level of sales related knowledge or proficiency at carrying out the specific tasks necessary to perform a sales job. Sales skills are proficiency levels that can change rapidly with learning and experience. [OCW]

sales territory: A group of present and potential customers that are assigned to a salesperson, branch, dealer, or distributor for a given period of time. Comment: The key word in the preceding definition is customers. "Good" sales territories are made up of customers who have money to spend and the willingness to spend it. While the key to sales territory design is customers, the notion of a territory is typically operationalized using geographical boundaries. In cases where products are highly technical and sophisticated, product specialists rather than geographic boundaries define sales territories. [OCW]

sales training: A formal or informal program designed to educate the sales force and convey management expectations of job responsibilities. Comment: Sales training provides managers with the opportunity to communicate high performance expectations through training and equip the force with the skills needed to reach high performance levels. A well designed training program moves beyond passive learning techniques and shows the salesforce how to sell. Behavior modeling is one successful approach to sales training. Some common objectives of sales training are to teach selling skills, increase productivity, improve morale, lower turnover, improve customer relations, and improve time and territory management. [OCW]

sales volume quota: A quota which emphasizes sales or some aspect of sales volume. Sales volume quotas can be expressed in dollars, physical units, or points (a certain number of points is given for each dollar or unit sales of particular products.) The point system is typically used when a firm wants to give selective emphasis to certain products in the line. [OCW]

salesperson: A person who is primarily involved in the personal or impersonal process of assisting and/or persuading a potential customer to buy a product or service to the mutual benefit of both buyer and seller. [BAW]

salesperson motivation: The amount of effort the salesperson desires to expend on each activity or task associated with the job. Job tasks include calling on potential new accounts, developing sales presentations, and filling out reports, etc. [OCW]

salesperson role: The set of activities or behaviors to be performed by any person occupying the position of salesperson in a firm. [OCW]

sample survey: Cross-sectional study in which the sample is selected to be representative of the target population and in which the emphasis is on the generation of summary statistics such as averages and percentages. Also called a field survey. [GAC]

sample: 1. (promotion) A small portion of a product which is made available to prospective purchasers to demonstrate the product's value or use and encourage future purchase. [DES] 2. (research) Selection of a subset of elements from a larger group of objects. [GAC]

sampling distribution: Distribution of values of some statistic calculated for each possible distinguishable sample that could be drawn from a parent population under a specific sampling plan. [GAC]

sampling error: Difference between the observed values of a variable and the long-run average of the observed values in repetitions of the measurement. [GAC]

sampling frame: List of sampling units from which a sample will be drawn, the list could consist of geographic areas, institutions, individuals, or other units. [GAC]

sampling units: Non-overlapping collections of elements from the population. [GAC]

satisficing: An action whose goal is to do something less than optimal, i.e., an action that is "satisfactory" and will get you by. [DLS]

satisfaction/dissatisfaction: A positive or negative reaction to a purchase decision or product after purchase. (See also **post purchase evaluation**.) [HHK]

scanner: Electronic device which records retail purchase data (prices, brands, product sizes, etc.) at the point of sale by means of reading universal product codes (UPC bar codes). [DES]

scanning: The process in point-of-sales (service) systems wherein the input into the terminal is accomplished by passing a coded ticket over a "reader" or having a hand-held "wand" pass over the ticket. In the food business, scanning is done by a non-human-readable bar code called universal product code (UPC), and in general merchandise the proposed format is human readable optical recognition characters. [WRD]

scenario: A narrative sketch, description of possible developments or outline of a conceivable state of affairs at some future period. It is designed to focus attention on future causal processes and decision points. [WL]

scrambled merchandising: A deviation from traditional merchandising which involves the sale of items not usually associated with a retail establishment's primary lines — e.g., supermarkets handling nonfood items, drug stores selling variety goods and sometimes, hardware. Also, scrambled retailing. [WRD]

screening of ideas: The step just prior to R&D and systems design in the product development process. It involves use of scoring models, checklists, or personal judgments, and is based on information from experience and various market research studies (including concept testing). Screening calls for judgments that predict the organization's ability to make the item and its ability to market the items successfully. It culminates in directions to guide technical personnel in their developmental efforts. [CMC]

script: A mental directory of appropriate actions in particular situations. [JPP/JCO]

S.D.-B.L. (sight draft—bill of lading): A sight draft is attached to the bill of lading and must be honored before the buyer can take possession of the shipment. Resembles C.O.D. terms and may be said to constitute one way of forcing them. [WRD]

SDR (special drawing rights): "Paper gold" created by the International Monetary Fund (IMF). The SDR is an international reserve asset which is exchanged by member countries of the IMF to offset trade surpluses and deficits. [WJK]

sealed-bid pricing: A mechanism for awarding a sale or contract. Confidential bids are due at a certain time and the award is normally made to the lowest bidder if his specifications conform to the request for quotation (RFQ). [GLL/DTW]

season dating: A form of advance dating allowed on merchandise of a seasonable nature, granted by a manufacturer to induce early buying of seasonable goods so as to keep the plant occupied in slack seasons. [WRD]

seasonal demand: A product demand that fluctuates and peaks at regular points in time. [DLS]

seasonal discount: A special discount to all retailers who place orders for seasonal merchandise well in advance of the normal buying period. [WRD]

seasonal variations: Regular changes occurring in the production or sales of products due to such factors as climate, vacations, holidays and customs. [WL]

secondary data: Statistics not gathered for the immediate study at hand but for some other purpose. [GAC]

secondary readers: (See **pass-along readers**.)

secondary shopping districts: Clusters of stores outside the central business district that serve a large population within a section or part of a large city; similar in character to the main shopping districts of smaller cities. [WRD]

security: An operating unit that is responsible for protecting merchandise and other assets from pilferage (internal or external). Those working in security may be employees or outside agency people. (See also **protection department**.) [WRD]

segmentation: (See **market segmentation**.)

selective advertising: Advertising that seeks to stimulate demand for a particular brand once primary, or generic, demand has been established; also can be used to maintain a brand position after primary demand stabilizes. [AMB]

selective distribution: A form of market coverage in which a product is distributed through a limited number of wholesalers or retailers in a given market area. [JRN]

selective exposure: A process by which people avoid stimuli in their environments, such as leaving the room while commercials are on TV. [JPP/JCO]

selective perception: The ability of the individual to protect himself or herself from the chaos and confusion of excessive and conflicting incoming stimuli. By selectively perceiving and organizing these stimuli, order is created. The needs, values, beliefs, opinions, personality and other psychological and physical factors are brought into play leading to selective attention, selective exposure, and selective retention, along with the ability to distort and add information to meet the needs of the perceiver to cognitively reorganize reality. [HHK]

self concept: 1. The ideas, attitudes, and perceptions people have about themselves. [JPP/JCO] **2.** The image one has of him or herself. Research indicates that the self concept is a relatively important variable in how a person judges and evaluates other persons or products. For example, the person with a self-concept of "upwardly mobile urban professional" may well prefer and purchase a different model or brand of automobile than the individual with a self-concept of a middle-aged "dowager". [HHK]

self reference criterion (SRC): The unconcious reference to one's own cultural values or one's home country frame of reference. [WJK]

self regulation: Refers to control of itself by a business organization independent of government supervision, laws or the like. [DC]

self selection: The method used in retailing by which the customer may choose the desired merchandise without direct assistance of store personnel. [WRD]

self service: A type of operation where the customer is exposed to merchandise that may be examined without sales assistance, unless the customer seeks such assistance. Usually accompanied by central or area checkouts or transaction stations. Typical of supermarkets and discount stores. [WRD]

self-fulfilling forecast: A forecast that motivates behavior causing the forecast itself to be realized. [WL]

self-liquidator: Gifts, premiums or other rewards offered to consumers by the seller at his net cost, generally including postage, handling, and taxes. [DES]

self-regulation: An industry or profession's internal efforts to establish standards of quality and truthfulness for its promotional efforts. [DES]

sell-and lease agreement: A term applied to an arrangement whereby a business enterprise owning and occupying real estate sells it to an investor, such as an insurance company, and makes a long-term lease on the property and often, in addition, an option or agreement to buy, effective at the termination of the lease. [WRD]

selling agent: An agent who operates on an extended contractual basis; sells all of a specified line of merchandise or the entire output of his principal, and usually has full authority with regard to prices, terms, and other conditions of sale. The agent occasionally renders financial aid to the principal. [WRD]

selling: The personal or impersonal process whereby the salesperson ascertains, activates and satisfies the needs of the buyer to the mutual, continuous benefit of both buyer and seller. [BAW]

semantic differential: Self-report technique for attitude measurement in which subjects are asked to check which cell between a set of bipolar adjectives or phrases best describes their feelings toward the object. [GAC]

semantic knowledge: The general meanings people have acquired about their world. (See also **episodic knowledge**.) [JPP/JCO]

semi-manufactured goods: Industrial goods that are at least one stage past being raw materials, and are sold for use as components of other products. They are comprised of parts and processed materials. [CMC]

sensitivity coefficient: The average percentage change in consumption corresponding to a 1 percent change in disposable income. [WL]

sequential sample: Sample formed on the basis of a series of successive decisions. If the evidence is not conclusive after a small sample is taken, more observations are taken; if still inconclusive after these additional observations, still more observations are taken. At each stage, then, a decision is made as to whether more information should be collected or whether the evidence is sufficient to draw a conclusion. [GAC]

served market: The business develops, manufactures, and markets products appropriate to a selected segment of the market. It should be noted that the market for which the product is developed (called the qualified market) and the market which is targeted in marketing efforts will often not overlap precisely. The overlap between the qualified market and the target market represents the served market. (See also **product-market definitions**.) [GSD]

service: (See **customer service**.)

service mark: A trademark for a service. [CMC]

service merchandiser: (See **rack jobber**.)

services: 1. Products, such as a bank loan or home security, that are intangible, or at least substantially so. If totally intangible, they are exchanged directly from producer to user, cannot be transported or stored, and are almost instantly perishable. Service products are often difficult to identify, since they come into existence at the same time they are bought and consumed. They are comprised of intangible elements that are inseparable, they usually involve customer participation in some important way, cannot be sold in the sense of ownership transfer, and have no title. Today, however, most products are partly tangible and partly intangible, and the dominant form is used to classify them as either goods or services (all are products). These common, hybrid forms, whatever they are called, may or may not have the attributes just given for totally intangible services. 2. Services, as a term, is also used to describe activities performed by sellers and others which accompany the sale of a product, and aid in its exchange or its utilization (e.g. shoe fitting, financing, an 800 number). Such services are either pre-sale or postsale and supplement the product, not comprise it. If performed during sale, they are considered to be intangible parts of the product. (See also **customer service**.) [CMC]

sets in use: The percentage of television or radio households that are tuned to the medium during a given time period; for television, the A.C.Nielsen Company, in their measurement of media audiences, refers to this as "Households Using Television—HUT." [AMB]

shaping: A process of reinforcing successive approximations of a desired behavior, or of other required behaviors, in order to increase the probability of the desired response. [JPP/JCO]

share of audience: The proportion of sets in use that are tuned to a particular broadcast station or network program during a given time period; share of audience (or "share") is computed by dividing the station (program) rating by the sets in use. [AMB]

shareholder wealth maximization (SWM): The assumed goal of the firm in financial economics. Comment: SWM is an assumption derived from certain axioms about individual behavior due to Von Neumann and Morgenstern. From these axioms it can be deduced that individuals will behave as if they were attempting to maximize an expected utility function. The empirical accuracy and ethical adequacy of SWM is an issue of some controversy. [PFA]

shelf life: The length of time a product can safely remain in storage between production and consumption. After this period, deterioration makes the product unfit for sale and/or consumption. Virtually every good has a shelf life, but services (if totally intangible) do not. Shelf life is not related to product obsolescence. [CMC]

shelf stock: In a complex distribution system, inventory occurs at the plant and at field locations. Shelf stock refers to inventory which has been accumulated for display at the point of final sale. [DJB/BJL]

shelf talker: Printed card or other sign used in retail stores to call attention to shelved products. Commonly attached to the shelves or railings of display cases. [DES]

Sherman Antitrust Act (1890): Prohibits contracts, combinations and conspiracies which restrain interstate or foreign trade, and prohibits monopolization, attempts to monopolize and conspiracies to monopolize. [DC]

shippers' cooperatives: Nonprofit organizations that pool members' shipments so that they can be moved at low carload or truckload rates instead of the more expensive L.C.L. or L.T.L. rates. [WRD]

Shipping Act (1984): Permits ocean common carriers to file agreements with the Federal Maritime Commission that fix or regulate transportation rates, pool traffic revenues, allot ports, and restrict the number of ships between ports. [DC]

shoplifting: The stealing of a store's merchandise by customers. (See also **pilferage**.) [WRD]

shopping center: A group of architecturally unified commercial establishments built on a site which is planned, developed, owned, and managed as an operating unit related in its location, size, and type of shops to the trade area it serves. [DLH]

shopping products: Products such as better dresses and hair treatments, for which the consumer is willing to spend considerable time and effort in gathering information on price, quality, and other attributes. Several retail outlets are customarily visited. Comparison of product attributes and complex decision processes are common. [CMC]

short delivery: A discrepancy in the amount of goods delivered, the number being less than shown on the purchase order or invoice. [WRD]

short run: (See **planning**.)

short-range plans: (See **tactics**.)

shortage: (See **inventory stock shortage**.)

shrink-wrap: A packaging process which allows the shipper to extend a clear plastic covering over a package or set of packages. The clear plastic is then circulated through a heat tunnel where the film "shrinks" to adhere closely to the package or collection of packages. [DJB/BJL]

shrinkage: The absence of book inventory. The presence of "shrinkage" suggests that there is less inventory than expected at some specific location in the channel. [DJB/BJL]

simple random sample: Probability sample in which each population element has a known and equal chance of being included in the sample and where every combination of n population elements is a sample possibility and is just as likely to occur as any other combination of n units. [GAC]

simple tabulation: Count of the number of cases that fall into each category when the categories are based on one variable. [GAC]

simulated test market: A form of market testing in which consumers are exposed to new products and to their claims, in a staged advertising and purchase situation. Output of the test is an early forecast of sales and/or market share, based on mathematical forecasting models, management assumptions, and input of specific measurements from the simulation. [CMC]

single column tariff: The simplest type of tariff which consists of a schedule of duties in which the tariff rate applies to imports from all countries on the same basis. [WJK]

situation analysis: The systematic collection and study of past and present data to identify trends, forces, and conditions with the potential to influence the performance of the business and the choice of appropriate strategies. The situation analysis is the foundation of the strategic planning process. The situation analysis includes an examination of both the internal factors (to identify strengths and weaknesses) and external factors (to identify opportunities and threats)—often referred to by the acronym, SWOT. [GSD]

situational involvement: Interest or concern with a product brought about by the situational context. For example, consumers may become situationally involved with buying a hot water heater if their old one breaks. (See also **enduring involvement**.) [JPP/JCO]

size lining: Related to concept of price lining; selection of predetermined size points at which merchandise will be offered. For assistance to customer selection, sizes should be according to customer behavior—e.g., junior sizes together. [WRD]

size scale: A chart of the proper quantity of an item to order in each size. [WRD]

skimming: (See **penetration pricing**.)

SKU: (See **stockkeeping unit**.)

sleeper effect: A controversial finding in the communications literature which asserts that the influence of advertising or other comminications material can increase once the message is no longer broadcast or presented to the subject. The research findings are divided on its existence with sufficient evidence to prove and to disprove the existence of the phenomenon depending on who is interpreting the findings. The belief is that the influence of advertising or other communications increases with number of repetitions. However, as repetitions increase, so does its noxiousness, lessening the effectiveness of the persuasion. Once the communication ceases to exist, its noxious character no longer exists and the prior repetition influence an increase in effectiveness. [HHK]

slipsheet: A materials handling devise usually composed of a flat piece of cardboard or board on which product is stacked. The multiple units of product are moved as a unit load in the transportation and distribution system. [DJB/BJL]

slogans: That part of an advertisement or commercial that provides an element of continuity for an advertising campaign, and/or crystallizes in a few memorable words the key idea or theme. [AMB]

small group theory: A set of conceptualizations and hypotheses relating to the behavior of individuals within a small group of psychologically interrelated individuals. It is the study of the influence of others in a small group of interdependent individuals on the beliefs, attitudes and behavior of the individual. [HHK]

snowball sample: Judgment sample that relies on the researcher's ability to locate an initial set of respondents with the desired characteristics; these individuals are then used as informants to identify still others with the desired characteristics. [GAC]

social accounting: (See **social audit**.) [WL]

social audit: A systematic assessment and report of some domain of a company's activities that have social impact; thus an assessment of social performance. [WL]

social class: A status hierarchy by which groups and individuals are classified on the basis of esteem and prestige. For example, one classification divides our society into Upper Americans (14 percent of the population), middle-class (32 percent of the population), working-class (38 percent of the population) and lower Americans (16 percent of the population). [JPP/JCO]

social consciousness: Refers to marketing management's concern for meeting social purposes, pursuing social benefits, and adhering to social criteria as compared with achieving the sales, profit and other wealth producing goals of capitalism. Social actions are often taken at the expense of immediate profits. [WL]

social cost: The cost to a society as a whole resulting from a firm's decisions and actions, such as the development and launching of a new product that impacts negatively upon the environment. [WL]

social engineering: Using the knowledge and techniques of social and behavioral sciences to improve the social systems in a community. [WL]

social factors in consumer behavior: Those variables other than individual psychological and cognitive factors that have an influence on the behavior of the consumer in the market place. It includes the small group, sub-culture such as ethnic groups, and social class among others. [HHK]

social impact of marketing: The external effects of the processes and outcomes of marketing on the well-being of society in general or of specific population segments. Comment: The economics term "externalities" connotes the same effects. The social impacts may be positive or negative. Examples of general impacts would be the effects on public health of the promotion of cigarette smoking. Segment impacts would be advertising portraying the elderly as forgetful, frightened and physically infirm; or racially discriminatory real estate marketing. These would be negative impacts. An example of a positive impact would be automobile commercials that portray drivers as always wearing seat belts. [ARA]

social indicators: Interrelated sets of social information in the form of statistical data and statistical series that can be used for "social accounting purposes." Data and information that facilitates the evaluation of how well a society or institution is doing in relation to social values and goods. [WL]

social influence: (See **personal influence** and **social factors**.) [HHK]

social man: A person whose buying decisions are highly influenced by sociological factors. [DLS]

social marketing: Marketing designed to influence the behavior of a target audience where the benefits of the behavior are intended by the marketer to accrue primarily to the audience or to the society in general and not to the marketer. Comment: Sometimes confused with **social impact of marketing**. Social marketing can be carried on by for-profit, public and private nonprofit organizations or by individuals. Examples would be attempts to influence individuals to stop smoking (by the private nonprofit American Cancer Society), report crimes (by the public U.S. Department of Justice), or donate to the Muscular Dystrophy drive (by the for-profit Southland Corporation (7-11 chain)). Attempts of one friend to influence another to go on a diet is also social marketing. (See also **social impact of marketing**.) [ARA]

social marketing: That branch of marketing that is concerned with the use of marketing knowledge, concepts and techniques to enhance social ends, as well as the social consequences of marketing strategies, decisions and actions. [WL]

social marketing perspective: That orientation or perspective that focuses on social purposes and reflects on whether or not a company should market a good or a service as compared to whether or not it can do so economically. [WL]

social marketing report: A report on those marketing activities that have social impact, usually in the form of disclosures to relevant publics, overall rating schemes or internal performance review. [WL]

social mobility: the ability of the individual to climb above, or slip below, the social class or position in society into which he or she was originally reared, through education, occupation or fortuitous circumstances. [HHK]

social motives: (See **psychological motives.**) [HHK]

social needs: (See **psychological motives.**) [HHK]

social responsibility: Refers to concern for the ethical consequences of a person's or institution's acts as they might affect the interests of others. Corporate social responsibility is seriously considering the impact of the company's actions and operating in a way that balances short-term profit needs with society's long-term needs; thus ensuring the company's survival in a healthy environment. [DC]

social stratification: (See **social class.**)

socialization: 1. A process by which an individual learns the values and appropriate behavior patterns of a group, institution, or culture. [JPP/JCO] 2. The process by which an individual is acculturated into the mores, norms, values and beliefs of a society or sub-division. Often applies to the learning and conditioning of children. [HHK]

socioeconomic: Refers to both the social and economic characteristics, status or relationships such as social class, education, profession, as well as income and wealth. [WL]

Soft Drink Interbrand Competition Act (1980): Permits the use of exclusive geographic areas by the soft-drink industry for bottling and distribution. [DC]

soft goods: Generally felt to be the clothing portion of nondurable goods. May also include bolt goods and notions. [CMC]

soft sell: The opposite of hard sell. (See also **high-pressure selling.**) [BAW]

solo coupon: A certificate for a price reduction or other inducement made for a single product or service. Commonly distributed separately from other products by media advertising, direct mail or other method. [DES]

sortation: Refers to the general process in material handling of sorting packages by origin or destination. Sortation is a generic word that describes a process of breaking down shipments into specific destinations. It is a process of sorting on customer locations or other destination designators. [DJB/BJL]

sorting: A function performed by intermediaries in order to bridge the discrepancy between the assortment of goods and services generated by the producer and the assortment demanded by the consumer. This function includes four distinct processes: sorting out, accumulation, allocation and assorting. [JRN]

sorting out: A sorting process that breaks down a heterogeneous supply into separate stocks which are relatively homogeneous. [JRN]

source credibility: The believability or veracity of the communication or source of a communication or advertising message. Although it is usually assumed that more credible sources will be of necessity be more believable and therefore more influential, research does not unequivocally support the contention. [HHK]

span of control (supervision):   The number of people a manager can supervise before managerial effectiveness declines. Comment: The number varies by the complexity of the positions supervised, but is generally thought to range from three to ten persons. When the span of control is exceeded it is usually necessary to insert another level of supervision. [VPB]

special drawing rights: (See SDR.)

special events: A sales promotion program comprised of a number of sales promotion techniques built around a seasonal, cultural, sporting, musical event or other activity. [DES]

specialty distributed coupons: Coupons distributed through non-traditional media, such as the back of cash register tapes, egg cartons, shopping bags, pizza boxes, etc. [DES]

specialty products: Products that have unique attributes or other characteristics which make them singularly important to the buyer. Multiple-store searching, reliance on brand, and absence of extensive product comparisons are the rule. Cigarettes, deodorants, and specialized insurance policies are examples. [CMC]

specialty stores: (1) Stores which handle a limited variety of goods, as compared to single-line stores. (2) Also used to refer to departmentized apparel stores, as distinct from department stores. (3) Increasingly used to refer to stores which cater to narrowly defined core customer target markets. [WRD]

specialty wholesalers (short-line distributors):   Those who stock a narrow range of products. [WRD]

speculation: This concept holds that changes in the form and movement of goods to forward inventories be made at the earliest possible time in the marketing process in order to reduce the costs of the marketing system. [JRN]

spiff: A cash payment made to salespeople at the retail level to influence them to promote and sell the manufacturer's brand or a specific item in the line rather than a competitive item. (See also **push money**) [DES]

split run: Two (or more) different advertisements from the same advertiser running simultaneously, and in similar positions, in alternate copies of the same print media vehicle; used to test and compare responses of alternative advertising approaches. [AMB]

split shipment: A vendor ships part of a shipment to a retailer and back orders the remainder because the entire shipment could not be shipped at the same time. [WRD]

spot broadcast: The purchase of radio and television commercials by a national or regional advertiser on a market-by-market basis; commercials are bought directly from a local station or cable system; contrasted to "network" broadcast in which the advertising purchase is for a group of interconnected stations. [AMB]

spot check: Used particularly in receiving operations when goods come in for reshipping to branch stores in packing cartons. Certain cartons are opened in the receiving area of the central distribution point and spot checked for quality and quantity. [WRD]

spot sale (or purchase): The sale or purchase of a commodity for immediate delivery, often on a cash basis. [WRD]

SPRINTER MOD III: A model for analyzing the response to a new product over time using test market data. It simulates product awareness, intention to buy, product search, brand choice, and postpurchase behavior. Besides facilitating a go/no go decision, the model is designed to help improve decisions regarding the level of marketing mix variables (Urban 1970). For other models predicting sales of new products, see ASSESSOR, LITMUS, NEWS, and TRACKER. [DCS/YJW]

staff authority: Includes two types of authority—advisory and functional. Advisory is implied authority based on the staff person's experience or expertise. A staff person with advisory authority cannot order something done but can recommend that it be done in a certain way. Functional is the authority held by functional managers (e.g. finance and personnel) to issue orders to people not under their direct (line) supervision; however, this authority encompasses only those functions designated by the chief executive. [VPB]

stages in the buying process: (See **buygrid framework**.)

stagflation: An economic condition characterized by a combination of slow growth (stagnation) and upward-creeping prices (inflation). [DLS]

Staggers Rail Act (1980): Allows competition and demand to establish rates for rail transportation; it prohibits predatory pricing and undue concentration of market power. [DC]

standard advertising unit (SAU): A system whereby newspapers offer national advertisers a number of standard size space units, resulting in a measure of uniformity for the advertiser buying different newspapers in an assortment of markets; a particular SAU has a prescribed number of columns in width and inches in depth. [AMB]

standard industrial classification (SIC): A system developed by the U. S. Department of Commerce to assign products and establishments to categories. It divides the U.S. economy into 11 divisions, including one for nonclassifiable establishments. Within each division, major industry groups are classified by two-digit numbers. Within each major two-digit SIC industry group, industry subgroups are defined by a third digit, and detailed industries are defined by a fourth digit. More detailed product categories range up to seven digits, as in the example below: [GLL/DTW]

D	Manufacturing
34	Manufacturers of fabricated metal products
344	Manufacturers of fabricated structural metal products
3441	Manufacturers of fabricated structural steel products
34411	Manufacturers of fabricated structural metal for buildings

Standard International Trade Classification: a numeric-based commodity code for products moving by air transportation. Developed by the United Nations and used by U.S. air carriers. [DJB/BJL]

standard metropolitan statistical area (SMSA): An integrated economic and social unit having a large population nucleus. [DLS] (An old term now replaced by **metropolitan statistical area (MSA)**, which see.)

standard package: In some trades, custom or law have stipulated one or several package sizes that the goods are customarily sold in. Bread and colas are typical, though few product categories today adhere only to the standard sizes. [CMC]

standardization: (See **grade labeling**.) [CMC]

standing order: An arrangement with a vendor to make shipments periodically in specified quantities in which the vendor may be authorized to ship a certain quantity each month or week for a set period. [WRD]

Stapel scale: Self-report technique for attitude measurement in which the respondents are asked to indicate how accurately each of a number of statements describes the object of interest. [GAC]

staple goods: Convenience goods such as sugar and potatoes that are bought often, and consumed routinely. Staples often offer little differentiation and are sold importantly on the basis of price. Sometimes called commodity products, but industrial goods can be commodities too. [CMC]

staple merchandise: That for which a fairly active demand continues over a period of years and which the retailer finds necessary to carry continually in stock. [WRD]

staple stock list: List of items that are to be carried regularly in stock. [WRD]

star: (See **growth-share matrix**.)

Statistical Abstract Of The United States: An annual publication of the U.S. Bureau of the Census, published since 1878 as the standard summary of statistics on the economic, social and political organization of the U.S. It is both a convenient statistical reference and a guide to other statistical publications. [WL]

statistical demand analysis: A method of sales forecasting that attempts to determine the relationship between sales and the important factors affecting sales, typically using regression analysis, and the use of that relationship to forecast sales for the future. [GAC]

statistical efficiency: Measure used to compare sampling plans; one sampling plan is said to be superior (more statistically efficient) to another if, for the same size sample, it produces a smaller standard error of estimate. [GAC]

status: The positioning of an individual within a group, organization or society. (See also **social class** and **social mobility**.) [HHK]

STEAM: A model for predicting the sales over time for a new frequently purchased consumer product based on panel data. The approach explicitly considers heterogeneity across households in their purchase behavior, and models repeat purchase as a function of the household's depth of repeat level (Massy 1969). For other models predicting sales of new products, see ASSESSOR, LITMUS, NEWS, SPRINTER MOD III, and TRACKER. [DCS/YJW]

stimulus response sales approach: A selling approach that emphasizes the importance of saying the right things at the right time by means of a well-prepared sales presentation (stimulus) in order to elicit the desired response (sale). [BAW]

stochastic model: Strictly speaking, any model having a stochastic, i.e., probabilistic or random, component. This component can stem from a variety of sources. It arises in models for a single individual making a single decision (e.g., to represent the effect of uncertainty). Randomness also is incorporated in modelling multiple events for a single individual (e.g., to represent the effect on each event of omitted variables — i.e., factors that have an impact but that are not explicitly part of the model). Finally, a probabilistic component can be used in modelling a single event for each of several individuals. Here the randomness represents the (unmeasured) heterogeneity across individuals. In each case the result is a process that, from the standpoint of the observer, appears to have a random component. Often the term "stochastic model" denotes a more narrow subset of models; namely probability mixture models (Lilien and Kotler 1983; Massy, Montgomery and Morrison 1970). [DCS/YJW]

stock balance: Concerned with planning and controlling merchandise investment so that it is balanced with expected sales. The three perspectives from which one can view stock balance are: (1) stock width (breadth), (2) stock support (depth), and (3) total dollars invested in stock. [WRD]

stock bin control: A system for maintaining assortments of staple goods by reordering periodically on a basis of empty spaces or observed low stock conditions in bins or on stock shelves. [WRD]

stock control: All the activities that are carried on to maintain a balance between inventories and sales. [WRD]

stock depth: The number of units in individual merchandise items needed to meet sales of each assortment factor. [WRD]

stock or inventory control: A system or approach to the management of material which is received, stored and distributed within the firm and between the firm and its vendors or customers. [DJB/BJL]

stock rotation: A term used in inventory management to describe the process of moving stock to insure freshness and shelf life of inventory. [DJB/BJL]

stock shortages: All unexplained or unrecorded shrinkages in the value of merchandise available for sale; the amount by which a physical inventory is short of a book inventory figure. [WRD]

stock turnover: An index of the velocity with which merchandise moves into and out of a store or department; the "rate of stock turnover" is the number of times during a given period that the average inventory on hand has been sold and replaced; computed by dividing sales by average inventory, with both stated in comparable valuations, either cost or selling price. [WRD]

stockkeeping unit (SKU):   A specific unit of inventory which is carried as a separate identifiable unit. A pint bottle and a quart bottle of the same product would be separate SKUs for inventory purposes. [DJB/BJL]

stock-out: A situation in which a retail store does not have enough items of a particular kind in stock to meet customer demand; thus, the product is not available to consumers. [WRD]

stockouts: When buyers are unable to fulfill their purchase intentions in a specific buying situation. [DJB/BJL]

stock-sales ratio: The ratio between the stock on hand at the beginning or end of a period and the sales for that period; determined by dividing stock, preferably at the beginning of the period, by sales; distinguished from inventory or stock turnover which is a ratio or an average for a period of time. [WRD]

stockturn: (See inventory turnover.)

store atmosphere: In-store emotional states that consumers experience but may not be fully conscious of when shopping. [JPP/JCO]

store brands: Private brands that are owned by retailers. [CMC]

store image: What consumers think about a particular store. [JPP/JCO]

store layout: Interior retail store arrangement of departments or groupings of merchandise. Should be organized to provide for ease of customer movement through the store and to provide for maximum exposure and attractive display of merchandise. [WRD]

store loyalty: The degree to which a consumer consistently patronizes the same store when shopping for particular types of products. [JPP/JCO]

store patronage: The degree to which a consumer shops at a particular store relative to competitive outlets. [JPP/JCO]

storyboard: The sequence of visual units drawn to portray the copy, dialogue, and action planned for a television commercial; akin to "layout" for the print media. [AMB]

straight commission: A compensation plan which uses commissions as the sole basis for pay. A commission is payment for achieving a given level of performance. Sales people are paid for results. Usually, commission payments are based on the salesperson's dollar or unit sales volume. However, they may be based on the profitability of sales to motivate the salesforce to expend effort on the most profitable products or customers. [OCW]

straight rebuy: (See **buyclasses**.)

straight salary: A compensation plan which relies exclusively on salary as a financial reward for sales personnel. A salary is a fixed sum of money paid at regular intervals. The amount paid to the salesperson is a function of the amount of time worked rather than any specific performance. Comment: Two sets of conditions favor the use of a straight salary compensation plan. These are (1) when management wishes to motivate people to achieve objectives other than short-run volume, and (2) when the individual salesperson's impact on sales volume is difficult to measure in a reasonable time. [OCW]

strategic business planning: (See **strategic market planning.**)

strategic business unit (SBU): From a strategy formulation point of view, diversified companies are best thought of as being composed of a number of businesses (or SBUs). These organizational entities are large enough and homogeneous enough to exercise control over most strategic factors affecting their performance. They are managed as self-contained planning units for which discrete business strategies can be developed. [GSD]

strategic management process: An approach to management which incorporates the following elements: (1) focusing planning processes on the search for competitive advantage; (2) the integration of strategic planning with operational and functional levels; (3) orientation towards funding and implementing strategies rather than discrete projects; and (4) greater emphasis and continued focus on strategic issues. [GSD]

strategic market planning: The planning process that yields decisions in how a business unit can best compete in the markets it elects to serve. Strategic market decisions are based on assessments of product market and pertain to the basis for advantage in the market. The plan that is the output of the process serves as a blueprint for the development of the skills and resources of a business unit and specifies the results to be expected. In many companies these are called strategic business plans. (See also strategic planning.) [GSD]

Strategic Planning Institute: (See **PIMS program.**)

strategic planning: The consideration of current decision alternatives in light of their probable consequences over time. The practice of strategic planning incorporates four distinguishing features: (1) an external orientation; (2) a process for formulating strategies; (3) methods for analysis of strategic situations and alternatives; and (4) a commitment to action. [GSD]

strategic sales program: A program which organizes and plans the company's overall personal selling efforts and integrates these with the other elements of the firm's marketing strategy. The strategic sales program should take into account the environmental factors faced by the firm. [OCW]

strategic window: The limited time period in which the fit between the factors critical for success in a market and the distinctive competences of a business competing in that market is at an optimum. The implication is that businesses should prepare for and respond appropriately to the "opening" and "closing" of strategic windows. [GSD]

strategy: Describes the direction the business will pursue within its chosen environment, and guides the allocation of resources and effort. It also provides the logic that integrates the perspectives of functional departments and operating units, and points them all in the same direction. The strategy statement for a SBU is composed of three elements: (1) a business definition that specifies the area in which the business will compete; (2) a strategic thrust that describes whether a competitive advantage is to be gained by focusing the scope or by exploiting an asymmetry in the position of the business; and (3) supporting functional strategies which are activities designed for consistency and comparability with other activities and the strategic thrust. [GSD]

stratified sample: Probability sample that is distinguished by the two-step procedure where (1) the parent population is divided into mutually exclusive and exhaustive subsets, and (2) a simple random sample of elements is chosen independently from each group or subset. [GAC]

STRATPORT: A decision support system for the allocation of a firm's financial resources across its strategic business units (SBU's). The approach models the impact of general marketing expenditures on both market share and on the firm's cost structure. Given a specific portfolio strategy, the system can evaluate the profit and cash flow implications of following that strategy over time. Alternately, the approach can determine the optimal allocation of marketing expenditures across SBU's in order to maximize net present value over a specified time horizon (Larreche and Srinivasan 1981, 1982). [DCS/YJW]

strengths and weaknesses analysis: (See **situation analysis**.)

strict liability: 1. A doctrine under which a seller is held liable for injury caused by a defective product even though the seller exercised all possible care in the preparation and sale of his product and the user had not bought the product from or entered into any contractual relation with the seller. [DC] 2. An extreme variant of product liability (in common practice today) in which the producer is held responsible for putting a defective product on the market. Under strict liability, there need be no negligence, sale no longer has to be direct from producer to user (privity of contract), and no disclaimer statement relieves the producer of this responsibility. [CMC]

string-street location: A location on a major thoroughfare upon which various kinds of stores are strung for a number of consecutive blocks. [WRD]

strip-type shopping center: One in which stores are aligned along a thoroughfare, usually set back some distance from the street to permit front parking. [WRD]

stub control: A perpetual inventory system of unit control in which sales information is obtained from stubs of price tickets rather than from saleschecks. [WRD]

style: A distinctive mode of presentation or performance in any art, product, or activity. Styles may be permanent, but move into and out of fashion. [CMC]

style-out: A method of pinpointing the determinants of consumer demand for fashion merchandise, whereby the buyer and merchandise manager physically inspect fast-selling and slow-selling items to determine their customer-attracting features. [WRD]

subculture: Segments within a culture that share distinguishing values and patterns of behavior that differ from those of the overall culture. [JPP/JCO]

subject: A person from whom information is secured in a marketing research study, either by questioning or by observing him or her in some way. [GAC]

subliminal perception: A psychological view that suggests that attitudes and behaviors can be changed by stimuli that are not consciously perceived. [JPP/JCO]

substantiation: An FTC requirement that advertisers have a reasonable basis for their advertising claims. [DC]

substitute products: Products which are viewed by the user as alternatives for other products. The substitution is rarely perfect, and varies from time to time depending on price, availability, etc. [CMC]

suggested retail: A recommended list price submitted by a manufacturer or other vendor to a retailer. [WRD]

summated ratings: Self-report technique for attitude measurement in which the subjects are asked to indicate their degree of agreement or disagreement with each of a number of statements; a subject's attitude score is the total obtained by summing the scale values assigned to each category checked. [GAC]

supermarket: A large departmentized, retail establishment offering a relatively broad and complete stock of dry groceries, fresh meat, perishable produce, and dairy products, supplemented by a variety of convenience, non-food merchandise and operated primarily on a self-service basis. [WRD]

superstation: A television station in a particular market that sends its signal via satellite to subscribing cable systems throughout the country; the cable system, in turn, disseminates the signal to subscriber homes by coaxial cable. A home equipped with a satellite antenna ("dish") also can receive a superstation's signal, provided the signal is not "scrambled;" if scrambled, a special signal decoder is required. [AMB]

superstores: Very large stores that are typically outgrowths of supermarkets and offer a wide range of the expected routine nonfood purchases of the mass market. [WRD]

supplement: A special, preprinted section of a newspaper, typically produced in magazine format, that is distributed by the newspaper to its circulation; supplements contain both editorial content and advertisements, can be produced by a national organization (syndicated supplements) or the local newspaper, and often are distributed in the Sunday edition of the paper; also called "magazine supplement" or "newspaper-distributed magazine." [AMB]

supplier management: The process whereby industrial buyers make suggestions about the suppliers' policies, procedures and strategies to improve the quality of products and services furnished. [WL]

supplies: Industrial goods that are consumed in the process of producing other products. They facilitate the production process, and do not go into the product itself. Frequently referred to as MRO, maintenance, repair, and operating supplies. [CMC]

supply: 1. (economic definition) A schedule of the amounts of a good that would be offered for sale at all possible prices at any one instance of time. 2. (business definition) the number of units of a product that will be put on the market over a period of time. [DLS]

supply house: Middleman selling industrial goods to manufacturers or other business or institutional users; generally "distributor," "wholesaler" or "jobber." [WRD]

supply-pushed innovation: Innovation that is based at least partly on the abilities and outputs of technical engineering and R&D functions. Making what the organization is able to make. Commonly called technology-driven innovation, and contrasts with demand-pulled innovation. (See also **demand-pulled innovation**.) [CMC]

surcharge: An additional charge for performing service which is assessed over and above the base rate. [DJB/BJL]

sustainable growth rate: A measure of the capacity of a business to grow within the constraints of its current financial policies. The maximum sustainable growth rate, which reflects the ability of the business to fund new assets needed to support increased sales, is estimated by:

$$ \text{SGR} \quad = \quad \frac{P\,(1 - d)(1 + L)}{t - P\,(1 - d)(1 + L)} $$

where:

$P =$ profit margin after tax

$d =$ dividend payout ratio (for a business unit this is computed from the corporate overhead charge plus any dividend paid to corporate)

$L =$ debt to equity ratio

$t =$ ratio of assets (physical plant and equipment plus working capital) to sales. [GSD]

sweepstakes: The offering of prizes to participants, where winners are selected by chance and no consideration is required. [DES]

symbolic meaning: The psychological and social meanings products have for consumers that go beyond functional attributes. [JPP/JCO]

syncratic decision making: A pattern of decision making within a family in which most decisions are made jointly by both spouses. [JPP/JCO]

syndicated research: Information collected on a regular basis that is then sold to interested clients (for example, Nielsen Television Ratings). [GAC]

synectics: The joining together of different and seemingly irrelevant elements and people into a problem-stating and problem-solving group. [WL]

systematic sample: Probability sample in which every kth element in the population is designated for inclusion in the sample after a random start. [GAC]

systems selling: An approach aimed at providing better service and satisfaction to customers, through the design of well-integrated groups of interlocking products, together with the implementation of a system of production, inventory control, distribution and other services, to meet major customers' needs for a smooth-running operation. [BAW]

tabulation: Procedure by which the number of cases that fall into each of a number of categories are counted. [GAC]

tactics: Short term actions undertaken to achieve implementation and broader strategy. (See also **implementation**.) [GSD]

take one pads: A packet of coupons, refund blanks or other promotional offers attached to or placed near the product being promoted. [DES]

take transaction: Sale of goods that are turned over to the customer immediately upon closing the sale rather than delivered. [WRD]

takeover: The process by which a firm or group of investors acquires control of a corporation via merger or a tender offer. The empirical evidence suggests that both the shareholders of the acquired firm and the bidding firm or group gain in the transaction on average—although the major portion of the gain goes to the "target" firm's stockholders. [PFA]

tare: Weight of a container deducted from gross weight of package to determine net weight and allowance for freight. [WRD]

target market: 1. (general) Particular market segments or groups of customers which the marketing organization proposes to serve, or whose needs it proposes to satisfy, with particular marketing programs. [PDB] 2. (retailing) The particular segment of a total population which the retailer focuses its merchandising expertise on to satisfy that sub-market in order to accomplish its profit objectives. [WRD]

tariff: A published set of rates for transportation and distribution services. [DJB/BJL]

tariff systems: The system of duties applied to goods and services from foreign countries. It may be a single rate of duty for each item applicable to all countries or two or more rates applicable to different countries or groups of countries. [WJK]

task forces, in new product development: Established for a new product idea to shepherd it through the various development stages until it is abandoned or approved for commercialization. The task force is composed of personnel (on loan, full or part time) from departments such as marketing, R&D, and finance. Other specialists may join the task force as needed. The task force disbands when the project is abandoned or when commercialization is authorized. Comment: The advantage of the task force is that disagreements among functional specialists are more readily resolved when members must work together to achieve goals. Also they have direct communications with their own functional departments which have new product assignments. The disadvantage is that there may not be enough competent people to staff the task forces assigned to the many new product projects going on at the same time. [VPB]

team selling: The practice of involving a group of people familiar with the viewpoints and concerns of key decision makers of the customer's organization to sell and service a major account. Comment: This is especially prevalent in the sale of complex industrial products, where a particular salesperson cannot be an expert on all aspects of the purchase process. [BAW]

tear sheets: Advertisements torn from newspapers or magazines sent to an agency or advertiser as evidence of insertion. [WRD]

technical salespeople: (See **sales engineers.**)

technological forecasting: The prediction of innovations and advances in a particular technology. Both exploratory and normative methods are used, the former to project future developments based on the past, and the latter to focus more on planning, and planned technological innovation. [WL]

technological mapping: Gathering and analyzing information about the direction and timing of possible competitive technological developments. [WL]

technology: The purposeful application of scientific knowledge; comprises hardware, software and standards. [WL]

technology assessment: The analysis and evaluation of the potential impact on society of the introduction,modification or development of a technology, both direct and indirect, intended and unintended. [WL]

technology planning: Developing plans and procedures to implement technology transfer. [WL]

technology transfer: The transfer of a capability to use, modify, or adapt a process, among organizations or countries. [WL]

telephone interview: Telephone conversation between a representative of the research organization, the interviewer, and a respondent or interviewee. [GAC]

telephone selling: Selling that involves interacting with customers using a telephone. [BAW]

terminal values: One of two major types of values proposed by Milton Rokeach. Terminal values represent preferred end states of being or global goals that consumers are trying to achieve in their lives. (See also **instrumental values.**) [JPP/JCO]

terms of access: All the conditions that apply to the importation of goods manufactured in a foreign country such as import duties, import restrictions or quotas, foreign exchange regulations, and preference arrangements. [WJK]

territorial allocation or rights: Rights given to the wholesaler or retailer (by the manufacturer) to sell his product or brand in a defined geographic area which is, at least to some extent, removed, isolated or "protected" from other wholesalers/retailers also selling the manufacturer's items. [JRN]

territory management: The planning, routing and scheduling of selling activities directed toward customers in a territory aimed at maintaining the lines of communication, improving sales coverage, and minimizing wasted time. [BAW]

territory potential: An estimate of the maximum possible sales opportunities that could be realized in a sales territory. [BAW]

territory, sales: A segment of the firm's market assigned to a salesperson or group of salespeople. Comment: While territories are typically defined by customers within a geographic boundary, they can be defined by customer types. [BAW]

test market: Trading area selected to test a company's new or modified product, service, or promotion. [WRD]

test marketing: One form of market testing. Usually involves actually marketing a new product in one or several cities. The effort is totally representative of what the firm intends to do later upon national marketing (or regional rollout). Various aspects of the marketing plan may be tested (e.g. advertising expenditure levels or, less often, product form variants), by using several pairs of cities. Output is a mix of learning, especially a sales and profit forecast. In some areas, test marketing is currently being stretched to include scanner market testing, where the marketing activity is less than total, but the term is best confined to the full-scale activity. [CMC]

Textile Fiber Products Identification Act (1958): An act which applies to yarns, fabrics and household articles made from fiber other than wool, and requires that such products bear labels revealing the amount of each fiber they contain and forbids misbranding of such products. [DC]

third sector: Collectively, all private nonprofit marketers. (See also **independent sector.**) [ARA]

13-month merchandising calendar: A calendar in which each of 13 "months" is always a standard four-week period. [WRD]

time rate of demand: The quantity of product that the market will absorb at a particular price per period of time. [DLS]

time series analysis: An approach to sales forecasting that relies on the analysis of historical data to develop a prediction for the future. [GAC]

title: Legal evidence of ownership or right of possession. [WRD]

token order: Placing a small order with the possibility of a larger one in the future. [WRD]

total cost (TC): 1. The sum of total fixed cost and total variable cost for a given level of output. [DLS] 2. (physical distribution) In a physical distribution system, includes all the costs of transportation, warehousing, order processing, packaging, etc. [DJB/BJL]

total cost of goods sold: "Gross Cost" of goods sold plus alteration and workroom net cost, if any, less each discount earned on purchases. (Retail inventory method of accounting.) [WRD]

total fertility rate: The number of births that 1,000 women would have in their lifetime if at each year of age, they experienced birthrates occurring in the specified year. [WL]

TRACKER: A model using three waves of survey data to predict 12-month test market sales for a new consumer nondurable product. The approach views potential customers as proceeding sequentially through stages of awareness, initial product trial, and repeat purchase.

The overall prediction of sales over time is constructed by predicting the time trend of these three quantities (awareness, trial, repeat) using the survey data (Blattberg and Golanty 1978). The effectiveness of the model's product awareness predictions has been investigated by Mahajan, Muller and Sharma (1984). For other models predicting sales of new products, see ASSESSOR, LITMUS, NEWS, and SPRINTER MOD III. [DCS/YJW]

tractor-trailer: The power unit and the van of a motor truck. This term usually refers to the two units that are commonly used for over-the-road surface transportation. [DJB/BJL]

trade acceptance: A noninterest-bearing bill of exchange or draft covering the sale of goods, drawn by the seller on, and accepted by the buyer. [WRD]

trade advertising: (See **business advertising**.)

trade allowances: Short-term special offers, made by marketers to channel members as an incentive to stock, feature, or in some way participate in the cooperative promotion of a product. [DES]

trade area: a geographical area containing the customers of a particular firm or group of firms for specific goods or services. [DLH]

trade card: Special card issued to the customer as successive purchases are made; entitles holder to a prize or purchase credit when a certain total is reached; also, punch card. [WRD]

trade channel: (See **channel of distribution**.)

trade credit: Supplying goods (by wholesalers and manufacturers) on terms that are intended to permit sale by the retailer before payment is due. [WRD]

trade discount: The discount allowed to a class of customers (manufacturers, wholesalers, retailers) on a list price before consideration of credit terms; applies to any allowance granted without reference to the date of payment. Also referred to as a functional discount. [WRD]

trade name: A trademark that is used to identify an organization rather than a product or product line. [CMC]

trade premiums: Prizes, usually merchandise, given by jobbers' retailers for their cooperation in achieving sales. [WRD]

trade regulation rule: Rules which are issued by the Federal Trade Commission and state that particular practices are unfair or deceptive acts within the meaning of Section 5 of the FTC Act. The Magnuson-Moss Act gave the FTC the power to promulgate substantive trade regulation rules, that is, rules having the force of law as opposed to interpretive rules merely stating the FTC's interpretation of its statutory mandate. [DC]

trade sales promotion: Marketers' activities directed to channel members to encourage them to provide special support or activities for the product or service. [DES]

trade salespeople: Salespeople employed by the manufacturing firm whose primary responsibility is to sell to channel members. [BAW]

trade show: A periodic gathering where manufacturers, suppliers, and distributors in a particular industry, or related industries, display their products and provide information for potential buyers (retail, wholesale, or industrial). [DES]

trademark: A legal term meaning the same as brand. A trademark identifies one seller's product and thus differentiates it from products of other sellers. A trademark also aids in promotion, and helps protect the seller from imitations. A trademark may be eligible for registration, as it is in the United States through the Patent and Trademark Office of the Department of Commerce. If registered, the trademark obtains additional protection, mainly exclusive use, but special efforts are necessary to keep the registration and the exclusive use. [CMC]

trading area: A district the size of which is usually determined by the boundaries within which it is economical in terms of volume and cost for a marketing unit or group to sell and/or deliver products; also, shopping radius. [WRD]

trading stamps: A type of continuity program where a consumer collects stamps or certificates issued with each purchase at participating retail stores. Stamps are generally redeemed for prizes from a catalog. [DES]

trading-up: (1) Seller's practice of handling and promoting more expensive or higher-grade merchandise in order to elevate the prestige of the firm. (2) Salesperson's effort to interest customer in better-grade and more expensive goods than the customer expects to buy. [WRD]

traffic (customer): When applied to retailing, refers to those people who frequent the store (or the shopping area) within a particular period of time. Traffic may be heavy, light, or medium. [WRD]

Traffic Audit Bureau: An organization that audits freight bills tendered to the buyer of the transportation service for accuracy. If inaccurate, a claim is filed by the payer of the transportation service to recover cost of over- charges. [DJB/BJL]

traffic items: Consumer products in demand and high replacement frequency which regularly bring traffic to a store or department. [WRD]

traffic management: A corporate function that is responsible for determining the mode of transportation and utilization of transportation equipment as well as general administration of the movement of goods by the firm. A traffic manager usually heads the traffic management function. [DJB/BJL]

trailer-on-flatcar (TOFC): Shipments of truck trailers on rail flatcars. Shipments moving as TOFC receive special rates. (See also **Piggyback**.) [DJB/BJL]

transactions cost analysis: An approach to analyzing the economics of vertical relationships. The basic premise is that firms will internalize those activities they are able to perform at lower cost, and will rely on the market for those activities where other providers have an advantage. The costs of transactions are determined by the frequency with which they recur, the environmental uncertainty surrounding them, and the specificity of the assets they require. [GSD]

transfer pricing: The pricing of goods and services which are sold to controlled entities of the same organization, e.g. movements of goods and services within a multinational or global corporation. [WJK]

transfers (interdepartmental merchandise): An intrafirm transaction accounting for the movement of merchandise from one selling department or location to another, which is a transfer-in for the department or other selling unit receiving the goods and a transfer-out for the department or location sending the goods. [WRD]

transit rate: Allows the through shipment of goods to be interrupted for intermediate processing. Even though the goods are stopped enroute to the ultimate destination, a through rate is charged similar to a rate that would be charged if the goods had not stopped enroute to their ultimate destination. [DJB/BJL]

transportation: A marketing function that adds time and place utility to the product by moving it from where it is made to where it is purchased and used. Includes all intermediate steps in the process. [DJB/BJL]

transportation modes: A specific class of related carriers such as truck, rail, air, or water. A generic class of transportation carrier. [DJB/BJL]

trend analysis: The use of analytical techniques, such as time series analysis, to discern trends. [WL]

trend extrapolation: Projecting patterns identified in data about the past into the future. [WL]

trial: A psychological term denoting the number of a practice run or a series of repetitions of a learning experience. Also used to imply a sampling or trial of a product before repurchase. [HHK]

trial close: An attempt made by the salesperson to close the sale. [BAW]

truckload: Shipment by truck of a full load. Usually qualifies for lower freight rate than smaller shipment. [DJB/BJL]

Truth-in Lending Act (1968): Requires full disclosure of terms and conditions of finance charges. (See also **Consumer Credit Protection Act**.) [DC]

TSR: An abbreviation that is used for a telephone sales representative. [BAW]

turnkey operation: Also called **system selling**, is a complete system solution, where the seller provides the buyer with a complete working operation, including all equipment, assembly, operating expenses, personnel training, and the like. It is common in foreign licensing where a firm provides experts to set up a foreign company, ultimately turning the operation over to the host entirely. [GLL/DTW]

turnover table: (See **brand-switching matrix**.)

turnover: (See **inventory turnover**.)

twig: Store (smaller than a branch) that specializes in a particular category or few categories of merchandise. Usually placed into a market area to combat some specific competition within the area, and the firm does not believe an entire branch in that market is reasonable (e.g., a home furnishings twig). [WRD]

two column tariff: A system of tariffs where the initial single column of duties is supplemented by a second column of duties which shows reduced rates agreed through tariff negotiations with other countries. [WJK]

two step flow of communication: The belief that the process of influence of communications material is not directly from the communicator to the audience or interpreters, but rather influence is a two step process from the mass communications such as advertising to the opinion leader in the group and from the opinion leader to the individual. [HHK]

tying agreements: (See **contracts, tying**.)

tying clause: Limitation in a contract requiring price maintenance or exclusive purchase of certain products from one party by the other. [WRD]

tying contracts: (See **contracts, tying**.)

Type I error: Rejection of a null hypothesis when it is true; also known as alpha error.

Type II error: Failure to reject a null hypothesis when it is false; also known as beta error.

ultimate consumers: Those who buy goods for personal or family use or for household consumption. [WRD]

UNCTAD (United Nations Conference on Trade and Development): An organization set up by the United Nations to assist the less developed nations. It seeks to accelerate the growth rate of the Less Developed Countries (LDCs) to not less than 5 percent per annum. [WJK]

underdeveloped countries: Those countries where 1987 GNP per capita ranged from $500 to $1000. These countries exhibit the symptoms of the first stages of industrialization which are: (1) small factories are erected to supply the domestic market with such items as batteries, tires, footwear, clothing, building materials and packaged foods; (2) the proportion of the population engaged in agricultural activities declines and the degree of urbanization increases; and (3) the available educational effort expands and literacy rises. (See **also pre-industrial countries, developing countries, industrialized countries,** and **post-industrialized countries.**) [WJK]

undifferentiated oligopoly: An oligopoly that produces and markets standardized products, e.g., cement or paperboard boxes. [DLS]

uneven exchange: An exchange of goods made by a customer when the value of the new goods received is different from that of the goods returned. [WRD]

unfair competition: 1. Business practices which are not considered ethical in a trade or industry; according to Federal and other laws, certain situations and/or practices which unduly injure competitors and work contrary to the public interest as interpreted in the business community and the nation's laws. [WRD] 2. Rivalry among sellers through the use of practices deemed to be unfair by judicial, legal or administrative agencies such as selling products below cost to drive a competitor out of business, or dumping goods in foreign markets. Defined in antitrust legislation as acts to mislead and confuse consumers, such as the deceptive substitution of one product for another in order to gain unfair advantage over competitors. [WL]

unfair trade practices acts: These are sales-below-cost statutes that vary widely from state to state and most frequently prohibit the sale of branded and unbranded goods below cost where the intent is to destroy competition or to injure a competitor. [DC]

Uniform Commercial Code: Adopted by most states, and provides consistency in commercial law and deals with all the aspects of a commercial transaction as well as other commercial matters such as bulk sales, investment securities and the bank collection process. [DC]

uniform communications system (UCS): A communications standard adopted by the food industry for electronic transmission of information between buyer and seller. [DJB/BJL]

uniform freight classification: A system which allows the grouping of related products into specific rate categories. These ratings are based on handling characteristics, bulk, value and perishability of the product. These ratings are used as the basis for standardized rates for classes of products. [DJB/BJL]

unique selling proposition (USP): An approach to the development of advertising messages that focuses on the differentiating qualities of the product or service; includes the ideas that an advertisement must make a proposition to the consumer, that the proposition must be one that the competition either cannot or does not offer (must be "unique" either in the brand itself or the claim made), and that the proposition is strong enough to move new customers to the brand. [AMB]

unit control: The control of stock in terms of merchandise units rather than in terms of dollar worth. [WRD]

unit load: A shipment which contains multiple units but moves as a single entity. For example, shipments which are palletized or slipsheeted or containerized are unit load shipments. [DJB/BJL]

unit packing: Packing merchandise in selling units (by the manufacturer) so it can be sold from sample and delivered to the customer without repacking at the store. [WRD]

unit pricing: Under unit pricing, products offered for sale include the price per unit such as per pound or quart, in addition to the price of the product. [WRD]

unitary price elasticity: A special situation where a cut in price increases quantity just enough that total revenue remains unchanged. [DLS]

United Nations (UN):   An international organization founded in 1945 of countries whose mission is to promote the cause of peace, prosperity, and human rights for all people. [WJK]

universal product code (UPC):   1. A national coordinated system of product identification by which a ten-digit number is assigned to products. The UPC is designed so that at check-out counter an electronic scanner will read the symbol on the product and automatically transmit the information to a computer which controls the sales register. The code is called OCR - font B. [WRD] 2. A set of bars or lines, printed on most items sold in supermarkets and other mass retailing outlets, that permits computers at checkout counters to retrieve the price of the item from its memory or data base. The data generated can be used for a wide variety of marketing decisions such as inventory control, allocation of shelf space, advertising, pricing and so on. [WL]

unsought goods: Products which the consumer does not seek, either from lack of awareness or lack of interest in the particular attributes they have. Since most products are both sought and unsought, by different persons, this category is not part of the basic classification of goods. [CMC]

urban population: Comprises all persons living in places of 2,500 or more inhabitants incorporated as cities, villages, boroughs, or areas designated as such by the Census, with some exceptions. [WL]

urbanized area: An area consisting of a central city or core together with contiguous closely settled territories that have a combined total population of at least 50,000. [WL]

user: (See **buying roles**.)

users' expectations method: A method of forecasting sales that relies on answers from customers regarding their expected consumption or purchases of the product. Also known as buyers' intentions method. [GAC]

utilitarian reference group influence: Compliance of an individual with perceived expectations of others in order to achieve rewards or avoid punishments. [JPP/JCO]

utility: 1. (general definition) The state or quality of being useful. 2. (economics definition) the usefulness received by consumers from buying, owning, or consuming a product. [DLS]

validity: Term applied to measuring instruments reflecting the extent to which differences in scores on the measurement reflect true differences among individuals, groups, or situations in the characteristic which it seeks to measure, or true differences in the same individual, group, or situation from one occasion to another, rather than constant or random errors. [GAC]

VALS: An acronym standing for values and life styles. VALS is a psychographic segmentation approach developed at SRI International. [JPP/JCO]

value: The power of any good to command other goods in peaceful and voluntary exchange. [DLS]

value added: 1. An economic concept referring to the value that a firm adds to the cost of its inputs as a result of its activities, thereby arriving at the price of its outputs. [WL] 2. A measure of the contribution to a product's worth by any organization which handles it on its way to the ultimate user. Value added is measured by subtracting the cost of a product (or the cost of ingredients from which it was made) from the price that the organization got for it. For resellers, this means the firm's gross margin; for manufacturing firms, it means the contribution over cost of ingredients. Presumably whatever work that firm did is reflected in the higher price someone is willing to pay for the product, hence that firm's value added. [CMC]

value added by marketing: The increase in value due to performance of marketing activities by a firm. Value added is computed by subtracting the market value of purchased goods from the market value of goods sold. [DLS]

value analysis: 1. An analytical procedure to study the costs versus the benefits of a currently purchased material, component, or design in order to reduce the cost/benefit ratio as much as possible. It is also called **value engineering**. When performed by a seller, it is often referred to as **value-in-use analysis**. [GLL/DTW] 2. A systematic study of a product, wherein the analyst keeps asking, "Can the cost of this part, this subassembly, or this step be reduced in any way, or even eliminated?" Value analysis is usually performed by engineers who are seeking new, less expensive, ways to design or create the product being studied. [CMC]

value chain analysis: An approach to assessing the positions of competitive advantage. A value chain first classifies the activities of a business into the discrete steps performed to design, produce, market, deliver and service a product. Supporting these specific value creation activities are firm-wide activities such as procurement, human resource management, technology and the infrastructure of systems and management that ties the value chain together. To gain advantage a business must either perform enough of these activities at a lower cost to gain an overall cost edge while offering a parity product, or perform them in a way that leads to differentiation and a premium price. [GSD]

value engineering: (See **value analysis**.)

value expressive reference group influence: An individual's use of groups to enhance or support his/her self-concept. [JPP/JCO]

value-in use analysis: (See **value analysis**.)

values: Widely shared beliefs by members of a culture about what is desirable or good (nutritious food, Japanese cars, Free Speech or honesty) and what is undesirable or bad (arson, bigotry, escargot, spinach or deceit). If a value is accepted by the individual, it can become a major influence on his or her behavior. [HHK]

variable cost, total: The sum of all costs directly tied to the number of units produced and marketed. [DLS]

variable cost, average: The sum of all variable costs at a given level of production divided by the number of units. [DLS]

variable price policy: A policy of adjusting prices to different customers, depending on their relative purchasing power or bargaining ability. [WRD]

variety: Has to do with the number of different classifications carried in a particular merchandising unit; implies generically different kinds of goods. (See also **assortment**.) [WRD]

variety store: Establishments primarily selling a variety of merchandise in the low and popular price range, such as stationery, gift items, women's accessories, toilet articles, light hardware, toys, housewares, and confectionery. Frequently known as "5 to 10 cent" stores and "5 cents to a dollar" store, merchandise is usually sold outside these price ranges. [WRD]

vehicle: (See **advertising media**.)

vendor: An organization that supplies specific goods or services to the business/organizational marketplace. [GLL/DTW]

vendor analysis: 1. (retail) An analysis of sales, stocks, markups, markdowns and gross margin by vendors. [WRD] 2. (industrial) An organized effort to assess strengths and weaknesses of current or new suppliers to assure supplier quality. It is usually undertaken by the purchasing department. [GLL/DTW]

venture: A risky new product project or business start-up. Ventures are often staffed by managers who are pulled out of their regular functional jobs and assigned to the project. The venture may be totally in-house (located on the customary premises, close to the regular operation) or it may be spun-out (relocated at some point well apart from the on-going operation). If in cooperation with another firm, it becomes a joint venture. [CMC]

venture teams, in new product development: Similar to new product task forces with an important difference: teams are independent of any functional department. Members stay with the project until it is abandoned or commercialized. In the latter case they may become the management team responsible for running the new product as a separate business. The venture team is authorized to obtain assistance as needed from functional departments or to purchase external assistance. Venture teams usually report to a top corporate officer. Comment: Venture teams are appropriate for developing new products which are outside of the company's existing businesses. They are also appropriate for totally new products which usually require more time, expense, and risk than managers of current operating businesses are willing to support. They are more likely to be used for high technology industrial products than, for example, consumer packaged goods. They require long term commitment and support from corporate management. [VPB]

vertical business system: (See **value chain analysis.**)

vertical integration: 1. The combination of two or more separate stages in the channel through ownership, including mergers or acquisitions. [JRN] 2. Expansion by acquiring or developing businesses engaged in earlier or later stages of marketing a product. In forward vertical integration, manufacturers might acquire or develop wholesaling and retailing activities. In backward vertical integration, retailers might develop their own wholesaling or manufacturing capabilities. [WL]

vertical market: Situation where an industrial product is used only by one or a very few industry or trade groups; the market is narrow but deep in the sense that most prospective customers in the industry may need the article. [WRD]

vertical marketing system competition: Competition between two vertical marketing systems. For example, the total vertical marketing system of General Motors competing with that of Ford Motor Company. (See also **vertical marketing system.**) [WRD]

vertical marketing systems: Channel systems consisting of horizontally coordinated and vertically aligned establishments that are professionally managed and centrally coordinated to achieve optimum operating economies and maximum market impact. The three types of vertical marketing systemss are administered, contractual and corporate channel system. [JRN]

vertical mergers: The joining or combination of two or more companies at different stages in the production process, such as the combination of IBM, a manufacturer of computers, with Intel, a manufacturer of microprocessors. [WL]

vertical price-fixing: A conspiracy among marketers at different levels of the channel to set prices for a product. [DLS]

vertical restraints or restrictions: Arrangements between firms operating at different levels of the manufacturing or distribution chain that restrict the conditions under which firms may purchase, sell or resell. [JRN]

vertical structure of the sales organization: Defines clearly what managerial positions have the authority for carrying out specific sales management activities. It also provides for the effective integration and coordination of selling efforts throughout the firm. [OCW]

vicarious learning: Changes in an individual's behavior brought about by observing the actions of others and the consequences of those actions. [JPP/JCO]

Vidale-Wolfe model: An econometric model that represents the rate of change of sales as a function of the rate of advertising spending. The lagged effect of advertising is incorporated using a sales-decay term (Vidale and Wolfe 1957). The model allows the effect of advertising to have different rise versus decay rates. [DCS/YJW]

visual front: Open storefront design which has no vision barrier between the interior and exterior. [WRD]

visual merchandising: That in which reliance is upon the use of informative labels, descriptive signs, or a self-service type of display, as opposed to dependence upon a salesperson for information. [WRD]

visual system of stock control: Method of controlling the amount of stock on hand by systematic observation rather than by records. [WRD]

voluntary group or chain: A contractual marketing system where a wholesaler bands together its independent retail customers into a voluntary group. A complete range of services is offered to retail members including centralized advertising and promotion, store location and layout, training, financing and accounting. [JRN]

wagon distributor: A wholesaler whose inventory of merchandise is carried on trucks which are operated by driver-salespersons; retailer's requirements for merchandise are determined at the time of the sales call and orders are filled immediately from the stock carried on the truck. Somewhat archaic. (See also **rack jobber.**) [WRD]

want slip: A slip on which the salesperson records customer requests for items that cannot be supplied from stock. [WRD]

want-book: A notebook in which store employees record the name of items called for by customers but are not in stock. [WRD]

warehouse: A physical facility used primarily for the storage of goods held in anticipation of sale or transfer within the marketing channel. [DJB/BJL]

warehouse receipts: Those which every public warehouse issues to depositors for goods placed in storage. [WRD]

warehouse retailing: Retailing of certain types of merchandise, particularly groceries, drugs, hardware, home improvement, and home furnishings in a warehouse atmosphere; facilities are typically in low-rent isolated buildings with a minimum of services offered, and the consumer performs the bulk of the functions in a self-service mode. [WRD]

warehouses, automated: A facility where machine power such as conveyors, automatic sortation, ASAR, and other materials handling applications have been implemented to speed the receiving, handling, picking, and shipping of product within the facility. [DJB/BJL]

warehouses, contract: A facility where the user of the warehouse contracts with a third party for some mix of labor, management, and material handling capability over a specified contract period. The contract period usually exceeds one year. [DJB/BJL]

warehouses, private: A private, or corporate, warehouse is a facility which is operated by the buyer or the seller of the product. It may be used to store raw materials in anticipation of production, work in process, or finished goods awaiting shipment to the buyer. [DJB/BJL]

warehouses, public: A for-hire facility that is available to any business requiring storage or handling of goods. The public warehouse usually operates on a monthly contract and charges for storage plus a handling fee for receiving goods and moving goods out of storage. [DJB/BJL]

warranty: A statement or promise made to the customer that a product being offered for sale is fit for the purpose being claimed. The promise concerns primarily what the seller will do if the product performs below expectations or turns out to be defective in some way. The promise (warranty) may be full (complete protection) or limited (some corrective steps), under terms of the Magnuson-Moss Act of 1975. It may also be expressed (orally or in writing) or only implied, and it may have time restrictions. [CMC]

waybill: An official shipping document which identifies shipper and consignee, routing, description of goods, cost of shipment, and weight of shipment. [DJB/BJL]

weak products: (Rarely) used in reference to products in the decline stage of the product life cycle, or otherwise so short of market value that they are destined for early abandonment. [CMC]

wealth: 1. All material objects that have an economic value possessed by a nation. 2. The aggregate of all possessions of economic goods owned by a person. [DLS]

Weber's law: Product purchasers and users are more interested in the relative differences between products than in the absolute characteristics of products standing alone. [CMC]

weeks' supply method of stock planning: A method of stock planning whereby one plans for a certain number of weeks' supply. In utilizing this method, it is assumed that the same stock turnover can be maintained throughout the selling season; thus, inventory carried is in direct proportion to expected sales. [WRD]

wheel of retailing theory: A theory of retail institutional change, which explains retail evolution with an institutional life cycle concept. [WRD]

Wheeler Lea Act (1938): An amendment to the FTC Act which added the phrase, "unfair or deceptive acts or practices in commerce are hereby declared unlawful," to the Section 5 prohibition of unfair methods of competition, in order to provide protection for consumers as well as competition. [DC]

white goods: (1) Large kitchen appliances, or (2) sheets and other bedding items. [CMC]

wholesale establishment: A recognizable place of business that is primarily engaged in performing marketing functions, including the functions of exchange on the wholesale level of distribution. [WRD]

wholesale market centers: A concentration of vendors' sales offices or display rooms in one place, usually a city or an area within a city; sometimes identified by a concentration of production facilities, as well as sales offices. [WRD]

wholesale merchants (distributors): Establishments primarily engaged in buying and selling merchandise in the domestic market and performing the principal wholesale functions. [WRD]

wholesale price index (WPI): A relative measure maintained by the U.S. government of average price changes in commodities sold in wholesale markets in the United States. [DLS]

wholesaler: Merchant establishment operated by a concern that is primarily engaged in buying, taking title to, usually storing and physically handling goods in large quantities, and reselling the goods (usually in smaller quantities) to retailers or to industrial or business users. [WRD]

wholesaler sponsored cooperatives: A form of contractual vertical marketing system which is an example of forward integration; retailers achieve vertical system advantages by affiliating with a sponsoring wholesaler. [WRD]

wholesaling: (1) All transactions in which the purchaser is actuated by a profit or business motive in making the purchase, except for transactions that involve a small quantity of goods purchased from a retail establishment for business use, which is considered at retail. (2) For U.S. Census of Business purposes, include the foregoing as based on the institutional structure of business establishments primarily engaged in wholesale trade. [WRD]

will-call: Products ordered by customers in advance of the time delivery is desired. [WRD]

WOM: An acronym standing for word-of-mouth, as in word-of- mouth communication. [JPP/JCO]

Wool Products Labeling Act (1939): Administered by the FTC, and requires labels be affixed to products containing wool showing the percentages of new wool, reused or reprocessed wool, and other fibers or fillers that are used. [DC]

workable competition: An economic model of a market where competition is less than perfect, but adequate enough to give buyers genuine alternatives. [DLS]

workload analysis: A procedure for determining the total amount of sales effort required to cover each territory, after considering the sales potential and the number of accounts to be served. Comment: The number of calls to be made on each, the duration of each call and the estimated amount of nonselling and travel time are explicitly considered. [BAW]

workrooms: Service departments such as apparel alterations, drapery manufacture, furniture polishing and repair, and carpet workroom. [WRD]

zero defects: A condition where a production unit makes every product without defect. Usually only a theory or a reference point, but actually sought in such categories as aerospace, serums, U.S. mint, and others. [CMC]

zero order model: A probabilistic model in which the probability of occurrence of any given outcome at a particular point in time does not depend on any previous outcomes of the process. Models of this kind are often used to represent brand choice behavior or media exposure patterns (Lilien and Kotler 1983). Evidence that this simple zero order assumption for brand choice behavior cannot be rejected, given empirical choice patterns, has been provided by Bass, Givon, Kalwani, Reibstein and Wright (1984). [DCS/YJW]

zip code: A geographical classification system developed by the U.S. government for mail distribution. A nested, numeric code with a range of five to nine digits. [DJB/BJL]

zone of rate freedom (ZORF):   A zone within which a carrier can raise or lower rates without regulatory or other administrative action. [DJB/BJL]

zone pricing: Delivered cost based on factory price plus averaged freight rate for section or territory to which goods are shipped (same delivered cost to all in the zone). [WRD]

REFERENCES

Aaker, D. A. (1975), "ADMOD: An Advertising Decision Model," *Journal of Marketing*, 12 (February), 37-45.

Assmus, G. (1975), "Newprod: The Design and Implementation of a New Product Model," *Journal of Marketing*, 39 (January), 16-23.

Bass, F. M. (1969), "A New Product Growth Model for Consumer Durables," *Management Science*, 15, 215-227.

Bass, F. M., M. M. Givon, M. U. Kalwani, D. J. Reibstein, and G. P. Wright (1984), "An Investigation into the Order of the Brand Choice Process," *Marketing Science*, 3, 267-287.

Bell, D. E., R. L. Keeney, and J. D. C. Little (1975), "A Market Share Theorem," *Journal of Marketing Research*, 12, 136-141.

Blackburn, J. D., and K. J. Clancy (1982), "LITMUS: A New Product Planning Model," in A. A. Zoltners (ed.) *Marketing Planning Models*, TIMS Studies in the Management Sciences, Vol. 18., New York: North-Holland, pp. 43-61.

Blattberg, R. C., and J. Golanty (1978), "Tracker: An Early Test Market Forecasting and Diagnostic Model for New Product Planning," *Journal of Marketing Reasearch*, 15, 192-202.

Chakravarthi, D., A. A. Mitchell, and R. Staelin (1981), "Judgement Based Marketing Decision Models: Problems and Possible Solutions," *Journal of Marketing*, 45, No. 4, 13-23.

Corstjens, M. L., and D. A. Gautschi (1983), "Formal Choice Models in Marketing," *Marketing Science*, 2, 19-56.

Currim, I. S. (1982), "Predictive Testing of Consumer Choice Models Not Subject to Independence of Irrelevant Alternatives," *Journal of Marketing Research*, 19, 208-222.

Daganzo, C. (1979), *Multinomial Probit: The Theory and Its Application to Demand Forecasting*, New York: Academic Press.

Day, G. S. (1986), *Analysis for Strategic Market Decisions*, New York: West Publishing Co.

Dubin, J. A. (1986), "A Nested Logit Model of Space and Water Heat System Choice," *Marketing Science*, 5, 112-124.

Ehrenberg, A. S. C. (1972), *Repeat-Buying: Theory and Applications*, Amsterdam: North-Holland.

Fudge, W.K., and L. M. Lodish (1977), "Evaluation of the Effectiveness of a Model Based Salesman's Planning System by Field Experimentation," *Interfaces*, 8, No. 1, Part 2, 97-106.

Goodhardt, G. J., A. S. C. Ehrenberg, and C. Chatfield (1984), "The Dirichlet: A Comprehensive Model of Buying Behavior," *The Journal of the Royal Statistical Society; Series A*, 147, 621-655.

Green, P. E., J. D. Carroll, and S. M. Goldberg (1981), "A General Approach to Product Design Optimization via Conjoint Analysis," *Journal of Marketing*, 45 (Summer) 17-37.

Green, P. E., and A. M. Krieger (1985), "Models and Heuristics for Product Line Selection," *Marketing Science*, 4, 1-19.

Green, P. E., A. M. Krieger, and C. M. Schaffer (1985), "Quick and Simple Benefit Segmentation," *Journal of Advertising Research*, 25 (June/July), 9-17.

Greene, J. D. (1982), *Consumer Behavior Models for Non-Statisticians*, New York: Praeger Publishers.

Guadagni, P. M. (1983), "A Nested Logit Model of Product Choice and Purchase Incidence," in F. S. Zufryden (ed.) *Advances and Practices of Marketing Science*, Providence, RI: The Institute of Management Sciences, pp. 90-100.

Hauser, J. R. (1986), "Agendas and Consumer Choice," *Journal of Marketing Research*, 23, 199-212.

Hauser, J. R., and S. P. Gaskin (1984), "Application of the 'Defender' Consumer Model," *Marketing Science*, 3, 327-351.

Hauser, J. R., and S. M. Shugan (1983), "Defensive Marketing Strategies," *Marketing Science*, 2, 319-360.

Hess, S. W., and S. A. Samuels (1971), "Experiences With a Sales Districting Model: Criteria and Implementation," *Management Science*, 18, No. 4, Part II, 41-54.

Huff, D. L. (1964), "Defining and Estimating a Trading Area," *Journal of Marketing*, 28 (July), 34-38.

Jeuland, A. P., F. M. Bass, and G. P. Wright (1980), "A Multibrand Stochastic Model Compounding Heterogeneous Erlang Timing and Multinomial Choice Processes," *Operations Research*, 28, 255-277.

Kahn, B. K., M. U. Kalwani and D. G. Morrison (1986), "Measuring Variety Seeking and Reinforcement Behavior Using Panel Data," *Journal of Marketing Research*, 23, 89-100.

Kalwani, M. U., and D. G. Morrison (1977), "A Parsimonious Description of the Hendry System," *Management Science*, 23, 467-477.

Kuehn, A. A. (1962), "Consumer Brand Choice—A Learning Process," *Journal of Advertising Research*, 2 (December), 10-17.

Larreche, J.-C., and V. Srinivasan (1981), "STRATPORT: A Decision Support System for Strategic Planning," *Journal of Marketing*, 45, No. 4, 39-52.

Larreche, J.-C., and V. Srinivasan (1982), "STRATPORT: A Model For the Evaluation and Formulation of Business Portfolio Strategies," *Management Science*, 28, 979-1001.

Lattin, J. M., and L. McAlister (1985), "Using a Variety-Seeking Model to Identify Substitute and Complementary Relationships Among Competing Products," *Journal of Marketing Research*, 22, 330-339.

Lilien, G. L. (1979), "Advisor 2: Modeling the Marketing Mix for Industrial Products," *Management Science*, 25, No. 2, 191-204.

Lilien, G. L., and P. Kotler (1983), *Marketing Decision Making: A Model-Building Approach*, New York: Harper and Row.

Little, J. D. C. (1970), "Models and Managers: The Concept of a Decision Calculus," *Management Science*, 16, B466-B485.

Little, J. D. C. (1975), "BRANDAID: A Marketing Mix Model, Part I: Structure; Part II: Implementation," *Operations Research*, 23, 628-673.

Little, J. D. C., and L. M. Lodish (1966), "A Media Selection Model and Its Optimization by Dynamic Programming," *Industrial Management Review*, 8 (Fall), 15-23.

Little, J. D. C., and L. M. Lodish (1969), "A Media Planning Calculus," *Operations Research*, 17, 1-34.

Little, J. D. C., and L. M. Lodish (1981), "Commentary on 'Judgement Based Marketing Decision Models'," *Journal of Marketing*, 45, No. 4, 24-29.

Lodish, L. M. (1971), "CALLPLAN: An Interactive Salesman's Call Planning System," *Management Science*, 18, No. 4, Part II, 25-40.

Luce, R. D. (1977), "The Choice Axiom after Twenty Years," *Journal of Mathematical Psychology*, 15, 215-233.

Mahajan, V., P. E. Green, and S. M. Goldberg (1982), "A Conjoint Model for Measuring Self- and Cross-Price/Demand Relationships," *Journal of Marketing Research*, 19, 334-342.

Mahajan, V., E. Muller, and S. Sharma (1984), "An Empirical Comparison of Awareness Forecasting Models of New Product Introduction," *Marketing Science*, 3, 179-197.

Mahajan, V. and Y. Wind (1986), *Innovation Diffusion Models of New Product Acceptance*, Cambridge, Mass.: Ballinger Publishing Co.

Massy, W. F. (1969), "Forecasting Demand for New Convenience Products," *Journal of Marketing*, 6, 405-412.

Massy, W. F., D. B. Montgomery, and D. G. Morrison (1970), *Stochastic Models of Buying Behavior*, Cambridge, MA: MIT Press.

McFadden, D. (1986), "The Choice Theory Approach to Market Research," *Marketing Science*, 5, 275-297.

Montgomery, D. B., A. J. Silk, and C. E. Zaragoza (1971), "A Multiple-Product Sales Force Allocation Model," *Management Science*, 18, No. 4, Part II, 3-24.

Moorthy, K. S. (1985), "Using Game Theory to Model Competition," *Journal of Marketing Research*, 22, 262-282.

Morrison, D. G., and D. C. Schmittlein (1981), "Predicting Future Random Events Based on Past Performance," *Management Science*, 27, 1006-1023.

Nakanishi, M., and L. G. Cooper (1974), "Parameter Estimation for a Multiplicative Competitive Interaction Model—Least Squares Approach," *Journal of Marketing Research*, 11, 303-311.

Parfitt, J. H., and B. J. K. Collins (1968), "Use of Consumer Panels for Brand Share Prediction," *Journal of Marketing Research*, 5, 131-146.

Parsons, L. J., and R. L. Schultz (1976), *Marketing Models and Econometric Research*, Amsterdam: Elsevier Scientific Publishing.

Pringle, L. G., R. D. Wilson, and E. I. Brody (1982), "NEWS: A Decision Oriented Model For New Product Analysis and Forecasting," *Marketing Science*, 1, 1-30.

Rubinson, J. R., W. R. Vanhonacker, and F. M. Bass (1980), "On 'A Parsimonious Description of the Hendry System'," *Management Science*, 26, 215-226.

Silk, A. J., and G. L. Urban (1978), "Pre-Test Market Evaluation of New Packaged Goods: A Model and Measurement Methodology," *Journal of Marketing Research*, 15, 171-191.

The Hendry Corporation (1970), *Hendrodynamics: Fundamental Laws of Consumer Dynamics*, Chapter 1, Hendry Corporation.

The Hendry Corporation (1971), *Hendrodynamics: Fundamental Laws of Consumer Dynamics*, Chapter 2, Hendry Corporation.

Thurstone, L. L. (1927), "A Law of Comparative Judgment," *Psychological Review*, 34, 273-286.

Tversky, A. (1972), "Elimination By Aspects: A Theory of Choice," *Psychological Review*, 79, 281-219.

Tversky, A., and S. Sattath (1979), "Preference Trees," *Psychological Review*, 86, 542-573.

Urban, G. L. (1970), "SPRINTER Mod III: A Model for the Analysis of New Frequently Purchased Consumer Products," *Operations Research*, 18, 805-853.

Urban, G. L., and G. M. Katz (1983), "Pre-Test-Market Models: Validation and Managerial Implications," *Journal of Marketing Research*, 20, 221-234.

Vidale, H. L., and H. B. Wolfe (1957), "An Operations Research Study of Sales Response to Advertising," *Operational Research Quarterly*, 5, 370-381.

Wind, Y., V. Mahajan, and R. Cardozo (1981), *New Product Forecasting Models*, Lexington, MA: Lexington Books.

Wind, Y., and T. L. Saaty (1980), "Marketing Applications of the Analytic Hierarchy Process," *Management Science*, 26, 641-658.

Yellott, J. I., Jr. (1977), "The Relationship Between Luce's Choice Axiom, Thurstone's Theory of Comparative Judgement, and the Double Exponential Distribution," *Journal of Mathematical Psychology*, 15, 109-144.